THE POLITICS
OF RACE IN BRITAIN

THE
POLITICS OF
RACE IN BRITAIN

Zig Layton-Henry

University of Warwick

London
GEORGE ALLEN & UNWIN
Boston   Sydney

George Allen & Unwin (Publishers) Ltd,
40 Museum Street, London WC1A 1LU, UK

George Allen & Unwin (Publishers) Ltd,
Park Lane, Hemel Hempstead, Herts HP2 4TE, UK

Allen & Unwin, Inc.,
9 Winchester Terrace, Winchester, Mass. 01890, USA

George Allen & Unwin Australia Pty Ltd,
8 Napier Street, North Sydney, NSW 2060, Australia

First published in 1984

British Library Cataloguing in Publication Data
Layton-Henry, Zig
   The politics of race in Britain.
1. Great Britain—Race relations   2. Great Britain—Politics and
government—1945–
I. Title
323.141   DA125.A1
ISBN 0-04-323026-1
ISBN 0-04-323027-X Pbk

Library of Congress Cataloging in Publication Data
Layton-Henry, Zig.
   The politics of race in Britain.
1. Racism—Great Britain.   2. Great Britain—Race relations.
3. Great Britain—Politics and government—1945–   I Title.
DA125.A1L39   1984   323.1′1′0941   84-6265
ISBN 0-04-323026-1
ISBN 0-04-323027-X (pbk.)

Set in 10 on 11 point Plantin by Phoenix Photosetting, Chatham
and printed in Great Britain by Billing and Sons Ltd,
London and Worcester

FOR MY PARENTS

CONTENTS

LIST OF TABLES

PREFACE AND ACKNOWLEDGEMENTS

One of the most important social and political developments in postwar Britain was the migration and settlement of hundreds of thousands of people from the New Commonwealth. This migration has created within Britain a large, distinctive minority population and this has considerable consequences for the political system. Race relations and immigration issues have for some time been important political issues and the introduction of strict immigration controls, the creation of new institutions like the Commission for Racial Equality, and the passage of a new Nationality Act in 1981 have in no way reduced the salience of race as a political issue. In fact, by drawing attention to the racial dimension it could be argued that they have had the opposite effect and have increased its salience. The riots of 1980 and 1981, the Scarman Report and the growing support in the Labour Party for policies of positive discrimination will ensure that race relations issues will remain highly controversial and of considerable importance.

Political scientists have been strangely remiss in neglecting the political consequences of New Commonwealth immigration, despite the political controversy it has aroused and the important implications for political integration that are involved. Will the British state and its institutions be able to generate the legitimacy and loyalty of its new non-white citizens in the same way as it has among previous groups of immigrants and their descendants? Economists, sociologists and historians have been more prominent in examining the implications of New Commonwealth immigration than political scientists, although most studies contain some political analysis. Major contributions to our understanding have been made by scholars like E. J. Rose and N. Deakin in *Colour and Citizenship*, and by S. Castles and G. Kosack in *Immigrant Workers and Class Structure in Western Europe*. John Rex and his collaborators in *Race, Community and Conflict* and *Colonial Immigrants in a British City*, and D. Lawrence in *Black Migrants, White Natives*, have examined in detail the problems of settlement and integration in major urban centres. The best-known political study is probably Paul Foot's *Immigration and Race in British Politics*, though this stimulating book has long been out of print. Ira Katznelson's *Black Men White Cities* and more recently Gary Freeman's *Immigrant Labor and Racial Conflict in Industrial Societies* have made valuable contributions. There have also been numerous studies of the National Front. However, there does appear to be a need for a general, up-to-date text on the politics of race in Britain covering the changing policies of the major parties, parliamentary developments, the politics of violence and the electoral consequences of the growing population of black Britons. This is the gap which I have attempted to fill.

The writing of any book involves numerous debts and it is impossible to mention them all. I am grateful to the Social Science Research Council for a personal research grant in 1979–80 which enabled me to spend a year at the Research Unit on Ethnic Relations at the University of Aston developing my knowledge of the political history of race relations in Britain. I wish to thank John Rex for his friendship and encouragement over many years even when, as a student in Birmingham, I had research interests far removed from his own. The work of Donley Studlar has been a source of inspiration in my teaching and research and I am obliged to him for reading and commenting on the manuscript and for his friendly encouragement. My thanks go also to Paul Rich for his helpful suggestions and also to Nicholas Deakin, Sheila Patterson and Stan Taylor. Michael Holdsworth and John Whitehead of Allen & Unwin must take some responsibility for suggesting the book and sustaining its production. It would be impossible to fulfil teaching and administrative commitments and pursue research without considerable family support and I am indebted to Jennifer and Alison for their tolerance and to my wife Barbara for her support and for typing the manuscript despite other pressing commitments. I must take the blame for any errors that appear.

For some of the chapters I have drawn on, though substantially revised, articles which have appeared in various journals. I am grateful to the editors and publishers for allowing me to make use of the material first presented there. These are 'Race, electoral strategy and the major parties', *Parliamentary Affairs* (1978), published by Oxford University Press; 'Commission in crisis', *Political Quarterly* (1979), published by the Political Quarterly Publishing Co. Ltd; 'Racial attacks in Britain', *Patterns of Prejudice* (1982), published by the Institute of Jewish Affairs; and 'Immigration and race in British politics: political aspects', nos 1–8, *New Community* (1978–81), published by the Commission for Racial Equality.

Z. Layton-Henry
Kenilworth, June 1983

INTRODUCTION

One of the most important but unforeseen results of the upheavals caused by the Second World War and the postwar economic boom in Europe, fuelled by reconstruction and American investment, has been the creation of substantial immigrant communities in most Western European countries. In Britain the migrant workers attracted by these economic opportunities were predominantly people from the West Indian colonies and the recently independent ex-colonies of India and Pakistan. These migrants and their families have created a substantial, diverse and distinctive minority population of non-white Britons and have transformed the country into a multi-racial society. Similar processes have also occurred in other European countries with migrant workers drawn from a wide range of different countries. These social and economic processes are unique in a number of respects and raise major political questions. Traditional European patterns of emigration have been reversed, long-accepted notions of citizenship have been challenged and many European states have been forced to search for new bases of political legitimacy in order to integrate and reconcile native citizens with the new migrants, some of whom as colonials or ex-colonials have the citizenship of their new country, while many others have foreign nationality. Similar processes and questions have also occurred in the United States, even though it has long been a country of immigrants. Mexican, Cuban and other Latin American migrants have caused Americans to compare their postwar experience with that of Europe.

These processes of migration and settlement have not been easy or peaceful. The British case is particularly interesting as most of the migrants have citizenship rights and therefore were legally and politically in a better position than most European 'guestworkers' or migrants to the United States. However, the difficulties have proved to be just as intractable as those in other countries, if not more so. The migration of hundreds of thousands of West Indians, Indians and Pakistanis to Britain after the war was neither anticipated nor welcomed by British policy-makers. From an early stage policy-makers were concerned about the social and political consequences but took no action, partly because the migrants were helping to alleviate the serious labour shortages which were holding back economic expansion and the provision of welfare services. Equally important was the priority British politicians gave to foreign affairs. They were used to playing a major role in world affairs and after the war were preoccupied with maintaining a world role for Britain and managing the withdrawal from Empire as gracefully as possible. Few anticipated the dramatic decline in Britain's world role, and politicians struggled unsuccessfully to maintain Britain's position as a world power and to cope with economic crises partly caused by trying to sustain this role. It is therefore not surprising that British politicians failed to appreciate the magnitude of the social and political problems which might develop if strong positive action were not taken to assist the integration and settlement of Commonwealth citizens. In particular, little effort was made to publicise the positive contribution that New Commonwealth settlers were making to the economy and social welfare services of the country, and few resources were devoted to assist their integration and settlement. This major group of new citizens was left to fend for itself and little was done to welcome the newcomers.

Immigration on any scale is resented by those who find themselves in competition with newcomers for jobs, housing and welfare services. It was, perhaps, inevitable that, without strong political leadership and the commitment of scarce resources, resentment and frustrations should build up and be expressed in discrimination, demands for immigration control and even violence. Immigration thus became a major political issue and politicians were forced to act when the race riots of 1958 alerted them to the potential seriousness of further neglect. The controversy over the passing of the 1962 Commonwealth Immigrants Act and the defeat of Patrick Gordon-Walker at Smethwick in the General Election of 1964 politicised the issue even further. After these shocks, national politicians desperately attempted to defuse the issue and keep it out of the political arena. Immigration and race relations were seen as emotional, irrational and intractable matters not amenable to the reason, negotiation and compromise which character-ised economic and class issues. British politicians were uncomfortable and inexpert in dealing with issues related to race relations and racism and wished to avoid or suppress them. They were much more expert at dealing with economic and class issues which in any event they considered to be more fundamentally important. But the uncomfort-able, irrational and unpredictable issues of immigration and race refused to fade away and policies of benign neglect proved increasingly inadequate. Populist politicians, the media and extremist parties like the National Front resurrected these issues time and time again. However, since major politicians and parties failed to develop long-term strategies to deal with these issues, they were often forced to react to particular crises, like the Kenyan Asians crisis in 1968, with hasty, ill-conceived measures which further politicised the very issues they wished to defuse.

In recent years the major parties have begun to develop longer-term strategies and policies. The Conservative Party's policies are based on the assumption that New Commonwealth immigration is largely over and that the crucial issues concern the integration of the second and third generations and the need to forge new bases of loyalty and legitimacy to integrate black Britons. This was the message the Conservative Party was attempting to convey in their poster 'Labour Says He's Black. Tories Say He's British' which caused so much controversy in the 1983 General Election campaign. The Labour Party is more ambivalent about tough immigration controls and is committed to eliminating those parts of the controls which are racially discriminatory. It is equally concerned about integration and more willing than the Tories to support tough anti-discrimination measures and to consider positive action. The riots in Brixton and Toxteth in 1981 heavily underlined the need to tackle discrimination in employment, housing and education more effectively than hitherto, and some Labour local authorities and Labour politicians have become converted to strategies which involve positive action or discrimination. The Liberal/SDP Alliance has adopted policies very similar to those of the Labour Party and in the General Election of 1983 made a particular appeal to black voters. The response of white citizens to the substantial introduction of such policies is difficult to predict. The riots also highlighted the hostile relations between sections of the black community and the police. Lord Scarman himself described the riots as anti-police riots and made a number of recommendations for the reform of police training and procedures. Some of this has been resisted by the Police Federation and other groups within the police, particularly his proposal that the police disciplinary code be amended to make racially discriminatory behaviour a specific offence. The Federation representatives argue that the code already covers such offences. There is a major dilemma in the pressure to contain crime and prevent riots in a situation where the legitimacy of police actions is being questioned by sections of the black community who feel harassed by police campaigns to prevent crime and also that they are not protected enough from racist attacks.

This book is an attempt to provide an accurate and up-to-date analysis of the politics of race in Britain and to throw light on the questions raised above. A detailed analysis of the processes and developments in Britain may help analysts and policy-makers in Europe and America to see the similarities and differences between their situation and the British case. A further reason for writing the book is that a considerable mythology has been created about many of the events and processes which are described here. The role of the major parties, of politicians and of legislation has often been subject to varied and conflicting interpretations. The role of the 1948 Nationality Act, the controversies over the 1958 riots and the 1962 Commonwealth Immigrants Act are cases in point. Such controversies have continued and recently have surrounded the 1981 Nationality Act, the 1981 riots and the Scarman Report. In the recent General Election of 1983 the importance of the black vote, the Conservative appeal to black electors and the problems facing black candidates in gaining parliamentary nominations and securing election have all been the subject of heated debate. This book will attempt to explain clearly and accurately how the politics of race in Britain has reached its present state and what is likely to happen in the immediate future. The analysis will concentrate on the major developments and particularly on the role of the major political actors and institutions. However, no historical analysis of the politics of race in Britain can ignore the causes of the migration and the legacy of slavery and imperialism which provide the enormously important historical context within which the migration took place. It is therefore sensible to begin the analysis with an examination of the imperial legacy and the causes of the migration before examining the political response and subsequent developments.

CHAPTER 1

The Imperial Legacy

It is impossible to comprehend the origins and development of race relations in Britain without recognising the crucial importance of the legacy of the slave trade and of the British Empire. The history of slavery and imperialism provides the context within which conditions were created which led to the postwar migration of thousands of West Indians and South Asians from the colonial periphery to the metropolitan mother country. The imperial connection determined in important ways the nature of the migration and the civic and legal rights of the migrants, most importantly their right of access to and settlement in Britain. It influenced their expectations regarding their reception and future in Britain and their views regarding the obligations of the mother country towards them. This historical legacy of the conquest and enslavement of African, Indian and other peoples left an indelible mark on both the conquerors and the conquered. The images, feelings and behaviour of native white British people towards the black and brown migrant workers were influenced by the knowledge that these migrants had been subject peoples of the British Empire. In turn colonial migrants were influenced in their attitudes, personality and culture by their legacy of subjection. As hostility to New Commonwealth immigration grew, the imperial connection, particularly the legacy of *Civis Britannicus sum* and the Commonwealth ideal, exerted surprisingly powerful constraints upon British policy-makers when they considered the introduction of immigration controls. They were also concerned with the problems of achieving decolonisation as smoothly and peacefully as possible. For those migrants, perhaps a large majority, who met with discrimination and disappointment, the history of slavery, racism and exploitation in the Empire provided powerful explanations for their failure to realise their expectations and a justification for resentment, alienation and revolt.

THE DEVELOPMENT OF THE SLAVE TRADE

European empires were gained over many centuries, starting at the end of the fifteenth century with the voyages of discovery of the Portuguese, who were followed by the Spanish, Dutch and English. From the first contact with the inhabitants of West Africa, Englishmen found blackness a peculiar and important point of difference between themselves and these people who appeared so far removed from themselves that they seemed to be almost opposites (Walvin, 1973). Some writers have emphasised the unfortunate cultural legacy in Europe which associates whiteness with goodness, cleanliness and beauty and blackness with evil, dirtiness and ugliness (Milner, 1975). Africans were black, primitive, polygamous, heathen, technologically backward and militarily inferior. Initial fascination with and curiosity towards Africans, which were the first natural reactions to the discovery of such different peoples, were quickly followed by feelings of superiority and disdain towards African culture and attributes, feelings which intensified as the slave trade developed. In 1554 John Lok brought slaves from West Africa to England and sold them as household servants (Little, 1948), and in 1562 Sir John Hawkins transported his infamous cargo of 500 slaves from West Africa to the New World and sold them to Spanish colonists in the West Indies (Williams, 1964). Thus began British involvement in an enormously lucrative trade which provided substantial profits for European traders and merchants and fabulous wealth for the owners of West Indian sugar plantations. As Britain acquired her own plantation economies in the West Indies and on the American mainland she became more and more heavily involved. The seizure of Jamaica from Spain in 1665, during Cromwell's protectorate, was a major early development. In 1713, under the Treaty of Utrecht, Britain gained the monopoly of supplying slaves to the Spanish colonies and quickly became the leading slave-trading nation and the centre of the Triangular Trade exporting manufactured goods to West Africa, slaves to America and the West Indies, and importing sugar, tobacco, indigo and cotton from the plantations in the New World. Britons and British cities grew rich from the profits of the Triangular Trade, notably Bristol, Liverpool, London and later Glasgow. The sugar islands in the West Indies were regarded as the jewels of empire and their wealth and stupendous prosperity were based on slave plantations. Many of the leading families in the country were enriched by their involvement in the trade and absentee West Indian planters were familiar figures in eighteenth-century English society. It is ironic to note that John Gladstone, the father of the great Liberal Party leader and opponent of Disraeli, made his large fortune in the West Indian trade and as a slave-owner in the West Indies. It is even more ironic that not only the wealth and descendants of the plantocracy returned to Britain, but many of the descendants of the transported slaves are today native-born British citizens.

Slavery therefore is part of Britain's history, and the profits obtained provided one of the sources of capital accumulation which helped to finance the industrial revolution. However, the British legacy from slavery in some ways is not as traumatic as it has been for other nations such as the Americans and South Africans. Few slaves came to Britain and British involvement in the trade was ended peacefully by judicial decisions and parliamentary legislation in 1807. The most famous judicial case was the Somersett judgement in 1772 when Chief Justice Lord Mansfield freed a negro slave, James Somersett, on the grounds that slavery was not recognised in English law; but it is disputed whether this judgement was as far-reaching as it is often portrayed (Shyllon, 1974). The action of Parliament, however, was decisive. In fact, after abolition British governments played a creditable role in ending the West African slave trade, paying some £20 million in compensation to British slave-owners in the colonies, making cash payments to Spain and Portugal for their consent to the abolition of the trade and signing some fifty treaties with African chiefs who were also compensated. The Royal Navy even attempted to enforce abolition by maintaining patrols off the West African coast (Baumgart, 1982).

However, one of the most disastrous legacies of slavery was the development of racist theories and ideologies to justify the treatment of African men and women as beasts of burden who could be owned as goods and chattels. Early stereotyping of Africans as savage, heathen and uncivilised intensified as the major contact with West Africans involved enslavement. Comparisons between negroes and chimpanzees, who also inhabited West Africa, became more frequent, as did the portrayal of Africans as having lustful and unrestrained appetites (Jordan, 1974). Biological theories of racial inferiority were clearly needed to justify such an abhorrent and anti-Christian trade and to salve the consciences of those European traders and plantation-owners who were reaping such rich rewards from slavery. Africans were thus caricatured as being more beast than man, sub-human, more akin to the apes and monkeys than to the rest of humanity. They were described, for example, by Thomas Carlyle as 'indolent two-legged cattle' (Carlyle, 1849). Religious backing was given to slavery by citing God's curse on Ham and his descendants who, it was prophesied, would be 'a servant of servants to his brothers' (Genesis 8 and 9). The Christian churches themselves were involved in slavery and the ownership of slaves (Lewis, 1978).

The disseminators of these racist views in the eighteenth century caricatured the African as sexual, musical, stupid, indolent, untrustworthy and violent. These attributes were often forced upon negroes by the conditions they experienced on the plantations and elsewhere. In London, for example, negroes found it difficult to gain employment and were often forced into roles as street musicians or 'idlers'. Writers such as Carlyle, Trollope and many others spread and reinforced these stereotypes. Even when slaves rebelled against their inhuman treatment and conditions this was used as further evidence of their untrust-worthiness and violence. The Jamaican rebellion of Morant Bay was brutally suppressed in 1865 and this suppression was supported by such well-known writers as Ruskin, Tennyson, Kingsley, Dickens and Carlyle, though others, notably J. S. Mill, spoke out against it. The rebellion resulted in the removal of the franchise from the 'ignorant and irresponsible rabble and the imposition of Crown colonial rule' (Walvin, 1973).

THE IMPACT OF EMPIRE

While the legacy of slavery is crucially important for understanding white attitudes and fears concerning blacks, it was only part of the global picture of European expansion and domination in the eighteenth and nineteenth centuries. This period saw not only the expansion of the slave trade and then its abolition, but also widespread privateering, commercial expansion and colonial wars between European powers fighting for trade and possessions. Race theories and racism became more pronounced as Europeans pursued policies of conquest and domination throughout the world (Kiernan, 1969).

The nineteenth century saw the emergence of Britain as the leading imperial power. The French Revolution towards the end of the eighteenth century was followed by the revolutionary and Napoleonic wars which prevented continental Europe for pursuing overseas adventures and enabled Britain to compensate from the loss of her American colonies by expanding her dominions in India and Africa at the expense of her European rivals. By the end of the Napoleonic wars Britain had established herself as the major imperial power and her unchallenged naval supremacy enabled her to assert her economic and political leadership in the world.

This vast Empire which Britain accumulated over 200 and more years was sustained not only by British technological superiority and military power, especially sea power; it also rested on a large number of myths, some of which it created and others of which it sustained and reinforced. The Empire boosted national pride and encouraged beliefs in the greatness of Britain, particularly England, its leading nation. It also encouraged beliefs in the superiority of the Anglo-Saxon race. Cecil Rhodes, for example, was not alone in his sentiments when, wandering across the South African veld, he mused 'As I walked, I looked up at the sky and down at the earth, and I said to myself this should be British. And it came to me in that fine, exhilarating air that the British were the best race to rule the world' (Huttenback, 1976). These xenophobic and racist beliefs were so strong that by the end of the nineteenth century it was widely assumed that the British were born to rule, that they were a nation of officers, singularly endowed by God with initiative, inventive genius, courage and leadership. These notions were not simply racist in the sense of asserting the superiority of white Europeans over non-white native peoples, though this formed part of it. A strong strain of nationalism and chauvinism existed too. The victories of Marlborough, Wolfe, Wellington and Nelson seemed to prove the innate superiority of the English over continental Europeans as well as non-Europeans who were accorded an even lower place in the hierarchy of national groups which was assumed to exist by so many Victorians. The denigration of the Irish in the nineteenth century shows how racially identical but economically and militarily weaker people can be attributed innately inferior characteristics by those who have greater wealth and power (Curtis, 1968).

Thus the British in the heady days of Empire looked down upon all other nationalities and races, and were often uninhibited in expressing their paternalistic and racist views. Sir Frank Fox provides an example of both such views. Giving advice on how to handle Africans he wrote, 'Be stern and prompt in punishment, but just, and you are all right. But you have to keep up a stern attitude or there will be trouble' (Cross, 1968). On the Chinese, whose ancient civilisation had been long admired in Europe and who were admired more than other non-white races, Fox was unequivocally denigrating: 'The Chinaman is not a desirable citizen. Economically he is undesirable because he can always undercut the white worker. Socially he is undesirable because, for all his good qualities, his outlook on life is so utterly different from that of white civilisation that he brings a deep taint of degradation to the white people with whom he comes into contact.'

In the nineteenth century the English had acquired enormous self-confidence and feelings of superiority based on their military, economic and technical achievements. This not only enabled them to acquire and rule a vast Empire but also to administer it with a relatively small investment in terms of soldiers and officials. Vast provinces were ruled with the co-operation of local chiefs and leaders. Naval power meant that reinforcements could be transported to any part of the Empire threatened by internal rebellion or external attack but, as such reinforcements might take weeks to arrive, the Empire was sustained by the confidence of the rulers and the awe and fear they inspired in the ruled. Huxley describes this mixture as respect. She wrote:

Respect was the only protection available to Europeans who lived singly or in scattered families among thousands of Africans accustomed to constant warfare and armed with spears and poisoned arrows, but had themselves no barricades and went about unarmed. This respect preserved them like an invisible coat of mail, or a form of magic and seldom failed; but it had to be very carefully guarded.

The least rent or puncture might, if not immediately checked and repaired, split the whole garment asunder and expose the wearer in all his human vulnerability. Kept intact, it was a thousand times stronger than all the guns and locks in the world – challenged it could be brushed aside like a spider's web. (Cross, 1968)

This respect was inspired by European military and technological success and was the temporary by-product of early European industrialisation and imperial expansion. It did not last but was sustained well into the twentieth century. The myth of European invincibility – the coat of respect – was only brushed aside by European defeats at the hands of the Japanese in the Second World War, for the British the defeats in Singapore and Burma being the most dramatic.

The position of the British in the territories of the Empire reinforced their feelings of superiority over and contempt for the subject native peoples. A whole class of soldiers, administrators and officials were required to administer and defend the Empire. India alone provided great opportunities for wealth, employment and adventure. Service in the East India Company, the Indian army, and the Indian civil service provided employment, income and excitement for generations of younger sons of upper- and middle-class families. The wider Empire and newly discovered territories beyond provided further opportunities for trade, settlement, booty and power. The fruits and profits of the Empire fell disproportionately to a small section of the population but the hope of adventure, freedom and wealth inspired millions of Britons to migrate overseas or seek work in the service of the Crown. Hundreds of thousands of jobs in Britain were created by and dependent upon supplying markets in the Empire and hardly a family in the country could have not been involved directly or indirectly in the imperial experience.

Those people most directly affected were those whose jobs or inclinations took them overseas as soldiers, sailors, traders, settlers, administrators or rulers. Generally the position of Britons overseas in the colonies reinforced their feelings of superiority over non-white peoples. Their contact with native peoples was generally in superior positions as representatives of the greatest world power at whose feet crouched over 100 million Hindus (Kiernan, 1969). No doubt many who went to work in the Empire were imbued with attitudes and feelings of superiority before they left Britain, but experience of and contact with native peoples reinforced these views and bred at best paternalism and at worst racism. The racial and class prejudices of Victorian England were strengthened in the colonies where Britons had greater power, higher status and more servants than they could command at home. As British rule was consolidated in new dominions, stricter separation of Europeans and natives was generally enforced and rigid codes of behaviour developed to maintain white superiority and prevent members of the white community 'going native'. The European clubs – exclusively reserved for officers and gentlemen – were well-known examples of the racial and class prejudice of the time (Orwell, 1935). They could be found all over the Empire and similar examples of social segregation can still be found in areas where European companies operate overseas. These small segregated outposts fostered exaggerated ideas of exclusiveness and superiority to which newcomers quickly learnt to conform. It was thus exclusive contact with the overseas white community rather than contact with native culture which fostered extreme racialist views.

It was not only the middle and upper classes who were involved in imperialism. The imperial legacy affected the whole nation. British workers at home and in the Empire were elevated by virtue of their membership of the ruling power. Class distinctions remained important among the British in colonial territories but working-class Britons, usually soldiers or sailors, were entitled to status and superiority *vis-à-vis* the natives. A common identity and solidarity had to be maintained between the rulers and against the ruled. Moreover, British workers overseas, though often experiencing harsh conditions, had a far higher standard of living compared with native people and usually compared with their domestic situation at home. Many could aspire to higher status by emulating those higher class Britons with whom they came into closer contact in the colonial situation.

The prejudices and attitudes of superiority most strongly bred in the colonial situation were further disseminated among the population in Britain through the press and popular literature, especially comics which were often extremely nationalistic and racist. Contacts with relatives and friends who had served overseas was another source of information about life in the colonies. It was naturally a matter of great pride to belong to a country which ruled an Empire which straddled the globe. Imperial success contributed to feelings of patriotism and xenophobia which could then be exploited by press barons and politicians, as they were during both the Boer War and the First World War. These values, prejudices and stereotypes were taught and reinforced in schools, through subjects like history, geography and religious instruction. History became a procession of British victories over European and native peoples all over the globe. Geography was a means of learning the topography, fauna and products of Britain and the more exotic countries which made up the Empire and Common-wealth. Religious instruction enabled British children to learn about the work of missionaries and martyrs who struggled to take the light of the gospel to God's heathen children in central Africa, the islands of the South Pacific or elsewhere in the Empire. Missionaries played a major role in pioneering British intervention in Central and East Africa where, at great cost in lives due to the climate, they were campaigning against Arab slavers and inter-tribal warfare (Cairns, 1965). Both the Church Missionary Society and the Church of Scotland were extremely active in missionary work.

A considerable literature developed applauding Britain's imperial role and glorifying the enterprise, leadership and success of British explorers, soldiers and adventurers. Boys particularly were encouraged to admire and emulate such heroes as Clive of India and Woolfe of Quebec. Livingstone was admired for his explorations in Africa as much as for his missionary endeavour and Cooke for his discoveries in the South Pacific. Hundreds of books on the Empire provided exotic backgrounds for masterly adventure stories like *Prester John*, *King Solomon's Mines* and *Kim*. Writers like Henty, Ballantyne, Stevenson, Kipling and Buchan enjoyed enormous popularity. Popular comics made such heroes and adventures very widely available to children from all classes and in the scouting movement drew thousands of young boys and girls into a massively popular youth movement whose inspiration came from an imperialist adventure. Even in the era of imperial decline after the Second World War the myths and values of Empire have continued in a spate of films applauding the heroism and triumphs of the age of British imperialism, and the 'public school' Victorian virtues that they represented. These films have included *Lawrence of Arabia*, *Zulu*, *55 Days at Peking*, *Khartoum* and a host of lesser-known ones such as *The Four Feathers*.

However, while the indirect impact of the Empire through monuments, buildings, museums, ceremonies, literature, education and entertainment was considerable, it is worthwhile emphasising once again that substantial numbers of Britons had direct experiences of the Empire and Commonwealth. This was particularly true of the social and political élite who provided the governors, generals, administrators and missionaries, but it was also true of the working class who provided the 'footsoldiers of imperialism' (Rex and Tomlinson, 1979). Hundreds of thousands of families had members who had served in the army in India, the Far East, Egypt, Africa and the Americas. The navy and the merchant navy took seamen to every part of the globe. The two world wars illustrate the closeness in historical time of imperial influences. Hundreds of thousands of conscript British soldiers fought in Africa, the Middle East and the Far East as well as in Europe with African, Indian and other Commonwealth troops. They were part of the armed forces of a great world power which emerged from both world wars with the prestige of victory even though other powers shared the honours, allies without whom victory would not have been possible. These experiences tended to confirm opinions of British greatness among British troops even though British politicians were well aware of the economic and military weakness of the country after the wars.

A further legacy of Empire has been the migration and settlement of British families all over the world. The hope of adventure, wealth and a better future inspired millions of Britons to migrate overseas to North America, Australasia and Africa. Few British families can have been untouched by these massive movements of emigration. People of British descent can be found in the most far flung corners of the world, some of whom, like the Falkland islanders, have played a surprisingly important role in recent British politics. By the end of the nineteenth century migration had become a conscious part of Britain's imperial policy and it was felt that encouraging migration to various parts of the Empire (and Commonwealth) would assist the economic development of Dominion territories, strengthen the ties with Britain and increase the power of the Empire. Land grants and assisted passages were used to encourage people to migrate. After the First World War the self-governing Dominions became more selective in their demands for migrants, requiring skilled workers rather than agricultural workers, but there was no halt in the outward flow and between 1919 and 1930 2 million people emigrated from Great Britain and Northern Ireland. By this time it was widely recognised by British politicians that Britain's position as a world power depended upon her ability to command through loyalty or control the resources of her Empire and Commonwealth. Britain's own economic and military strength alone could not sustain her pre-eminent position in world affairs.

There has been considerable debate over whether the Empire existed solely for the enrichment and glorification of Britain or whether positive benefits were bestowed upon the subjects of the Empire. Some writers have viewed the British Empire as a benevolent trusteeship on behalf of less fortunate, backward peoples. One American wrote:

> Two blades of grass have grown where one grew before. Britain's flag wherever it has advanced has benefited the country over which it floats and has carried with it civilisation, the Christian religion, order, justice and prosperity. England has always treated a conquered race with justice and what under her law is the law for the white man is the law for his black and yellow brother . . . if injustice is done to him, the English courts are open to him for redress and protection as speedily and impartially as to any white man. (Huttenback, 1976)

This view of the Empire is too positive. The Empire originally developed so that Britons and Britain could be enriched, but once it had become established it developed a rationalising myth which caused British governments to be drawn into overseas commitments which were often expensive and which they strongly wished to avoid. The rationalising myth was that 'the role of the British Empire was to lead the world in the arts and civilisation, to bring light to dark places, to teach the true political method, to nourish and protect the liberal tradition. It was to act as trustee for the weak and to bring arrogance low' (Cross, 1968). It was an arrogant but a powerful myth which inspired many young Britons to seek positions in far distant places. It is impossible not to admire the missionaries who went to Central Africa with their families despite their knowledge that they were facing an environment likely to result in a speedy death, before which they were unlikely to have any impact on an indifferent African population. Many who volunteered for service as district officers and commissioners were inspired by positive motives. To read *A Pattern of Islands*, for example, is to read about a well-intentioned, benevolent administrator – a paternalistic and just ruler of the islanders of whom he had charge (Grimble, 1952). However, he was also a British administrator who ensured that British mining interests benefited from the discovery of bauxite and allowed commercial considerations to prevail over the long-term interests of those Pacific islanders.

The myth, moreover, had a powerful influence on many of those subject to British rule. Mahatma Gandhi, even after his experiences in South Africa in conflict with white settlers, maintained considerable admiration for the British Empire, which he believed was founded on spiritual rather than material foundations. 'I have always believed there is something subtle and fine in the ideals of the British constitution. Tear away those ideals and you tear away my loyalty to that constitution, keep those ideals and I am for ever a bondsman' (Huttenback, 1976). The ideals could not easily be sustained as Indians aspired to the highest administrative and political positions in their country and were forced to agitate more and more vigorously for independence.

The civilising role of European imperialism was much more strongly emphasised in the French imperial tradition. The French believed totally in the superiority of their culture, language and civilisation and made it a central part of their imperial policy to transform Senegalese, Taihitians, Algerians and Vietnamese into French men and women as far as possible. Thousands of French teachers were employed to teach the overseas French the language and culture of France. In turn representatives of the overseas departments were able to sit as deputies in the French parliament.

In the British Empire generalisations are difficult as British rule was an incredible hotch-potch of different forms and arrangements, cheap to run but inefficient in terms of developing an overall policy (Cross, 1968). Policies for economic development and educational advance were little developed before the First World War or, in most places, before the Second World War. Native populations were administered, not educated and trained. Often education was left to missionary activity. Administration was relatively efficient, law and order relatively fairly upheld and many officials displayed high degrees of honesty and service; but there was little investment except in areas where returns were high, such as mining, farming and forestry. As Marxist theories of imperialism gained support in the twentieth century there developed on the left widespread feelings of guilt at having been associated with the neglect of the colonies, and even more guilt at having been associated with and having benefited from the exploitation of colonial peoples.

In an important sense the colonies were the economic peripheries of the metropolitan colonial power. There was free movement of capital within the Empire and considerable movement of labour, though once it became clear that Asians were prepared to move and look for work all over the Empire the self-governing white Dominions quickly enacted legislation to control immigration (Huttenback, 1976). Nevertheless, Indians were recruited to work on the sugar plantations in the West Indies, Mauritius and Fiji, to build railways in East Africa, and to work on plantations in Australia and South Africa. The economies of the peripheral colonies were geared to the economic needs of the mother country and these economic links forged strong ties. Education in the colonies, for those who received any, focused on the language, history, religion and political values of the colonial power, thus reinforcing the economic and political links that already existed. These economic and cultural links were to provide powerful reasons for the later postwar migration from the colonial periphery to the metropolitan centre.

'CIVIS BRITANNICUS SUM'

Another factor that was to be of crucial importance to the migration of West Indians and Asians after the Second World War and which facilitated this migration was the common citizenship which all British subjects in all parts of the Empire enjoyed. In a formal sense there was no legal definition of British citizenship and nationality before the twentieth century. As Britain extended her rule to new territories and colonies the people in these new Dominions of the king became new subjects owing him allegiance. It had been decided in the Calvin case (1607) that a subject's allegiance was owed personally to the king and not to the kingdom. This feudal interpretation of allegiance overcame the political problem which was created after the Union of the Crowns in 1603 when the two kingdoms of England and Scotland were united under one king (Dummett, 1976). As the Empire was created and expanded the law of England was considered to apply to the colonies as well as to Britain. There was no distinction between the 'subject' status of Britons at home or overseas. Even when some of the overseas

Dominions were granted home rule, like Canada and Australia, and began to govern themselves, their inhabitants retained the status of British subjects. They did not acquire by their independence any new citizenship or nationality. This was the case until 1946, when Canada passed its own citizenship law. Thus in the heyday of Empire British subjects populated a quarter of the world. Many of these were native Britons and their descendants who had migrated and settled throughout the Empire, but many more were natives of the territories conquered by Britons and annexed to the Empire. These people were British subjects and shared a common allegiance to the monarch because they had been born in His Majesty's Dominions, but they were not British by birth or descent. This allegiance involved powerful obligations and duties such as obedience to established authority and to English law, and commitments to the mother country, such as service in war. In return the monarch had obligations to protect his subjects and provide good government. These obligations and allegiances were not a meaningless facade. When war was declared in 1914 the whole Empire was committed to the war and there was a remarkable demonstration of imperial solidarity. India sent four divisions in the first weeks of the war to join the British Expeditionary Force and by the end of the war a million and a quarter Indians had seen service outside India. Even after four years of conflict Indian support was undiminished. On 29 April 1918 Gandhi was still writing to Lord Chelmsford, 'It is clear to me that we should give the Empire every available man for its defence' (Tinker, 1976, p. 31).

As English law made no distinction between subject and citizen, all subjects were in law citizens. The distinction that was made was between subjects and aliens. Aliens were those who owed no allegiance to the British Crown. Gradually the fact that any British subject, no matter what his or her colour or creed, could come to the mother country, serve in the armed forces or public service, stand for Parliament and enjoy the same rights and obligations as any other Briton came to be subsumed under the grandiose notion '*Civis Britannicus sum*' and became part of the ideology which legitimised British rule in the Empire.

However, within the Empire all British subjects were not treated equally, and as the self-governing white colonies moved towards self-government they demanded the right to determine the composition of their populations. By the mid-nineteenth century there was already agitation in Australia, South Africa and Canada to control Asian immigration and various devices were invented to secure this control (Huttenback, 1976). The question of common immigration policy was raised at the Imperial Conference which met in 1911 but only Britain was in favour of the free movement of people within the Empire and it was agreed that each Dominion should be allowed to decide for itself which elements it desired to accept in its population (Tinker, 1976, p. 28). Britain's support for free movement was partly because it felt this was incumbent upon it as the centre of the Empire and Commonwealth, but also in the expectation that the major movement would continue to be an outflow from Britain.

By 1948 the Labour government had granted independence to India, Pakistan, Burma and Ceylon. It was clear that these countries would wish, like Canada, to enact their own citizenship legislation whether they remained in the Commonwealth or not. In order to clarify the whole question of British citizenship and nationality the government introduced a British Nationality Bill. This Bill proposed two classes of British citizen: first, citizens of independent Commonwealth countries and secondly, the remainder, who were called citizens of the United Kingdom and Colonies. It is interesting to note that the subjects of independent Commonwealth countries who now had their own citizenship were to remain British citizens as well and would continue to have the rights of *'Civis Britannicus sum'*. The government wished that the links and unity developed during the history of Empire could be continued, albeit more on a basis of partnership, as the Empire evolved into the Commonwealth. In fact the Conservative opposition attacked the Bill as unnecessary and as undermining the unity of the Commonwealth because, by giving primacy to local citizenship, the derivative British nationality would gradually decline in importance and eventually lapse. Sir David Maxwell Fyfe, who led Tory opposition to the Bill, reserved the opposition's right to revert to the old common citizenship if this should be the wish of the other Dominions and member states of the Commonwealth. He was also concerned lest the provisions for separate categories of citizens might be used to discriminate against Commonwealth citizens, arguing that there would be no point in these new categories unless there was some intention of dropping the idea of the common status of all British citizens and our proud boast of the open door. 'We are proud', he stated, 'that we impose no colour bar restrictions making it difficult for them when they come here . . . we must maintain our great metropolitan tradition of hospitality to everyone from every part of our Empire' (*Hansard*, 7 July 1948, col. 405).

This debate took place shortly after the end of the Second World War at a time when the Conservative Party still considered itself to be the party of the Empire. While India, Pakistan, Burma and Ceylon had gained their independence, all expect Burma had remained in the Commonwealth – accepting the king as head of the Commonwealth. Moreover, while these were all fairly advanced countries with educated leaders and competent administrations, it was thought that other colonies were very far from independence. A United Nations Trusteeship Committee report which recommended that Britain should prepare Tanganyika for independence envisaged the earliest realistic date as being 1985. In fact Tanganyika was granted independence in 1961. Indian claims to independence were widely accepted even by the Conservatives who realised that India's contribution to the war, some 2 million men under arms, deserved at least Dominion status. Nevertheless, even in 1949 in a pamphlet on imperial policy the Conservative Party could state that 'The Empire and Commonwealth is the supreme achievement of the British people and the most successful experiment in international relations that the world has ever known' (Conservative Central Office, June 1949a).

The Conservative Party, which was to return to power in 1951, was therefore committed to common citizenship for all British subjects in the Empire and to freedom of movement for both labour and capital. A Conservative policy document also published in 1949 stated: 'There must be freedom of movement among its members within the British Empire and Commonwealth. New opportunities will present themselves not only in the countries overseas but in the mother country and must be open to all citizens' (Conservative Central Office, July 1949b). It was of course assumed that the major movement of population would continue to be an outward one from Britain to the Old Dominions and to the climatically suitable parts of Africa such as Rhodesia and the Kenyan highlands, but it was emphasised that a welcome should be extended to all those who wished to come from the Dominions and colonies to live and work in Britain. As was stated by Henry Hopkinson, Minister of State for the Colonies, 'In a world in which restriction on personal movement and immigration have increased we can still take pride in the fact that a man can say *'Civis Britannicus sum'*, whatever his colour may be, and we take pride in the fact that he wants to and can come to the mother country' (*Hansard*, 5 November 1954, col. 827).

CONCLUSION

It is extremely hard to assess the legacy of over 300 years of British imperialism. The legacy is at the same time intangible and all-pervasive. It affects the West Indian migrants to Britain and their descendants whose African origin is clear but whose forefathers' culture was destroyed by slavery and who were brought up in the culture of the slave-owners and colonial rulers. It influences the Asians who were encouraged to migrate to all parts of the Empire as coolie labour but were refused admission by the Old Dominions once they were perceived as settlers. In East Africa their economic success caused first resentment and then expulsion as decolonisation removed the protection they had enjoyed from the imperial power. Finally the

British citizenship they had retained as security in case of anti-Asian action by the new regimes was devalued when it was most needed. The legacy of imperialism continues to affect the view British citizens have of the worth of different national and racial groups. A survey carried out by the Colonial Office in Britain in 1948 of public attitudes towards the colonies found both a widespread lack of knowledge and widespread perceptions that coloured people were primitive, uncivilised and pagan (Little, 1948). A more recent survey investigating attitudes of the British to other people found that 65 per cent thought the British were superior to Africans, 61 per cent thought they were superior to Asians, 36 per cent thought they were superior to other Europeans and 33 per cent thought they were superior to Americans (Rose *et al.*, 1969). While nationalism is clearly involved in these responses, the Victorian view of a hierarchy of different races in the world seems to be reflected as well.

Since the Second World War, decolonisation has proceeded at an extremely rapid rate but it is clear that the attitudes associated with imperialism are far harder to emancipate than the colonies themselves. By 1981 Britain had divested herself of almost all her colonies save a handful of islands. However, the same government which granted independence to Zimbabwe, the last major colony in Africa, could still go to war over barren islands over 8,000 miles from Britain. Moreover this war, which was fought in defence of less than 1,000 kith and kin who had been subject to invasion from Argentina, evoked a considerable emotional response from a people who had apparently quietly accepted the rapid decline of Britain as a world power in the postwar period. The sailing of the naval task force to the South Atlantic clearly struck a strong nationalistic chord in a nation used to being a great naval power but starved of recent military or economic success. The Falklands war, though highly expensive, played a major role in re-establishing the credibility of a government losing popular esteem in a world recession but which, after victory was secured, proceeded to secure re-election with a substantial majority.

CHAPTER 2

Migration to Britain

It is always difficult to pinpoint historical causes and turning points, and the origins and causes of New Commonwealth immigration to Britain are no exception. Many writers on this migration take as their starting point the arrival of the *Empire Windrush* in June 1948 which docked at Tilbury with 492 intending migrants from Jamaica (Braham, 1982). Others argue that the origins go back to the 1930s when the depression and consequent high levels of unemployment led to considerable unrest and rioting in Jamaica, Barbados and Trinidad. As a result of these disturbances a Royal Commission was established in 1938 to investigate social and economic conditions in the West Indies. It concluded that considerable expenditure was needed on social services and economic development and recommended that the British government should also encourage investment to help to alleviate poverty and unemployment (*West Indian Royal Commission 1938–39*, 1945). Years of economic neglect had finally erupted into violence and the colonial government would have had to take drastic action in response to these manifestations of frustration and resentment if the Second World War had not broken out.

Certainly the preconditions for migration existed in the West Indies. The prosperity and expansion of the sugar industry which had made Jamaica and the other islands the jewels of Empire in the seventeenth and eighteenth centuries had required a very substantial labour force to work the plantations. This labour force was first made up of African slaves and their progeny and later of indentured labour imported from India. The prosperity of the British sugar islands was undermined in the nineteenth century by free trade which ended their privileged access to the British market and exposed them to competition from other sugar producers, especially Cuba and Brazil. Towards the end of the nineteenth century the growth of the sugar beet industry in Europe and North America also undermined the economic position of the islands. As the West Indies fell into relative economic decline they were left with populations which were too large for their economies to support easily. Only Jamaica and mainland Guyana with their bauxite industries and Trinidad with its oil were in a position to sustain significant rates of economic growth. Generally the islands were characterised by high population densities, high levels of unemployment, low gross domestic product per capita and low rates of economic growth.

Jamaica, which was by far the largest British island, had long had a tradition of migration. Jamaicans migrated to Panama to help to build the railways in the 1850s and between 1880 and 1921 a considerable emigration took place as opportunities for work occurred in other parts of the Caribbean region. Jamaicans found work on the construction of the Panama Canal and on the sugar and banana plantations on the central American mainland. Many others sought work in the USA and Venezuela. The depression of the 1920s and 1930s limited opportunities for employment and between 1921 and 1941 no net emigration took place (Peach, 1968).

It has been argued that push factors were the primary cause of migration from the West Indies to Britain after the war (Glass, 1960, pp. 6–7): such factors as unemployment, population growth and the cutting off of alternative outlets for migration such as the Walter-McCarren immigration act of 1952 which for a time almost halted West Indian emigration to the United States. It is more likely that while these push factors, namely poverty, unemployment, population growth and lack of opportunities, were necessary conditions for migration to take place, they were not sufficient. These conditions had existed before in the 1920s and 1930s when little emigration took place. Moreover these conditions varied considerably between the islands (and British mainland territories) even from year to year, but once the migration flow was under way the trends from the different areas showed great similarity. It is therefore likely that they were reacting to a strong external stimulus, namely labour shortage in Britain (Peach, 1968). It appears therefore that it was the pull factors of job vacancies, better opportunities and prospects of a higher standard of living which were decisive in attracting West Indians and later Asians to Britain. This analysis is strengthened by the finding that migration from the West Indies to Britain in the 1950s was closely linked to job vacancies. Migration rose and fell according to the labour needs of the British economy. There was a slight time lag of three months and, as one would expect, male immigration was the most sensitive to changes in labour market conditions.

The crucial factors initiating the migration to Britain were the Second World War and the experiences of many West Indians stationed in Britain. The continuing shortage of labour after the war stimulated and sustained the migration. This was due to the postwar reconstruction and the great boom in the European economies which occurred in the 1950s and 1960s. These factors combined to create the crucial conditions necessary for migration.

Before the First World War very few black people lived in Britain, though black people, often brought to England as slaves or servants, had been common in earlier times (Walvin, 1973). During the First World War, however, many colonial seamen served in the merchant navy and some settled in such seaport towns as Liverpool, Cardiff, London and North and South Shields. However, these communities suffered high levels of unemployment, partly because of the economic depression, but more so on account of racial prejudice. They were usually confined to the most run-down parts of the towns and relations with the rest of the local population were often antagonistic. There were a number of quite serious racial disturbances immediately after the war (Ministry of Labour, 1948; May and Cohen, 1974). However, the postwar depression and continuing heavy unemployment between the wars provided no incentive for further immigration and these settlements remained small.

The outbreak of the Second World War in 1939 caused a dramatic change in the whole situation. Black colonial workers were recruited and brought to Britain to help in the war effort. Others came voluntarily. The major examples of official government recruitment schemes were first, a group of 1,200 British Hondurians who were recruited to fell timber in Scotland; secondly, about 1,000 West Indian technicians and trainees who were recruited for service in war factories in Merseyside and Lancashire (Mr Leary Constantine, later Lord Constantine, was employed by the Ministry of Labour as welfare officer to look after this group of men during their war service); thirdly, 10,000 West Indians recruited for service in the Royal Air Force to work in Britain as ground crews; and fourthly, some thousands of colonial seamen either recruited or enlisted in the merchant navy. Large numbers of them were engaged to fill casual vacancies and not all were based at British ports (Cabinet Papers, 1950).

After 1941 there had also been a substantial increase in the number of colonial stowaways who came mainly from West Africa and the West Indies, as well as colonial passengers and seamen coming to Britain. In 1942 it was made easier for colonial subjects to enter Britain as restrictions on landing without documentary evidence of British nationality were lifted after representations from colonial governments. It was felt that all British subjects were contributing equally to the war effort and that there should not be restrictions on particular groups. Due to the shortage of labour caused by the war these colonial migrants had no difficulty in finding employment.

The war was a crucially important catalyst for postwar migration. Large numbers of colonial peoples were uprooted from their home communities. Men serving abroad had their horizons widened and they saw opportunities for work in Europe. Those colonial servicemen who saw war service in Britain did so under particularly favourable conditions. They were well received and well treated by members of the British public who saw them as allies in the struggle for national survival. Colour prejudice and discrimination in housing and employment which had been a serious factor facing black people already settled in the seaport towns was greatly reduced during the war.

Most of those men recruited under the special schemes were eligible for gratuities and repatriation at the end of the war, but although persistent efforts were made to induce as many of them as possible to return home, a substantial number preferred to remain in Britain (Cabinet Papers, 1950). Nearly half the British Hondurians, for example, preferred to settle in Scotland and the north of England and one-fifth of the West Indians who were repatriated to Jamaica, finding themselves unemployed and with little prospect of finding jobs, spent their gratuities on returning to Britain on troopships repatriating later colleagues.

It is clear that the British government was not enthusiastic at the prospect of recruiting substantial numbers of colonial workers even though the economy was suffering substantial labour shortages. In fact the government was making considerable efforts to recruit workers from the displaced persons camps in Germany and from Italy. It was even persuading German ex-prisoners of war to stay to work in Britain. The Polish Resettlement Act established a Polish Resettlement Corps to help the Polish soldiers who did not wish to return to Poland to find jobs and to settle in Britain. These 120,000 Poles were, despite union opposition, quickly absorbed into the labour market although often in jobs far below their skills and education. The European Volunteer Workers Scheme was an arrangement by which male and female workers were recruited from displaced persons camps in Germany under rather harsh conditions which the Labour government adopted to mollify union fears of competition for employment. These conditions were that European volunteer workers who came to Britain had to be assigned to particular jobs where serious labour shortages existed; they could not change jobs without permission; they had to belong to the relevant trade union; they could not be promoted over British workers; they would be the first to be made redundant if lay-offs occurred; and they could be deported immediately if they became unemployed, injured or disabled. These conditions could be lifted after four or five years. These tough conditions in fact rarely needed to be enforced as the postwar labour shortage continued, but even so many European volunteer workers further migrated to North America (Tannahill, 1958). There was also some recruitment of Italian workers at this time and considerable immigration from Ireland, which was uncontrolled. However, all these sources of labour were quickly absorbed and in fact were offset by the emigration of Britons to Commonwealth countries and to the United States.

Some colonial governments believed that British manpower requirements could be met by recruiting workers in those colonies which suffered high levels of unemployment, and pressed their views on the British government. In October 1948 an inter-departmental working party was established 'to inquire into the possibilities of employing in the United Kingdom surplus manpower of certain colonial territories in order to assist the manpower situation in this country and to relieve unemployment in those colonial territories (Ministry of Labour, 1948). The committee noted the serious unemployment situation in Jamaica and the shortage of labour in the United Kingdom, but was uncertain whether there was much scope for further recruitment as some 180,000 foreign workers (mainly Poles, Ukrainians and German ex-prisoners of war) had been allocated to vacancies in undermanned industries. The committee seemed to prefer European volunteer workers as these were subjected to strict labour controls and could be prosecuted or deported if they broke their conditions of recruitment. Colonial workers, being British subjects, were free from labour controls and could not be deported if they left the 'essential' jobs for which they were recruited. There was also a fear that colonial workers might find unemployment benefits so generous compared with earnings in the West Indies that there would be little incentive for them to seek employment at all (Ministry of Labour, 1948, para. 14).

The arrival in June 1948 of the *Empire Windrush* and its 492 unaided Jamaican immigrants was considered by the committee. These migrants had been warned before leaving Jamaica of the difficulties they were likely to meet in finding work and accommodation in the UK. Many of them had made no arrangements and their only plans were to land and then seek work. Owing to the size of the influx special steps were taken officially by members of the Colonial Office to meet them and give them assistance. As most of the men were skilled or semi-skilled the finding of work was not difficult and all the men were placed in jobs within three weeks. Temporary accommodation was provided, for those who had made no arrangements, at the Deep Shelter at Clapham South tube station. In September the *Orbita* arrived in Liverpool with 108 migrants from Jamaica and again they quickly found work. Although no one realised it at the time, a largely spontaneous migration of people had begun.

Despite the ease with which these migrants had found jobs, the inter-departmental committee was not convinced that colonial labour should be encouraged and in fact recommended that no organised large-scale immigration of male colonial workers should be contemplated (Ministry of Labour, 1948, para. 27). However, the committee noted that there were serious shortages of female workers in the textile industries and domestic employment, and felt that accommodation could be more easily arranged than in the case of male workers. There were also serious shortages of hospital domestic workers and 54,000 vacancies for nursing staff, but while the committee recommended the recruitment of a limited number of colonial workers as hospital domestics it did not recommend the recruitment of nursing staff, as the colonies themselves were short of such workers (paras 17–27).

In view of the continuing migration a further inter-departmental meeting was held at the Home Office on 18 February 1949 to consider what action should be taken by the relevant departments, namely the Colonial Office, the Home Office, the Ministries of Labour, Health and Transport, and the National Assistance Board. It was decided to concentrate action on the following recommendations:

(a) to press colonial governments to reduce the flow at source by making it known that jobs and accommodation in the United Kingdom are not too easily found, by not issuing passports to persons who cannot pay their passages or are obviously of the type who do not welcome regular employment and by imposing greater controls at the ports to prevent stowing away.

(b) to stiffen up immigration practice at UK ports by a return to the pre-1942 practice of requiring all arrivals from any destination to produce satisfactory evidence of British nationality.

(c) to set up a working party of representatives of the government departments concerned to tackle the problem of those colonials already here by dispersal, by finding employment and accommodation and by arranging for voluntary repatriation of the misfits. (Cabinet Papers, 1950, para. 11)

In March 1950 the Cabinet requested a memorandum from the Secretary of State for the Colonies on the immigration of coloured people from British colonial territories. It was presented to the Cabinet on 18 May. Coloured immigration was seen as causing problems in the areas of accommodation, employment and law and order, and the remedy was seen as discouraging the migrants, but the Secretary of State concluded:

My department has been under some pressure from parliamentary and public sources to take special action in the way of setting up clubs and providing welfare officers to attend to the needs of these people. It would, however, be a wrong policy to treat the colonial residents as a class apart from the community in general, though it must be recognised that they do need special guidance. Apart from the settled colonial community only some three or four thousand persons are involved and by careful and continual attention to their needs I am confident that the problem can be kept within bounds without out resort to any drastic measures. (Cabinet Papers, 1950, para. 13).

The concern of the Labour government with coloured immigration can also be seen by the request of the Cabinet to the Prime Minister at its meeting on 19 June 1950 to arrange for a further review of the means by which coloured people from British colonial territories might be checked and the implications of introducing control legislation (Cabinet Papers, 1951). This time the ad hoc committee set up under the Home Secretary's chairmanship was more positive in its conclusions. It argued that as the immigration of coloured people from British colonial territories was on such a small scale and as the issues of policy involved in control legislation were so important and controversial, no such legislation should be introduced. Even legislation to control the entry of stowaways would mean a break in the traditional policy of giving all British subjects the right to enter the UK and to enjoy the same rights and privileges as were given to UK citizens. It concluded that a very large increase in migration in the future might make legislation for control essential but that this was not justified at the present time (Cabinet Papers, 1951).

This rather discouraging attitude of the Labour government and its civil service advisers to colonial immigration is surprising given the fact that the economy was being held back by a serious shortage of labour and the government was attempting to alleviate this by a number of schemes to recruit European workers. It can partly be explained by the fears of Labour politicians and trade union leaders that the postwar boost in employment caused by postwar reconstruction and economic recovery might be shortlived as happened after the First World War. This also explains the hostility among the unions to the employment of Poles and European volunteer workers immediately after the war.

The establishment of a significant ethnic minority population in Britain was neither planned nor anticipated by policy-makers. The Royal Commission which published its report on population needs in 1949 had been concerned with the disadvantages of a falling population, especially as it did not wish to recommend discouraging British emigration to other parts of the Commonwealth, but it concluded that 'a systematic immigration policy could only be welcomed without reserve if the migrants were of good human stock [presumably European] and not prevented by religion or race from intermarrying with the host population and becoming merged with it' (Royal Commission on Population, 1949, pp. 226–7). The Commission doubted the capacity of an established society like Britain to absorb immigrants of an alien race and religion. The ability of colonial workers to integrate with and be accepted by the native population was a matter which had concerned the Colonial Office in recruiting such labour during the war but wartime conditions had facilitated their acceptance and integration. Once New Commonwealth immigration developed after the war the government proved very reluctant to intervene with either a policy of management or control. On the one hand the government did not wish to be seen to be encouraging such immigration; on the other hand policies of control would have disrupted relations with colonial and Commonwealth governments.

THE GROWTH OF IMMIGRATION

As can be seen from Table 2.1, migration from the West Indies gradually built up during the 1950s and was quickly followed by migration from the Indian sub-continent. As in the case of the West Indies, many of the early pioneers were seamen and servicemen. Once they found they could find work and establish themselves, they then informed relatives and friends of the opportunities available (Anwar, 1979). Once a tradition of migration is established it tends to gain a momentum of its own and people become drawn in through patronage and sponsorship by the early settlers and by imitation of and persuasion by friends. In the West Indies emigration to Britain caught the imagination of large numbers of the islanders and some islands quickly began to suffer labour shortages themselves. In India and Pakistan effective migration chains were established with the migration being based on sponsorship by friends and relatives. Indians, particularly those in the Punjab, had long had a tradition of migration for work and in the nineteenth century had settled all over the Empire. The Second World War, the violent and disruptive partition of India at independence and, in the early 1960s, the construction of the Mangla Dam uprooted hundreds of thousands of Punjabis and made them more willing to migrate (Anwar, 1979). Once migration to Britain was under way it was encouraged by the sponsorship of the early migrants and their reports of employment opportunities available and also by the operation of travel agents who made a good living encouraging migration (Deakin, 1970).

The historical links between Britain and the countries from which

Table 2.1 *Estimated Net Immigration from the New Commonwealth 1953–62*

	West Indies	India	Pakistan	Others	Total
1953	2,000				2,000
1954	11,000				11,000
1955	27,500	5,800	1,850	7,500	42,650
1956	29,800	5,600	2,050	9,350	46,800
1957	23,000	6,600	5,200	7,600	42,400
1958	15,000	6,200	4,700	3,950	29,850
1959	16,400	2,950	850	1,400	21,600
1960	49,650	5,900	2,500	−350	57,700
1961	66,300	23,750	25,100	21,250	136,400
1962*	31,800	19,050	25,080	18,970	94,900

* First six months up to introduction of first controls.
Source: House of Commons Library, 1976.

the migrants came meant that many of the migrants had knowledge of the English language, education system, cultural traditions and history. This was most obviously the case in the West Indies where the language, religion, educational system, culture and sport owed so much to centuries of British influence. The impact of British culture was much less pervasive in India and Pakistan but many of the early Asian migrants to Britain had experience in the British armed forces and some knowledge of the English language.

New Commonwealth immigrants came to Britain in search of work, a higher standard of living and better prospects for their children. The expansion of the British economy in the 1950s and 1960s created substantial shortages of labour, particularly in the relatively stagnant sectors of the economy, for example textiles, metal manufacture and transport, where low pay, long hours and shift work made the jobs unattractive to native workers. These industries were unable to compete with expanding sectors for native workers in short supply. In a few cases employers recruited directly; for example, Woolfe's in Southall recruited workers from the Punjab, London Transport set up an office in Barbados, and textile employers advertised in the Indian press. However, most migrants were not recruited directly but came unaided as voluntary migrants.

In periods of economic expansion the more prosperous regions of England with expanding industries quickly developed labour shortages which were partly filled by immigrant workers who concentrated in the major conurbations of Greater London, the West Midlands, Manchester, Merseyside and Yorkshire, where the best employment opportunities were to be found. Immigrant workers found work mainly as unskilled or semi-skilled workers. Research in the mid–1970s revealed substantial variations in the type of employment different groups occupied. In the extreme case of Pakistanis, 58 per cent of Pakistani men were found to be doing unskilled or semi-skilled work compared with 18 per cent of white men, while 8 per cent of Pakistanis compared with 40 per cent of whites were doing non-manual jobs. For Indians and West Indians the contrast was less extreme but still very great, with 36 per cent of Indians and 32 per cent of West Indians doing unskilled or semi-skilled manual work. All groups, particularly West Indians (59 per cent) were well represented in skilled manual grades but only Indians (20 per cent) and East African Asians (30 per cent) were well represented among non-manual occupations (Smith, 1977). New Commonwealth immigrants were found to be greatly over-represented in shipbuilding, vehicle manufacture, textiles, manufacturing in general and also in transport. West Indian women were heavily over-represented in the health service where there has been a long tradition of recruiting both nurses and domestic hospital staff from the West Indies. The health service has also recruited substantial numbers of New Commonwealth doctors, particularly from India, Pakistan and Bangladesh.

Immigrant workers thus formed a replacement labour force and found work mainly as semi-skilled and unskilled workers. They came in a period of labour shortage made more acute by the continuing willingness of Britons to emigrate overseas, particularly to Australia and North America. While the other major industrial countries of Western Europe were all recruiting very substantial increments to their labour forces from southern Europe, north Africa and Turkey to man their industries and fuel economic growth and expansion, Britain's gains to her labour force were more than offset by her even higher levels of emigration.

Table 2.2   *Net Migration to the United Kingdom*

1951–61	+12,000
1961–71	−320,000
1971–81	−306,000

Source: OPCS, 1982.

In Europe the migration of people from developing countries occurred later than in Britain, predominantly in the 1960s and 1970s. However, once it began, it continued on a substantial scale. It is estimated that the five major labour-receiving countries of France, Germany, the Netherlands, Sweden and Switzerland had over 4.5 million foreign workers in 1981. If their families were included, they had nearly 11 million foreign residents. These figures underestimate the numbers of immigrants because many migrant workers to France and the Netherlands came from colonies or former colonies and had French or Dutch citizenship. Furthermore, other countries such as Austria, Belgium and Luxembourg also had many migrant workers. Countries such as Germany which did not recruit from former colonies usually recruited foreign workers from countries with which they had close historical or geographical ties, for example Yugoslavia and Turkey in the German case.

One interesting contrast between Britain and other major European countries like France and Germany was lack of government planning and involvement in immigration policy once the migration developed. The French, of course, had a long tradition of concern about the size of their population and the need for people as a resource for military and economic needs. The enormous losses sustained by the French during the First World War led to policies to increase the birth rate and immigration, which latter involved labour contracts with countries like Poland and Italy, which were ended when the depression of the 1930s set in. French politicians and employers seem to have had a much better appreciation than the British of the economic importance of immigrant labour to create and sustain economic growth (Freeman,

Table 2.3   Foreign Workers in Europe by Country of Employment and Country of Origin 1981

(In thousands of country of employment)

Country of origin	Austria	Belgium	France	Germany	Luxembourg	Netherlands	Sweden	Switzerland
Algeria		3.2	382.1			0.2		
Austria				87.0				19.5
Finland				3.0			104.4	4.9
Greece				132.2		2.3	7.3	
Italy	2.1	90.5	157.6	316.1	9.2	10.5		234.9
Morocco		37.3	171.9			40.2		
Portugal		6.2	434.6	57.1	15.9	5.6		9.3
Spain	0.2	32.0	128.9	85.9	1.0	12.7		63.4
Tunisia		4.7	73.2			1.5		
Turkey	30.4	23.0		637.1		59.5		22.7
Yugoslavia	113.9	3.1		357.7	0.7	8.4	23.0	34.3
Other EEC	12.5	81.5	49.4	151.6	23.4	45.5	39.5	85.2
non-EEC	17.2	40.0	194.2	254.2	2.0	52.1	59.3	40.9
Total	176.3	332.2	1591.9	2081.9	52.2	238.5	233.5	515.1

Source: OECD Sopemi Report, 1982.

1979). Their government and employers co-operated to secure surplus value for France out of these cheap, insecure and dispensible workers. Even illegal immigration was encouraged as these workers were vulnerable to more ruthless exploitation. The French and German governments signed bilateral agreements with major labour-sending countries to secure the workers desperately needed by their expanding economies.[1] Some immigrants to France and Germany were of course citizens. In the German case immediately after the war millions of Germans came to the Federal Republic from lost German territories in the east and the German Democratic Republic. In the French case some migrant workers from the French colonies had French citizenship. But in countries like France and Germany foreign migrant workers were regarded as guestworkers, members of an industrial reserve army which enabled employers to keep their costs down, raise profits and contribute to higher living standards and economic growth. As they were predominantly young and fit they contributed more to the economy and social services than they took out and as foreigners were not entitled to full social and welfare benefits or to participate in politics. In the 1960s and 1970s, although there was evidence of racism in France, on the whole there was less hostility to immigrants than was the case in Britain as politicians and employers in France had been much more active in publicising the positive economic contribution of migrant workers and the economic necessity of importing them (Freeman, 1979).

CONCLUSION

British political leaders and civil servants appeared to be much less aware of the economic importance of migrant labour in creating and sustaining economic growth and prosperity than were their continental opposite numbers. They were much more aware of the problems of racial prejudice and discrimination that migrants might face: the difficulties of finding accommodation in the acute postwar housing shortage and the dangers of black immigrants being forced into ghettos. They were also aware that colonial immigrants were British subjects who could not be treated as a dispensible industrial reserve army like European volunteer workers or the foreign migrants to other European countries. Even though many migrant workers, particularly Asians, came as single men with every intention of making money and then returning home to buy land or businesses (Anwar, 1979), it was assumed by the government that many would wish to settle. As far as West Indian migrants were concerned, women formed a high proportion of migrants from the beginning of the migration (Peach, 1968), and settlement was therefore much more likely.

One of the most difficult problems early migrants faced was finding accommodation, and in the housing market, as in employment, the immigrants tended to fulfil a replacement role. They were forced to rent or buy cheap older housing in inner-city areas which were being vacated by native white families moving to new suburban housing estates away from city centres. They did not at first qualify, unless homeless, for local authority housing as these generally stipulated local residential qualifications (often five years' residence) which excluded new migrants. Gradually New Commonwealth immigrants achieved the residential qualifications necessary for local authority housing and this has resulted in a large movement of West Indian families into such housing. Nearly 50 per cent are now housed in this way. Asians have preferred to remain in owner occupation and continue to suffer from overcrowding, though this is declining (Home Office Research Study No. 68, 1981). Asian and West Indian children attend the same state primary and secondary schools as native children; however, because of the residential concentration of immigrant families, their children tend to go to schools where a high proportion of children are also Asian and West Indian (Rex and Tomlinson, 1979).

A considerable challenge was presented to the social services and local authorities by the gradual migration of substantial numbers of black immigrants from countries with rather different cultural traditions. The assumptions hitherto underlying services had provided for a homogeneous population with shared cultural and linguistic codes but these were rapidly eroded in areas of immigrant settlement. Moreover, the migration has been so substantial that integration is unlikely to be achieved as rapidly as with previous waves of migrants. Distinctive cultural patterns are likely to be maintained by such factors as childhood socialisation, residential segregation and as a result of reaction to the hostility and misunderstanding of the majority population. While in many respects immigrant families, because of their relative youthfulness, make less demands on the social services than the host population, they tend to live in areas of urban decline, their children may have special educational needs and they suffer high levels of unemployment, especially in periods of recession. Their cultural distinctiveness may require ethnically sensitive provision which some members of the majority may resent, feeling that immigrants should assimilate. Another danger is that special provision may also be seen as reducing scarce public resources and thus become a basis for resentment and political conflict (Ballard, 1979).

The response to colonial migration to Britain by politicians and policy-makers in the 1950s was hesitant and ambiguous, and little positive was done to assist their settlement, integration and acceptance. In contrast to the later migration of southern Europeans and Third World people to the continental countries, it was not welcomed as a response to manpower needs and a valuable asset in creating economic growth and sustaining higher living standards and prosperity. British policy-makers only tolerated it and would have liked to discourage it. They were aware from the beginning of the social and political costs of immigration, especially of the problems of racial prejudice that migrants would face and which might prevent the integration of black workers. The inter-departmental working party set up in 1947 had expressed concern at the possibility of an 'inassimilable minority' being created by migration and this is why it concluded that controls were the only practical solution (Deakin, 1972). What is surprising is that the Labour Cabinet did not believe that this prejudice could be overcome by a positive programme of public education, legislation or administrative action (Cabinet Papers, 1950, para. 12, iv). This sensitivity to the social and political costs of migration as well as the rather earlier arrival of colonial (or post-colonial) migrants partly explains why Britain moved to a position of instituting legislative controls rather earlier than other European countries. The economic gains, however, were also not as obvious as elsewhere. The growth in the British economy in the 1950s and 1960s was relatively slow compared with the other major European economies and was punctuated by crises over the balance of payments, the role of sterling as an international currency and by worries about inflation. It was also a period of rapid withdrawal from extensive imperial commitments overseas and a realisation by British leaders and people of declining world status. In this situation immigration was seen rather as an added burden than as a valuable asset. However, the major factor leading to the introduction of immigration controls was the popular hostility which manifested itself in a campaign for control. Given the private anxieties of policy-makers from the very beginning of New Commonwealth migration it could even be argued that controls were introduced more reluctantly and less quickly than might have been anticipated if these anxieties had been more widely realised. On the other hand a more positive early lead by the government and political leaders might have done much to assuage public anxieties. It is now appropriate to examine the popular reaction to New Commonwealth immigration and the development of the campaign for control which was eventually successful in politicising immigration as an issue and in obtaining immigration control legislation.

NOTE TO CHAPTER 2

[1] France signed agreements with Italy in 1946 and 1951, with West Germany in 1950, Greece in 1954, Spain in 1961, Morocco, Mali, Mauritania, Tunisia, and Portugal in 1963, Senegal in 1964, and Yugoslavia and Turkey in 1965 (Freeman, 1979, p. 74).

CHAPTER 3

The Campaign for Control

Explanations for the politicisation of the race issue and the success of the campaign for control of coloured immigration vary considerably. Some commentators have argued that politicians and the press stimulated popular concern over immigration and then used manifestations of such concern to justify the introduction of immigration controls (Foot, 1965; Dummett and Dummett, 1969; Rose *et al.*, 1969). The Dummetts in their passionate article on Britain's racial crisis place the blame squarely on successive Conservative and Labour governments whom they argue have allowed racists to set the terms of the debate and then have inflamed the situation even further by introducing racist immigration policies which have encouraged the racists to make further demands. Paul Foot takes a similar view when he argues that

> Commonwealth immigrants in Britain, before they become playthings of party politics, and despite a total lack of government concern or planning, were greeted with general friendliness and hospitality. Of course there was a colour bar in some pubs. Of course there was antagonism in some factories and bus garages. But these were exceptions. Overall the reaction was kind, even helpful. A considerate and co-ordinated effort by politicians to assist assimilation and to isolate and punish the racialist minority would have been decisive. (Foot, 1965, pp. 233–4)

In contrast, Donley Studlar has argued that while Britain has an élitist political system where policy-making is usually determined by an élite independent of and autonomous from the general public, on this issue public opinion has been so powerful and hostile to New Commonwealth immigration that policy-makers have had to concede to public demands. He argues that policy-makers, many of whom were liberal or socialist, have been reluctantly forced to give in to popular demands for immigration controls and then subsequently forced to introduce further controls once initial legislation came to be considered inadequate and ineffective (Studlar, 1974a, 1980; Hewitt, 1974). Some scholars have gone even further and argued that the general public widely believes that politicians responded too slowly to public concern over coloured immigration and allowed far too many immigrants into the country. Each tightening of immigration controls is thus seen as confirmation of the failures of past policies. Politicians have allowed, against the wishes of ordinary people, the creation of a substantial minority of British citizens who are widely seen as foreign intruders and illegitimate competitors for scarce resources. This, it has been argued, has made a considerable contribution to the general disillusionment with our party-political structure (Lawrence, 1978/9).

As has already been shown, the beginnings of the postwar migration of West Indians and other colonial workers to Britain did not pass unnoticed. Despite the serious labour shortage the Labour Cabinet and their civil service advisers were acutely aware of the social implications of a substantial immigration of black workers and had discussed how to prevent this happening even before the migration was substantially under way. The paper prepared for the Cabinet meeting in May 1950 by the Colonial Secretary had assumed that such a migration would be met by racial hostility, and the inter-departmental working party had also warned of the dangers of creating an inassimilable minority.

In public, however, there was little discussion. The arrival of the *Empire Windrush* was covered in the media and raised in the House of Commons by James Harrison who was concerned at the problems of accommodation and integration that the new migrants might face. He also raised the possibility of control but his concern was exceptional at this time (*Hansard*, 13 July 1948, col. 1160) and, as we know, the Labour Cabinet finally decided, three years after Harrison had raised the issue, that no action was necessary.

THE BEGINNINGS OF THE CAMPAIGN

When the Conservatives returned to office in 1951 there was a whole range of economic, social and foreign policy issues which appeared far more serious and urgent than the tiny level of immigration of black workers. However, a campaign against coloured immigration had already been initiated by Cyril Osborne, Conservative MP for Louth. His campaign was conducted in three arenas. First, he raised the matter in the House of Commons where he badgered government ministers with questions about disease and crime among black immigrants. Secondly, he campaigned within the Conservative Party where his views had considerably more support than they had in Parliament. Resolutions at the Central Council and the party conference demanding health checks on immigrants, the extension of powers of deportation and making Commonwealth immigrants subject to Aliens Acts were all passed in the mid-1950s. Thirdly, he attempted to galvanise public opinion by achieving maximum publicity for his views in the press. He was confident that his views commanded widespread support and gradually his sensationalist campaign achieved this latter aim (Pannell and Brockway, 1965).

In Parliament Osborne's questions were received coldly and with little consideration from Sir Anthony Eden, Harold Macmillan and other ministers who had to deal with them (*Hansard*, 24 January 1957, col. 392). Frequently in their replies ministers paid tribute to the contribution of West Indian nurses to the hospital service and of other immigrants to the manning of public transport and other industries. When the question of the need for immigration control was raised the response invariably was that the situation was under review but it was important to maintain the traditional ties between the United Kingdom and the Commonwealth (*Hansard*, 5 December 1958, cols 1579–80; Pannell and Brockway, 1965). The more Osborne pressed his campaign in the period 1952–8 the stronger became the government's public commitment to the principles of Commonwealth citizenship and the 'open door'. So in December 1958 David Renton could respond on behalf of the government to an Osborne motion by saying: 'This country is proud to be the centre of an inter-racial Commonwealth which, my Honourable Friend agrees, is the greatest assortment of peoples of all races, creeds and colours the world has ever seen. As a result of that we have always allowed any of the people in what was the Empire and is now the Commonwealth to come to this country and go from it as they please' (*Hansard*, 5 December 1958, cols 1579–80). The Cabinet thus gave every appearance of being determined not to interfere with the free movement of Commonwealth citizens.

This public stance was deceptive, however, as it is clear that some members of the Cabinet shared Osborne's concern and were in favour of control. Sir Winston Churchill reportedly told Sir Ian Gilmour in 1954 that 'Immigration is the most important subject facing this country but I cannot get any of my ministers to take any notice' (Bradley, 1978). Discussing Jamaican immigration to Britain with the Governor, Sir Hugh Foot, he said 'We would have a magpie society: that would never do' (Deakin, 1972). Harold Macmillan revealed in his memoirs that the problem of coloured immigration was brought to the attention of the Cabinet in 1954 and that early in 1955 after some rather desultory discussion it was agreed that a Bill should be tentatively drafted. 'I remember', he writes, 'that Churchill rather maliciously observed that perhaps the cry of "Keep Britain White" might be a good slogan for the election which we should soon have to fight without the benefit of his leadership' (Macmillan, 1973). In view of Churchill's earlier remarks it was perhaps only partly in jest, and illustrates the contradictory attitudes which permeated all levels of British society. The inter-departmental working party was reconvened yet again to consider ways in which controls would be introduced, but although it decided that a system of controls similar to those in operation for aliens was necessary, the Cabinet decided that no action should be taken. This decision was announced to the House in November 1955 (*Hansard*, 10 November 1955, col. 2005–6; Rose *et al.*, 1969, p. 209).

The reasons for this decision are quite clear. First, the level of West Indian and Asian immigration was very small; only a limited number of areas were affected and outside Parliament there was no pressure for control. Secondly, there remained a considerable shortage of labour and the balance of migration was negative, so that migrant workers were desperately needed. Thirdly, by the end of the 1950s it was clear that the transition from Empire to Commonwealth would proceed more quickly than Conservative leaders had earlier envisaged. A number of colonies were moving towards independence such as the Gold Coast which became independent, as Ghana, in 1957, and the Tory leadership realised that this transition would be hard for many Conservatives to accept. They hoped to cushion the decline of Britain's imperial role by emphasising her position as the leader of a great multi-racial Commonwealth. The Commonwealth ideal – the vision of a multi-racial partnership co-operating on terms of equality in political, economic and cultural matters – was to replace the old-fashioned and increasingly untenable myth of British imperial greatness. It was crucial for the success of this policy that Britain's relations with Commonwealth countries, and especially those colonial countries in Africa, Asia and the West Indies which would form an increasingly important majority in the evolving Commonwealth, should not be jeopardised. The colonies approaching independence, having no special ties of kinship or culture with Britain, had to be persuaded that membership of the Commonwealth was worthwhile and would not compromise either their independence or status as Third World countries. The imposition of immigration controls, particularly if seen to be racist, would have threatened Britain's moral authority as leader, or at least *primus inter pares*, of the Commonwealth. The fact that Britain alone in the Commonwealth kept to the principle of common citizenship and freedom of movement for all Commonwealth citizens appeared to give her a moral authority and a central position which Conservative leaders felt was too valuable to discard lightly. This view became the dominant view in the Colonial and Commonwealth Office and was strongly represented in the Cabinet by the ministers in charge of colonial and Commonwealth relations. These ministers consistently advocated the views of their departments and of the colonial governments they represented by opposing the imposition of controls whenever the matter was raised.

Other Commonwealth issues were less important but carried some weight. The imposition of controls would have hurt the West Indian economies and undermined the difficult negotiations preceding the ill-fated attempt to establish a West Indian Federation. Difficulties were also emerging over the future of the colonies in East and Central Africa, particularly with regard to their white settler minorities. Initial Labour Party support for the proposed Central African Federation which would have united Northern and Southern Rhodesia and Nyasaland was withdrawn because of fears that the white minority in Southern Rhodesia would retain political and economic control. Thus the bipartisan government and opposition approach to Commonwealth affairs appeared to be breaking down. In this situation a decision to control Commonwealth immigration would have been highly controversial (Rose *et al.*, 1969). The government therefore preferred informal arrangements, and when immigration from India and Pakistan began to rise after 1955 it negotiated directly with these governments to restrict the flow at source. Both the Indian and Pakistani governments agreed to do this by restricting the issuing of passports and requiring financial deposits from intending migrants (Hiro, 1973, p. 107).

THE POPULAR RESPONSE

Popular reaction to New Commonwealth immigration was originally confined to the areas of settlement which were mainly parts of London and major towns in the Midlands and north of England. In the employment sector there were attempts to exclude black workers from certain occupations or to restrict them to the lowest grades (Beetham, 1970), but these efforts were the actions of local work groups and trade union branches. Nationally trade union leaders gave a warmer welcome to black immigrants, presumably because they were British citizens, than they had to the Polish ex-combatants and European volunteer workers (Miles and Phizacklea, 1977b). No doubt they also wished to avoid accusations of racism. Gradually as the labour shortage continued and as employers and workers grew accustomed to working with black workers many of the early difficulties were overcome. But outside the work situation there was considerable resentment towards black immigrants, often associated with housing problems (Glass, 1960; Patterson, 1965; Deakin, 1965). The new black workers were being forced to settle in urban areas in decline. These inner-city areas were being vacated by white families moving to the suburbs and the white residents who remained behind often associated the falling status of their area with the new black residents (Foot, 1965; Patterson, 1965; Rex and Moore, 1967; Rex and Tomlinson, 1979). There were also accusations in some areas that landlords were using black tenants to push out whites in controlled tenancies to realise higher rents and property values (London Labour Party, 1955; Deakin, 1965). In 1957

Marcus Lipton, the Labour MP for Brixton, and a man who had worked hard for good race relations in his constituency, drew attention to these problems in an adjournment debate on the housing problem in London. He outlined some of the problems being experienced in his constituency: the general difficulty of West Indian immigrants in finding accommodation, and specific problems between neighbours and over controlled tenancies. Other London Labour MPs raised similar difficulties which were being experienced in their constituencies (*Hansard*, 22 November 1957, cols 743–5). Lipton himself was coming under pressure from his white, working-class constituents and was worried that local Conservatives might use the issue against him. The failure of central government to provide local authorities with additional funds to alleviate the shortage of housing and accommodation in areas of immigrant settlement was a factor contributing to inter-racial hostility.

THE 1958 RIOTS

The campaign for control gained considerable impetus in the latter half of 1958. The racial disturbances in Nottingham and Notting Hill in August and September dramatically publicised the problems of integration and apparent public hostility to continued coloured immigration. These were not, of course, the first incidents of inter-racial violence in the postwar period. In Birmingham in May 1948 a crowd of white men variously estimated at between 100 and 250 besieged and stoned a hostel where Indian workers were living. In August 1948 there were two days of mob violence and racial attacks in Liverpool and in July 1949 Deptford was the scene of a serious disturbance. In August 1954 there were two days of inter-racial violence in Camden Town (Glass, 1960). Sporadic attacks by white youths on black men were not uncommon in the 1950s and had given rise to the term 'Paki-bashing'. However, the violence in 1958 forcibly brought the issue of coloured immigration to the attention of the national press, politicians and the wider public living outside the areas of immigrant settlement. In both Nottingham and Notting Hill the disturbances lasted several days and involved many hundreds of people. Hostile crowds of 1,500 and 4,000 were reported to be involved in the Nottingham disturbances and crowds of 200, 400 and 700 participated in some of the Notting Hill attacks. In London some 140 people were arrested during the four main days of the disturbances between 30 August and 3 September 1958. Mr Norman Manley, Prime Minister of Jamaica, and Mr Carl Lacorbinière, Deputy Chief Minister of the West Indian Federation, flew to London for consultations and a tour of the riot areas. They rejected officials' suggestions concerning control of West Indian immigration at source, saying that control was a matter for the UK government.

There were two immediate reactions to the riots. First, there was widespread condemnation of the violence by politicians, church leaders and leader writers in the press; and generally young hooligans were blamed. Gaitskell wrote in *The Times* (4 September 1958), 'Whatever local difficulties there may be, nothing can justify the riots and hooliganism of the past few days'. There was also widespread satisfaction with Lord Justice Salmon's deterrent sentence on nine youths convicted for assault during the disturbances and his forthright condemnation of their actions: 'You are a minute and insignificant section of the population who have brought shame on the district in which you lived and have filled the whole nation with horror, indignation and disgust. Everyone, irrespective of the colour of their skin, is entitled to walk through our streets erect and free from fear. This is a right which these courts will always unfailingly uphold.' (Rose *et al.*, 1969, p. 214)

The second reaction to the riots was to assume that they were a response by host populations who felt under pressure from the new immigrant population and that the answer was immigration control. The numbers involved in the riots suggested that it was not only young thugs who were implicated and that they represented the most extreme manifestation of a more widespread resentment of, and hostility towards, coloured immigration. According to Glass (1960, p. 146), 'The trouble-makers of Notting Hill acted out tendencies which were latent in all social strata. They were shouting what others were whispering.' The local MP for Notting Hill, Mr George Rogers, put forward this view and called for controls. More significant was the statement of Sir Alec Douglas-Home, Minister of State for Commonwealth Relations, who, speaking in Vancouver, said that 'curbs will have to be put on the unrestricted flow of immigrants from the West Indies'. This was the first time a minister associated with Commonwealth affairs admitted that one of the major principles of Commonwealth policy would have to be abandoned. Later the same month (October 1958) the Conservative party conference passed a resolution favouring immigration control. The government, however, refused to be panicked into jeopardising the time-honoured principle of allowing free entry to Commonwealth and colonial subjects (*The Times*, 4 September 1958).

The riots had alerted the media to the news – or sensationalist – value of the immigration issue. A poll in the *Daily Express* (quoted by C. Osborne, *Hansard*, 5 December 1958, col. 1563) showed overwhelming public support for immigration control.

	For Control	No Action	Don't Know
Nationally	79.1%	14.2%	6.7%
London Area	81.5%	11.2%	7.3%

A Gallup poll taken immediately after the riots found that 92 per cent had read about the riots and while 27 per cent blamed whites for causing them and only 9 per cent blamed blacks, 35 per cent blamed both. This poll found less support than the *Express* poll for immigration control but a substantial majority appeared to favour some controls, with only 21 per cent opposed to any at all (Social Surveys, 1958). The Gallup poll did discover substantial levels of prejudice so that 71 per cent were opposed to mixed marriages, 61 per cent said they might or would definitely move if substantial numbers of black people settled in their neighbourhood and 54 per cent opposed the view that black and white people should be subject to the same conditions for entry on to council house waiting lists.

Cyril Osborne immediately stepped up his campaign for control. His parliamentary efforts had been supported since 1955 by Norman Pannel (Kirkdale), Martin Lindsey (Solihull) and Harold Gurden (Selly Oak), and they were encouraged in their efforts both by the riots and by their success at the Conservative conference in October, which passed a resolution, despite Butler's opposition, favouring immigration controls. Osborne raised the issue in the debate on the Queen's Speech in October and again in a private motion in December where Lindsey made it clear that it was coloured immigration and not immigration as such which should be controlled. 'We all know perfectly well that the core of the problem is coloured immigration. We must ask ourselves to what extent we want Great Britain to become a multi-racial community . . . A question which affects the future of our own race and breed is not one we should merely leave to chance.' David Renton, replying for the government, propounded the official policy which was that this country was proud to be the centre of an inter-racial Commonwealth and denied that there was any need for control (*Hansard*, 5 December 1958, cols 1579–80). However, the *Economist* (29 November 1958) reported shortly before the debate that the view in many civil service departments was that controls could not be long postponed.

Immigration was not an issue in the General Election of 1959 except in one or two local contests such as North Kensington where Sir Oswald Mosley attempted to exploit the tensions revealed by the previous year's riots. Mosley came bottom of the poll and lost his deposit despite a well-publicised campaign. The public pressure for control thus seemed to be minimal. However, one result of the General Election had been the election of a strong contingent of Conservative MPs from Birmingham, most of whom favoured controls, and these were to strengthen greatly the support for control inside Parliament. The government remained reluctant to take action. In the Cabinet Boyle and Macleod were the leading opponents of control and the Cabinet appeared unwilling to override their opposition. Most ministers still regarded the Commonwealth as a major asset to British standing and diplomacy in the world and were extremely reluctant to take any action which might undermine its unity and attractiveness, particularly to potential members, that is, those colonies which were rapidly moving towards full independence. There were also strong economic reasons favouring immigration as the most prosperous areas of the country in the West Midlands and the south-east continued to suffer from labour shortages which hindered economic expansion, and these were the areas to which immigrants were attracted.

In October 1960 no provision was made for a debate on immigration at the annual Conservative Party conference, although there were seven resolutions advocating control sent in from constituency associations. On 13 October the Birmingham Immigration Control Association was established and this strengthened the hands of those Birmingham MPs who were pressing for control. In December and again in January 1961 Harold Gurden organised a series of meetings of backbench MPs to discuss control and lobby the Home Secretary. In February Butler told Gurden he was prepared to consider controls but there was still no agreement in the Cabinet on the need for positive action. In reply to a Private Member's Bill introduced by Cyril Osborne on 17 February, David Renton said again to the House that the government refused to contemplate legislation which might restrict the historic right of every British subject regardless of race or colour freely to enter and stay in the United Kingdom (Hansard, 17 February 1961, cols 2009–19).

THE CAMPAIGN SUCCEEDS

By the summer of 1960 it was clear that a very substantial rise in West Indian immigration was taking place, and further attempts to persuade the Jamaican government to control the flow by passport restrictions were unsuccessful. Moreover in India the Supreme Court ruled that it was unconstitutional for the Indian government to refuse to issue passports to its nationals and this raised the possibility of substantial migration from a virtually limitless source. The growing political campaign for control in Britain was itself stimulating immigration as intending migrants rushed to beat the possible introduction of restrictions. In May 1961 the Gallup poll found that 73 per cent of the population favoured controls, 21 per cent free entry, with 6 per cent undecided. There were thirty-nine resolutions sent in from constituency associations for debate at the annual conference demanding control, and while Butler made no commitment to introduce a Bill in his reply to the debate on immigration, the strength of feeling at the conference and the dramatic rise in numbers coming in convinced the Cabinet that action was urgently needed. A Bill was hurriedly prepared, the decision to legislate was announced in the Queen's

Speech on 31 October and the Bill was published the following day.

Thus occurred the conversion of the Conservative Party from free entry for all Commonwealth citizens to the 'little England' policy of immigration control. The change coincided with the decline of Britain from being a great imperial power with world-wide territories and commitments to a European power which was making tentative efforts to join the EEC as the alternative vision of political, economic and cultural co-operation in a multi-racial Commonwealth faded. The withdrawal from Empire was sporadic and often difficult as the fighting in Cyprus, Kenya and Malaya showed. Nevertheless it proceeded rapidly after the Suez fiasco in 1956 and, surprisingly, under Conservative administration. The withdrawal from Empire was hard for some Conservatives to accept as their vision of the Commonwealth was as a perpetuation of the Empire with Britain continuing to act as the leader or at least as the focal point. For this reason many of these imperial Conservatives were reluctant to see any weakening of Commonwealth unity which might result from legislation against Commonwealth citizens. Lady Huggins, the wife of a former Governor of Jamaica, gave expression to this view when she said:

> The increase in West Indian immigration in recent years has created domestic difficulties in this country. But what is the Commonwealth worth? Is domestic difficulty here an adequate reason for abandoning the whole concept of the Commonwealth? If we are not prepared to pay that price we shall imperil our whole colonial policy and our whole Commonwealth ideal'. (Foot, 1965, p. 155)

Thus a commitment to the Empire and its successor, the Commonwealth, was felt by many Conservatives, especially those who had served as soldiers or administrators in the colonies. These Conservatives rather regretted Britain's imperial decline and opposed the move towards the EEC. However, during the 1960s they were to become increasingly disillusioned with the Commonwealth ideal as New Commonwealth members refused to show the loyalty and support which Britain had received in the past from the Old Dominions and the Empire. The Suez crisis in 1956, when Britain was strongly condemned by members of the New Commonwealth for the invasion, the withdrawal of South Africa in 1961 from the Commonwealth and the collapse of the Central African Federation in 1962–3 were important factors contributing to this disillusionment.

Conservatives on the liberal wing of the party had also opposed immigration controls but for rather different reasons from those who wished to maintain imperial traditions. They favoured the transformation of the Empire into the Commonwealth and hoped that a multi-racial Commonwealth would be an important influence and give

Britain greater moral authority in a world where Third World countries were playing a greater role. They were opposed to controls because they suggested racial discrimination and colour prejudice. They were also more aware of the economic value of immigrant workers. Those Conservatives who most strongly favoured controls appeared to be 'self-made' Conservatives, small businessmen and working-class Conservatives with popular-authoritarian views, who could be said to belong to the narrowly chauvinistic 'radical right' of the party. These Conservatives were stronger in the constituencies and the electorate than in Parliament or the executive committee of the National Union, where the progressives and the paternalistic patricians appeared to be strongly represented. In Parliament the views of the radical right were supported by MPs usually representing constituencies with substantial numbers of working-class Conservatives, often in areas feeling 'threatened' by an influx of immigrants. The newly elected MPs for Birmingham could be said to represent this section of the party (Foot, 1965).

The major factors contributing to the change in Conservative policy were first, the growing feeling among many ministers that increasing racial tension could only be avoided if controls were introduced (Butler, 1973, p. 208). The substantial increase in coloured immigration after 1959 raised more acutely the problems facing local authorities, but it was the possible reaction of the indigenous population against coloured immigration, if immigration remained uncontrolled, which concerned members of the government. Secondly, the pressure for control was building up strongly in the National Union of Conservative and Unionist Associations, to such an extent that party leaders felt concessions had to be made. Thirdly, the decision of the Indian Supreme Court, the failure of Jamaica to join the West Indian Federation and Britain's decision to apply for membership of the EEC all combined to reduce the importance of Commonwealth constraints. Finally, it appeared that legislation to control immigration would be electorally very popular, and while the party leadership was reluctant to make much of this, it was clearly an important consideration (Layton-Henry, 1980a).

THE 1962 COMMONWEALTH IMMIGRANTS ACT

Since control had been considered by the Cabinet as early as 1954, and since the Home Office had been asked to prepare draft legislation as early as 1955, it is remarkable that the Bill presented in 1961 was so rushed and poorly prepared. The government felt that the legislation would command general support and were astounded at the opposition the Bill received from the Labour and Liberal parties, from the churches and in the press. The Bill was also condemned by West Indian politicians and by Jawaharlal Nehru, the Indian Prime Minister.

Gaitskell's furious onslaught on the Bill, which he described as cruel and brutal anti-colour legislation, stunned the government. The Labour opposition at this time appeared demoralised and divided after their 1959 electoral reverse and racked by internal difficulties over unilateral disarmament, constitutional reform and Gaitskell's leadership. Macmillan had failed to anticipate that the Immigration Bill presented the opposition leader with a great moral issue with which he could unite the whole Labour Party behind his leadership. Moreover, the haste with which the Bill had been prepared and the reluctant acquiescence of some Conservative ministers for the Bill presented the opposition with an easy target. Gaitskell brilliantly exploited the ambiguities in the Bill and the mishandling of the Irish provisions by Macmillan. He argued that immigration was self-regulating and that the substantial increase in immigration had been caused by the wholly artificial conditions created by the growing campaign to introduce controls. The accusations that Commonwealth governments had not been properly consulted were very damaging to the government, especially when Gaitskell published a protest from Sir Grantley Adams, the West Indian Federal Premier (Williams, 1979, pp. 676–9). Gaitskell's speech on the second reading of the Bill won universal praise.

The government found it difficult to counter the opposition's onslaught, especially as they were accused of betraying the Empire and Commonwealth. The *Daily Express* headline (15 November 1961), 'Labour Spoke for the Empire', after the second reading vividly exposed their dilemma. Government leaders were reluctant to abandon the Commonwealth ideal which had been elevated into a major principle of Conservative policy and to disrupt relations with Commonwealth leaders. Accusations of racism were embarrassing to liberal Tories and damaging to the government's image abroad both in the Commonwealth and in the United Nations. Liberal Tories and Tory imperialists were thus both thoroughly unhappy about the Bill and the opposition gleefully pressed home their advantage in the second reading debate. James McCall argued, 'It is a shameful thing that a party who glorified in the sweets of Empire when they were profitable shows that it is hypocritical when it comes to repaying some of the debts' (*Hansard*, 16 November 1961, col. 778). The West Indian economies particularly had been shaped to serve Britain's convenience and controls would seriously worsen unemployment there. More soberly other Labour spokesmen argued that the Bill was an admission of the government's failure to take effective measures to deal with the social problems caused by immigration and would not help to resolve them (*Hansard*, 16 November 1961, col. 799).

In retrospect the Labour fury with the Tory betrayal of a hitherto sacred principle seems largely symbolic (Deakin, 1972), although it was extremely damaging to the government at the time. Labour opposition was not pressed at the committee stage of the Bill nor at the third reading. It was, however, sufficient to obtain substantial concessions from the government and the Bill was substantially amended: Denis Healey listed the opposition's successful amendments to the Bill in his speech on its third reading (*Hansard*, 27 February 1962, col. 1271). However, Labour's crusading enthusiasm for opposing the Bill was quickly dissipated. Patrick Gordon-Walker, who had made a powerful speech summing up the opposition's case on the second reading, found himself under considerable pressure from his constituents and took no further part in combating the Bill. A substantial minority of Labour MPs had always favoured controls and these also kept a low profile. In fact when it came to the vote on the third reading some 78 Labour MPs did not appear in the lobbies and this contributed to an easy victory for the government, whose majority of 84 on the second reading rose to 103 on the third reading.

The Commonwealth Immigrants Act which came into effect on 1 July 1962 was only a mild measure of control. A system of employment vouchers for Commonwealth immigrants was introduced. There were three categories of vouchers: category A for those migrants with a specific job to come to; B for those with special skills in short supply; and C for any intending migrant at all on a first come, first served basis, though priority was given to those with war service. Initially the impact of the Act seemed substantial as net immigration from the New Commonwealth fell from 94,900 in the first six months of 1962 to 16,450 in the last six months. However, the government had promised to administer the Act liberally and did so. In 1963, for example, over 30,000 category A vouchers were issued (Rees, 1979) and net migration from the New Commonwealth averaged over 50,000 per year between 1963 and 1966. In fact it was to continue at this level throughout the 1960s and 1970s although the immigrants were increasingly to be composed of the dependants of men already settled in Britain.

Public concern over immigration was not allayed for long by the Act and in fact the salience of immigration as an issue was greatly raised by its controversial passage. In January 1962 a smallpox epidemic broke out in Bradford and received widespread publicity. The *Observer* reported that 'the spread within days of an often fatal disease from Pakistan to Yorkshire has shocked people and frightened them' (14 January 1962). Sir Cyril Osborne used the outbreak to blame the opposition for opposing immigration controls (Foot, 1965, p. 141).

Between 1962 and 1964 the mood of the Conservative Party swung strongly in support of tougher controls. In July 1963 immigration was exploited as an issue in two by-elections at Deptford in London and

West Bromwich in the Midlands, but Labour easily retained the seats. In September the Southall Residents Association was formed to protest against the increasing numbers of Indians settling in the borough and the growing proportion of immigrant children in Southall schools. Less widely reported was the exploitation of the issue by local Conservatives in Patrick Gordon-Walker's constituency of Smethwick (Foot, 1965, chs 1–4).

In the 1964 General Election campaign immigration control was not an important issue in the national campaigns of the parties, although Sir Alec Douglas-Home, one of the early converts to immigration control in the Cabinet, raised the issue in speeches at Bradford and Birmingham, claiming credit for excluding a million coloured immigrants who would have come to Britain but for the Act (Butler and King, 1965, p. 363). The dramatic importance of the General Election of 1964 was, of course, the impact of Peter Griffiths's victory at Smethwick where he unseated Patrick Gordon-Walker after an anti-immigrant campaign. Griffiths captured the seat with a staggering 7.5 per cent swing to the Conservatives in the teeth of a national swing to Labour of 3.2 per cent. The result was to have a momentous effect. It appeared to confirm the worst suspicions of those who believed that the general public was deeply racially prejudiced and that if the issue were exploited by unscrupulous politicians it could evoke a massive popular response. The Smethwick result confirmed the self-appointed populists, Osborne and Pannel, in the rightness of their campaign, but it had a damaging impact on the Labour Party which was already moving away from Gaitskell's opposition to controls.

An analysis of Labour's response to New Commonwealth immigration is now appropriate, as for the next period of nearly six years Labour governments were to be responsible for the management of immigration control and the development of race relations policy. These Labour administrations determined in fundamental ways the shape of the race issue in British politics as it was to develop in the 1960s and 1970s. First we shall examine the response of the Labour Party to New Commonwealth immigration before it was elected in 1964, and then proceed to analyse the development of policy under the leadership of the new Prime Minister, Harold Wilson.

CHAPTER 4

The Labour Response 1945–1964

The challenge to the Labour Party posed by New Commonwealth immigration has been particularly pertinent. The new migrants have been poor, largely unskilled or semi-skilled and have migrated to Britain to become a replacement labour force filling those jobs which were too poorly paid or uncongenial to attract native workers in a situation of labour shortage. The Labour Party, although it is a broad coalition of diverse class, ideological, union and regional interests, is the major British political party which claims to espouse socialist principles and represent the interests of the working class to which the vast majority of the new immigrants belonged. It was natural therefore that the New Commonwealth immigrants should look to the Labour Party to defend their interests. Also the Attlee administration, which was in power at the very beginning of the migration, had created a considerable fund of good will among many of the migrants because of its record of sympathy with the aims and aspirations of independence movements in the colonies (Attlee, 1937; Gupta, 1975). Most important of all it had granted independence to India and Pakistan, the first of the New Commonwealth countries to achieve independence and from which a majority of future New Commonwealth migrants were to come.

However, many British workers and their families also look to the Labour Party to defend their interests. To some extent they see themselves in competition with immigrant workers for housing, jobs, health and welfare benefits, and in the past workers have brought pressure to bear on their representatives to control immigration (Garrard, 1971). Furthermore, as a party which aims to achieve power electorally and to form the government, the Labour Party must be responsive to public opinion and political pressure.

In examining the development of Labour Party policy with regard to New Commonwealth immigration it is worthwhile emphasising three major dimensions of the Labour Party. First, there is the importance of principle in a party which claims to be a socialist party incorporating the aims and ideals of democratic socialism. Socialists of all shades of opinion are opposed to racialism as discrimination on racial grounds contradicts basic socialist beliefs in the equality and brotherhood of men. The rise of fascism in the 1930s, the avowed racist beliefs of the German Nazis and the consequent extermination of millions of Jews made racialism one of the major evils all socialists opposed. Secondly, the Labour Party is a party representing the interests of organised labour and it has to be particularly sensitive to the interests of the trade unions which are affiliated to the party and provide such a large proportion of its financial and organisational strength. Thirdly, it is an electoral coalition, an organisation for mobilising votes in order to achieve a parliamentary majority and form a government.

These three dimensions of the party are not mutually exclusive and in practice the Labour Party embodies all three, but the pressures generated by these internal dynamics are often contradictory and the priority given to each plays an important role in determining the nature and content of party policy. This is clearly illustrated, as we shall see, in analysing the development of party policy in the area of immigration control and race relations legislation.

In the early postwar period the migration from the West Indies and later from the Indian sub-continent was largely seen in the context of colonial policy and relations with the Commonwealth. This was true for all the major parties. Labour's avowed colonial policy at this time was to transform the colonies of the Empire into fully independent members of the Commonwealth 'as each colonial people becomes ready for independence' (Labour Party, *Manifestos*, 1950, 1955). Labour Party policy in the early 1950s also emphasised the need to end the colour bar where it existed in colonial territories and the need for self-determination on the basis of equality for all races (Labour Party, 1956).

At home immediately after the war there was some concern in the Labour movement with Mosley's attempt to rebuild his New Union Movement and with occasional instances of the operation of a colour bar in sport and in some restaurants (Labour Party, *Annual Conference Report*, 1948, p. 179; 1949, pp. 114–15), but the Labour government of 1945–51 was overwhelmingly preoccupied with economic recovery and its heavy programme of nationalisation and health and social welfare legislation. It was also proud of its initiatives in foreign policy, claiming considerable credit for the granting of independence to India, Pakistan, Burma and Ceylon, and thus for launching the new multi-racial Commonwealth which was to succeed both the cosy white man's club of the Old Commonwealth and the Empire itself. The row over the banning by Patrick Gordon-Walker, the Colonial Secretary, of Seretse Khama from Bechuanaland after his marriage to an English girl early in 1951 showed the clash between party principles and practical expediency. Many Labour MPs believed that their Government had betrayed its principles and was too ready to appease South African racist sensibilities (Goldsworthy, 1971). In fact, after 1950 many on the left of the party were becoming increasingly concerned with the drift of Labour's colonial policy and at the consolidation of the power of white settler minorities in different parts of Africa. They felt that the policies advocated by the Fabian Colonial Bureau, which was very influential in developing Labour's postwar colonial policy, were too cautious. Many, like Fenner Brockway, became involved in movements like the Congress Against Imperialism, founded in 1948, and its successor, the Movement for Colonial Freedom (1954) in order to press the party in the direction of speedier independence for colonial territories. Their campaign for an end to the colour bar in the colonies and independence on the basis of equality for all races went together with opposition to racial discrimination at home and also to any legislation which might be construed as detrimental to the colonies or former colonies.

As we have already seen in Chapter 2, the Labour government was not too preoccupied with other matters to overlook the beginnings of New Commonwealth immigration, which it considered a worrying development which ought to be discouraged. In June 1948, in reply to questions from Tom Driberg about the sailing of the *Empire Windrush*, George Isaacs, the Minister of Labour, said, 'I hope no encouragement is given to others to follow their example' (*Hansard*, 8 June 1948, col. 1851). In October 1948 the Cabinet established the inter-departmental working party to examine the employment in Britain of surplus colonial labour (Ministry of Labour, 1948) and subsequently commissioned two further reviews, one from the Colonial Secretary (Cabinet Papers, 1950) and the other from the Home Secretary (Cabinet Papers, 1951). In spite of its concern and the advice of the working party, the Cabinet finally decided in February 1951 that legislation to control colonial immigration was not justified in view of the small scale of the immigration and the implications of breaking the traditional policy of allowing all British subjects free access to the UK. However, it is clear that it was not in principle opposed to control which it felt might become essential if there were a substantial increase in this immigration.

LABOUR IN OPPOSITION 1951–62

Between 1951 and 1958, with the Labour Party now in opposition, no positive or coherent policy with regard to New Commonwealth immigration was developed. In Parliament there were two types of intervention by Labour MPs concerned with race relations matters. First, there were those predominantly left-wing MPs who had a particular interest in colonial affairs and who were totally opposed to racial discrimination which they wanted abolished in the colonies

(*Hansard*, 20 June 1952, cols 492–3). The best examples are Reginald Sorenson and Fenner Brockway. They were also opposed to attempts to introduce a colour bar in Britain and introduced Bills to outlaw racial discrimination here as well, but were never able to gain enough support to get their Private Members' Bills transformed into legislation. They had some support on the National Executive Committee (NEC) and in 1953 the NEC in an early initiative invited Kenneth Little, an eminent academic, to prepare a memorandum on racial discrimination. He recommended legislation along the lines of the United States' Fair Employment Practices Commission, but these proposals were not followed up and the matter was allowed to drop (Deakin, 1972).

The second form of intervention in Parliament was by Labour MPs responding to increasing levels of public concern in their constituencies as these became areas of immigrant settlement. The first debate on West Indian immigration, for example, was initiated by John Hynd, a Labour member from Sheffield, on 5 November 1954. He was one of a small group of Labour members who openly favoured control. In the debate he complained bitterly about the influx of coloured immigrants from Jamaica and the effects on housing, social security and employment. He was also concerned about inter-racial sexual relationships. Henry Hopkinson, the Conservative Minister for the Colonies, showed no sympathy for Mr Hynd's views or anxieties (*Hansard*, 5 November 1954, cols 821–31).

At the local level the local government authorities, particularly Labour councils who tended to control the main areas of immigrant settlement, attempted to cope with the housing and welfare problems associated with immigration. In 1954 Marcus Lipton led a delegation from Lambeth Council to the Colonial Office to ask for help in integrating West Indian immigrants and this example was followed by Birmingham, but no extra assistance was forthcoming.

On 1 March 1955 the NEC issued a short report on colour prejudice arguing that the problems concerned with immigration were based on colour and suggesting four alternative courses of action: first, to call upon affiliated organisations to oppose racial discrimination: secondly, to seek Commonwealth discussions on immigration; thirdly, to request the TUC to establish a special committee to study problems of employment and union membership among immigrants; and fourthly, to call a conference of local authorities and coloured representatives to discuss the problem (Foot, 1965).

At the end of 1954 a joint sub-committee of the executive of the London Labour Party had been established 'to consider problems arising out of the recent influx of coloured people into London'. The report, *Problems of Coloured People in London*, was published in September 1955 and was concerned mainly with housing and other general welfare provision. It concluded:

We feel concern about the intensification of present problems that will come if the volume of immigration of coloured people continues to rise each succeeding year. The idea of our imposing any restraint upon the coming of coloured citizens of the Commonwealth is repugnant to the Labour movement and could only, if at all, be justified if it were certain that such immigrants were coming to conditions in this country which would be intolerable . . . finally we entirely agree that the problem can only be solved satisfactorily by ensuring to the West Indian peoples an economy which will give them prosperity and security at home. (London Labour Party, 1955)

In November 1957 five Labour Members, all from areas of immigrant settlement in London (Albert Evans [Islington South], Eric Fletcher [Islington East], B. J. Parkin [Paddington North], C. W. Gibson [Clapham] and Marcus Lipton [Brixton]), moved an adjournment debate on housing problems 'caused' by coloured immigration. They were especially concerned with the problems of overcrowding and complaints from white tenants forced to share facilities with immigrants. In some areas there were complaints that landlords were using black tenants as a means of putting pressure on white tenants in controlled tenancies to secure vacant possession (*Hansard*, 22 November 1957, cols 743–75). Other Labour Members were more concerned with the racial discrimination faced by the newcomers, and as early as 1953 Fenner Brockway had introduced a Private Member's Bill to outlaw racial discrimination in public places. This Bill failed to pass, but Brockway took up this cause and until 1964 his Private Member's Bills on this subject became almost an annual event.

In April 1958 the Labour MP for Accrington, Mr H. Hynd, brother of the Member for Sheffield, moved an adjournment debate on the motion that 'In the opinion of this House the time has arrived for reconsideration of the arrangements whereby British subjects from other parts of the Commonwealth are allowed to enter this country without restriction' (*Hansard*, 3 April 1958, col. 1415). The beginning of his speech outlined the dilemma facing those of the left who felt as he did. He said:

This is a difficult and not very pleasant subject to discuss. It is difficult because we are proud of our traditional open door, and we have been especially glad to welcome to these shores people from our own Commmonwealth. It is delicate because anyone who raises it is immediately open to suspicion of racialism or of arousing passions and prejudices which no one wants to arouse. It is no pleasant task, because as a trade unionist and as a socialist and something of an internationalist as well, my sympathy is with the underdog, particularly those who find it necessary to leave their country and earn a living. I would be the first to object to any kind of bar on the grounds of race, colour or creed. Indeed my object today is the very opposite. It is precisely because I am beginning to be afraid that these prejudices may develop . . . that I am introducing this motion. (*Hansard*, 3 April 1958, col. 1415)

This was a classic statement of the dilemma facing many politicians on the left. Their own personal convictions, whether Christian or humanist, as well as their political principles, demanded opposition to racism and its manifestations. On the other hand, as politicians they felt they had to be sensitive to the anxieties and feelings of their constituents which were often chauvinistic and prejudiced. A few Labour MPs at times did seem to share the prejudices of their constituents, though this could rarely be admitted in left-wing circles or in public. However, the clash between standing up for principles or responding to popular hostility to immigration was a dilemma which was to become more and more acute as the immigration of New Commonwealth citizens continued.

THE TRADE UNION RESPONSE

British trade unions have traditionally been suspicious of, and hostile towards, high levels of immigration. In the 1890s the TUC passed several resolutions demanding the control of Jewish immigration. After the Second World War strict conditions were imposed on the employment of European volunteer workers before the unions would agree to their recruitment. They had to join the appropriate union, be the first to lose their jobs in case of redundancy, and accept limited opportunities for promotion. In practice many of the conditions were never enforced as continuing economic expansion and full employment assuaged union fears of unemployment and wage cutting. Nevertheless in some industries like mining the employment of foreign labour proved to be impossible because of union opposition (Tannahill, 1958).

The reaction of the trade unions to New Commonwealth immigration was surprisingly positive, at least at the national level. The TUC Congress in 1955 welcomed the new migrants to Britain and deplored attempts to erect a colour bar against Commonwealth citizens (Trades Union Congress, *Report*, 1955). Clearly union leaders felt an obligation towards immigrants who they felt had been forced to come to Britain because of colonial exploitation and lack of investment in their territories. Moreover opposition might be interpreted as racist. However, trade union leaders were not confident about the reaction of their members to black workers. The working party on the employment of colonial labour reported:

The leaders of the Trade Union movement generally take the line that while they themselves have no objection in principle to the introduction of coloured workers from British territories, the decision whether or not to go on with a recruiting scheme must in every case be left to the local branch in the area of prospective employment. The local Trade Union officials usually say they would help if they could, but that the workers in their particular area are not prepared to accept coloured workers in their place of employment. (Ministry of Labour, 1948, para. 15)

There were efforts by local branches in the transport industry to exclude black workers, but concern about immigration was more widespread than this (Wright, 1968; Patterson, 1969; Beetham, 1970). In 1956 when tension rose Jack Jones, Midlands organiser of the Transport and General Workers' Union, suggested that coloured workers 'can form a pool of cheap labour which can be used to depress wage standards and fight the trade unions' (*Birmingham Mail*, 5 June 1956). In May 1955 the biennial conference of the Transport and General Workers' Union had called for the strictest control over all forms of immigration and in 1957 a motion calling for the government to exercise strict control over the number of coloured workers who were allowed to enter Britain was passed with executive support (Deakin, 1972). The new General Secretary, Frank Cousins, said in his winding-up speech, 'We cannot afford that these people should be allowed unrestricted entry into this country as a basis for the reduction of our bargaining powers' (*Manchester Guardian*, 11 July 1957).

Thus the response of the major working-class institutions to New Commonwealth workers up to 1958 was ambiguous. There was opposition in principle to racial discrimination but in practice there were no strong positive policies developed either by the Labour Party or by the trade unions. Those in the Labour movement who identified West Indian immigration as a problem which needed to be controlled had made as much of the running as those, like Fenner Brockway, who were advocating positive legislation against racial discrimination. This was the situation on the eve of the racial disturbances in Nottingham and Notting Hill.

THE IMPACT OF THE RIOTS

The race riots in Nottingham and Notting Hill in August and September 1958 proved to be a watershed in the formulation of Labour Party policy on immigration control. The immediate reaction of several Labour MPs was to demand control. Mr George Rogers, MP for North Kensington, which included Notting Hill, told the *Daily Sketch:* 'The government must introduce legislation quickly to end the tremendous influx of coloured people from the Commonwealth . . . overcrowding has fostered vice, drugs, prostitution and the use of knives. For years the white people have been tolerant. Now their tempers are up' (*Daily Sketch*, 2 September 1958). James Harrison (Nottingham West) and Maurice Edelman (Coventry North-West) also issued statements supporting control. But the overwhelming reaction on the left was to condemn the riots as hooliganism and illegitimate manifestations of racism. Gaitskell, of course, unequivocally condemned the riots and so did the NEC which rushed out a statement on racial discrimination at the end of September just in time for the party conference (Labour Party, 1958). This statement condemned the violence and expressed abhorrence at all manifestations of racial prejudice. It emphasised the importance of the Commonwealth ideal, the multi-racial nature of the Commonwealth and its unique opportunity to create racial understanding, confidence and co-operation in the world. It argued that if Britain were to remain the centre of the Commonwealth the welcome to Commonwealth citizens coming to Britain should be wholehearted and unreserved.

Tribune, the major paper on the left of the Labour Party, responded to the riots with a strong leader under the headline '*No Surrender to Prejudice*' (5 September 1958). The leading article strongly condemned the riots and all manifestations of racial discrimination. It also opposed any introduction of immigration controls. Most unusually this editorial position drew a hostile response from many readers and the majority of letters published opposed *Tribune*'s position. The response from *Tribune*'s normally radical readership suggested that concern about New Commonwealth immigration was widely felt even among those who usually considered themselves to be on the left (Gupta, 1975).

However, the riots for the time being crystallised official Labour Party policy to one of total opposition to immigration controls as any opposition to the open door might be seen as capitulation to the worst excesses of racism. The Labour Party was thus precipitated into a policy of upholding the Commonwealth ideal just at the point when the campaign for control in the Conservative Party gained considerable impetus. The violence manifested against black people was so appalling to Labour leaders that they were unable to see that the strength of public opinion on coloured immigration might have to be appeased if electoral losses were not to follow. However the riots, while highlighting the issue, seem to have prevented the Labour Party from developing a realistic policy on immigration which would have both reassured the public about the size and consequences of New Commonwealth immigration and at the same time been non-racist. The riots were regarded as ugly isolated incidents and not as part of a rising trend of opposition to black immigration which might have growing political significance.

Meanwhile the NEC statement was endorsed by the annual conference and the NEC also decided to establish a special committee on race relations, approaching the TUC to encourage them to set up a similar committee for joint discussion and action with the party. Legislative action to outlaw racial discrimination in public places became official party policy. In December 1959 the Labour opposition initiated a debate on racial intolerance and James Callaghan, party spokesman on colonial affairs, urged the government to introduce legislation to outlaw discrimination (*Hansard*, 7 December 1959, cols 115–16). In 1960 Fenner Brockway attempted unsuccessfully to introduce two Bills against racial discrimination, one in April and another in December, while on the other hand Francis Noel-Baker demanded to know why the Aliens Act should not apply to New Commonwealth citizens (*Hansard*, 12 April 1960, col. 1272; 7 December 1960, cols 1270–72).

THE COMMONWEALTH IMMIGRANTS BILL

In the Queen's Speech in October 1961 the government announced its intention to introduce a Commonwealth Immigrants Bill to control Commonwealth immigration (*Hansard*, 31 October 1961, col. 6). At the meeting of the parliamentary Labour Party which discussed the opposition response on 15 November a small group of MPs attempted to persuade the party not to embark on a course of total opposition to controls, but Gaitskell was determined to stand by Labour policy and to stage a massive display of opposition to the Bill. He routed the proponents of control and at the end of the meeting only twelve voted against his policy of total opposition (Foot, 1965, p. 171).

It has been argued in Chapter 3 (pp. 42 ff.) that the conflict between the main parties over the Commonwealth Immigrants Bill was largely symbolic (Deakin, 1968a), presumably in the sense that this opposition was merely a token stand in favour of party principle. However, it appeared very damaging to the Conservative government at the time and it marked a turning point in the fortunes of the opposition party which began to improve from this period. Butler and Macmillan were startled and dismayed by the savage attack unleashed by Gaitskell and Gordon-Walker against the Bill on its second reading. Gordon-Walker made a powerful speech in support of the opposition amendment which was

> that this House refuses to give a second reading to a Bill which, without adequate inquiry and without full discussion at a meeting of Commonwealth Prime Ministers, removes from Commonwealth citizens the long-standing right of free entry to Britain, and is thus calculated to undermine the unity and the strength of the Common-

wealth; gives excessive discretionary powers to the executive without any provision for appeal; will be widely regarded as introducing a colour bar into our legislation; and though providing for health checks and for the deportation of those convicted of certain criminal offences fails to deal with the deplorable social and housing conditions under which recent Commonwealth immigrants and subjects of Her Majesty are living. (*Hansard*, 16 November 1961, col. 687).

The opposition vigorously exploited the mishandling of the Irish provisions and the lack of consultation with Commonwealth Prime Ministers, and accused the government of capitulating to racial prejudice. At first the Irish were to be subject to controls so the government would be able to claim that the provisions were not racist. However, in the second reading debate the Home Secretary said that it was not practicable to include the Irish in the Bill and the opposition gleefully argued that this exposed the racist intentions of the Bill. Then, when winding up the debate, the Minister of Labour said that the government would have another look to see whether the Irish could be included under its provisions. The government front bench were enormously embarrassed by the opposition's concerted attack and their inadequate preparations to deal with it. The highlight of the debate was Gaitskell's speech. He made one of the most powerful and memorable speeches of his career though it was a speech which was to prove a most embarrassing legacy to his successors. He demanded:

What then is the reason for the Bill? The immigrants are healthy, law-abiding and are at work. They are helping us. Why then do the government wish to keep them out? We all know the answer. It is because they are coloured and because in consequence of this there is a fear of racial disorder and friction. This is the real question. Why do we have so much hypocrisy about it? Why do we not face up to the matter? There is a problem here. None of us has ever denied it. There are social problems and an appalling housing problem. We concede the existence of these problems in certain areas, but we do not believe for one moment that this Bill is the way to handle them. We do not believe that the Bill is justified by the facts. We think that probably it will not work at all. But at the same time we think that it will do irreparable harm to the Commonwealth. (*Hansard*, 16 November 1961, col. 796)

Michael Foot was to describe Gaitskell's performance in glowing terms in *Tribune* on 24 November:

No praise is too high for the manner in which it was done. Hugh Gaitskell in particular debated with a devastating passion which spread terror and shame along the government benches . . . The spectacle of the Labour party asserting its principles in the face of what is supposed to be the popular need of the moment, and resolving to withstand all the pressures of expediency, is something fresh and exciting, a new element on the political scene . . . The party is united, and not merely united but exhilarated' (*Tribune*, 24 November 1961, p. 5)

The impact of Gaitskell's performance on his party was greatly increased by the divisions and disunity which had rent the party since its electoral débâcle in 1959. The two years since then had seen hard fought and damaging battles over unilateral disarmament and the reform of the party constitution, in both of which Gaitskell had been heavily involved. In the Commonwealth Immigrants Bill, which was presented to Parliament a few weeks after the annual conference which reversed the unilateralist decision of the previous year but which refused to amend Clause IV, Gaitskell was presented with an issue of principle which he could use to reunite the whole party behind his leadership. His stand was all the more effective because it was on an issue on which he felt morally right. It may also have been partly influenced by his family background. His father was an Indian civil servant who served in Burma; this may have given Gaitskell a particular commitment to the Commonwealth ideal and the need to maintain the Commonwealth as a bridge between the rich white developed countries and the poor black or brown nations. Politically Gaitskell's intervention was enormously successful: the Labour Party was united and for the first time since their 1959 defeat moved strongly on to the offensive. The Conservative government, on the other hand, was demoralised, deeply embarrassed and divided.

The ferocity of the opposition's attack on the second reading and the hard work by a few Labour Members at the committee stage succeeded in achieving a number of substantial concessions in the Bill, such as the publication of the instructions to immigration officers and the fact that the Act would run for only eighteen months and then have to be reconsidered and renewed annually by Parliament. This ironically was to prove an embarrassment to the subsequent Labour government when it decided to renew the Act. The wholehearted opposition attack also had a marked impact on public opinion and the Gallup poll taken after the debate showed a fall in the proportion favouring control from 76 per cent to 62 per cent (Foot, 1965, p. 172). However, the figures still suggested that the party was substantially out of line with the majority of the public and Gaitskell had certainly identified the Labour Party with opposition to controls in the public mind and in the mind of the immigrants themselves, who identified the Labour Party as the champion of their rights.

The TUC supported the Labour Party's opposition to the Bill but, significantly, criticised the manner in which controls had been introduced rather than the principle of immigration controls against Commonwealth citizens (Miles and Phizacklea, 1977, pp. 14–15). However, after its success on the second reading, the Labour opposition failed to press home its advantage. The fight in committee was not led by the front bench but by a backbench Labour MP, Eric Fletcher, and by the third reading on 27 February, while the Bill was still attacked as racialist and discriminatory, Mr Denis Healey, winding up for the opposition, conceded that controls might be necessary but if they were they should be achieved through bilateral discussions and controls agreed with the Commonwealth countries (*Hansard*, 27 February 1962, col. 1271). This loss of impetus may have been due partly to government concessions but also to pressure put on MPs from their constituents. Patrick Gordon-Walker, for example, who led the opposition attack on the second reading found himself a major target of the anti-immigrant lobby in his constituency. The government thus carried the third reading with a substantially larger majority than it had on the second – 103 compared with 84.

THE RETREAT FROM PRINCIPLE

The change in Labour Party policy became clearer after Gaitskell's death in January 1963. Harold Wilson, the new leader, in a speech in Trafalgar Square on 17 March 1963, pledged the Labour Party to wholehearted support for Fenner Brockway's Bill against racial discrimination, a large-scale programme designed to educate public opinion on the race issue and the repudiation of those Labour clubs which persisted in applying a colour bar, but he was noticeably reticent on the party's position on immigration control. By the summer there had been a marked shift of opinion in favour of control and in the autumn, when the Commonwealth Immigrants Act came up for renewal, a majority of the Shadow Cabinet led by Patrick Gordon-Walker and Sir Frank Soskice were against opposition to renewal (Howard, 1963). They wished to allow the Act to be quietly renewed without taking a principled stand that might be electorally damaging. However, Harold Wilson and George Brown were agreed that some stand should be made and the compromise proposed by Denis Healey on the third reading was accepted. Labour would withdraw unilaterally imposed controls in favour of alternative ones negotiated bilaterally with the relevant Commonwealth countries.

In the debate on the Expiring Laws Continuance Bill on 27 November 1963 Harold Wilson proposed the opposition's compromise position. He argued that objections to the Commonwealth Immigrants

Bill had been first, because it was based on race and colour discrimination; secondly, because it discriminated against the Commonwealth; and thirdly, because it was imposed unilaterally (*Hansard*, 27 November 1963, col. 365). However, on the general issue of immigration control, he said 'We do not contest the need for immigration control'. Labour differed over the means not the ends and 'would be prepared to accept the negotiations with Commonwealth countries' (*Hansard*, 27 November 1963, col. 368). The government spokesman, Henry Brooke, convincingly argued that Labour's position was untenable as there was not the smallest chance of achieving effective voluntary control of immigration with Commonwealth governments. He announced that between July 1962 and 25 October 1963 applications for vouchers to work in Britain totalled 319,000 (284,000 from India and Pakistan) and of these, 59,000 vouchers had been issued and 260,000 applicants were still waiting for a decision. Applications were accumulating at the rate of 10,000 a week. Brooke argued that voluntary control was clearly impossible (*Hansard*, 27 November 1963, cols 373–5). The government had a majority of 50 after a poorly attended debate in which many of Labour's frontbench spokesmen were absent.

After this debate it was clear that the Labour Party did not have a logical or defendable policy on immigration control. It had a more coherent policy on racial discrimination where it was committed to legislation and the Society of Labour Lawyers prepared a draft Bill which was accepted by the committee established by the NEC to consider forthcoming Labour policy on race relations and immigration.

In the constituencies Cyril Osborne and some other Tories were arguing that controls were not tough enough and pointing to the level of applications for vouchers. In some constituencies the issue was becoming important. In September 1963 the Southall Residents Association was formed to protest against the increasing number of Indians settling in the borough and the growing proportion of immigrant children in Southall schools. In Smethwick the Midlands correspondent of *The Times* was already reporting the anti-immigrant campaign of the Conservative parliamentary candidate, Peter Griffiths, who, commenting on the slogan 'If you want a nigger neighbour, vote Labour', is reported to have said, 'I should think that it is a manifestation of the popular feeling. I should not condemn anyone who said that' (*The Times*, 9 March 1964).

Soon after the 1963 decision to oppose the continuation of the Commonwealth Immigrants Act, Transport House began to receive a small but steady stream of letters, mainly from Labour supporters, arguing that an idealistic policy would be electorally disastrous (Foot, 1965, p. 178). The Labour Party became more and more defensive on the issue and only a short item was included in the manifesto for the General Election. It stated that:

> a Labour government will legislate against racial discrimination and incitement in public places and give special help to local authorities in areas where immigrants have settled. Labour accepts that the number of immigrants entering the United Kingdom must be limited. Until a satisfactory agreement covering this can be negotiated with the Commonwealth, a Labour government will retain immigration control. (Labour Party, *Manifesto*, 1964).

THE GENERAL ELECTION OF 1964

During the election campaign the issue of immigration was frequently raised and in the latter stages of the campaign, in two major speeches in Bradford and Birmingham, Sir Alec Douglas-Home was claiming credit for excluding nearly a million people because of the Act (Foot, 1965, p. 148). Harold Wilson countered brilliantly in Birmingham by arguing 'We are not having the immigration question used as an alibi for the total Tory failure to handle the problems of housing slums, schools and education in this country' (Foot, 1965, p. 180). Other Labour candidates were not so positive and ironically were blaming the Tories for failing to control immigration effectively and for presiding over thirteen years of unrestricted inflow of Commonwealth immigrants (Deakin, 1972, pp. 232, 236).

Despite all the publicity the issue received during the campaign the electoral impact of the issue was unclear until the announcement of the result at Smethwick where Peter Griffiths dramatically unseated Patrick Gordon-Walker, the Shadow Foreign Secretary. It was a shattering result and a disaster for race relations as it appeared to show that racial prejudices could be effectively exploited for electoral advantage (Hartley-Brewer, 1965; Foot, 1965). It was then also noticed that in other areas where immigration was particularly salient as an issue Labour had done poorly, for example in Southall where Bean, the British National Party candidate, gained 3,410 votes, more than the Labour majority, which was reduced to 1,897 (Woolcott, 1965). In addition to Smethwick two seats which Labour should have won were Perry Bar in Birmingham, where the Birmingham Immigration Control Association helped the Tory candidate, and Eton and Slough where the indefatigable campaigner against racial discrimination, Fenner Brockway, lost his seat (Brockway, 23 October 1964).

The Labour Party was thus returned to office under the most inauspicious circumstances for developing strong positive policies on any controversial issue not excepting race relations. The result of the

General Election was widely held to be indecisive, rather similar to the electoral result in 1950, when the Labour government with an overall majority of six was harried into another election in less than two years, which it then lost. How would the new administration face the challenge of racism posed by the Smethwick result and at the same time protect its electoral vulnerability?

CHAPTER 5

Appeasement in Government: Labour 1964–1970

The members of the new Labour government were shocked and angry at the Smethwick result. They felt they had lost the seat as the result of an 'utterly squalid' campaign by the Smethwick Conservatives (Wilson, 1971, p. 55), and even worse this campaign had been successful in a working-class area apparently securely Labour. This was the first time immigration had played a significant role in a general election and it seemed to confirm that the immigration issue could be exploited by unscrupulous politicians for electoral advantage.

Labour leaders had been out of office for thirteen years and were naturally hungry for power. They had confidently expected to be returned with a substantial majority. The actual majority of five was a great disappointment and to lose even a handful of seats – and some felt it could have been rather more than this (Hattersley, 1972) – because of the exploitation of racial prejudice was an added insult. This combination of a small majority and the size of Griffiths's victory undermined the confidence of Labour politicians in handling the immigration issue. The new government, as all Labour governments are, was under considerable pressure to respond to what it saw as the practical realities and to abandon socialist principles for electoral considerations.

The nettle had to be grasped swiftly as the renewal of the Commonwealth Immigrants Act was one of the first measures confronting the new government. Harold Wilson, the new Prime Minister, had already made it clear that he was in favour of strengthening the Act in some respects (*Hansard*, 27 November 1963, cols 365–72) so a decision to renew the Act was predictable. Wilson moved quickly to respond to the Smethwick setback, raise the morale of socialists in the party and nail his anti-racist colours to the mast, with a spirited but largely ritualistic attack on Peter Griffiths on the first day of the new

Parliament. He called on Sir Alec to repudiate the victor of Smethwick who 'until a further general election restores him to oblivion will serve his term here as a parliamentary leper' (*Hansard*, 3 November 1964, col. 71). Labour fury over Smethwick continued during the Expiring Laws Continuance Bill when Michael Foot and Tom Driberg made notable attacks on Peter Griffiths (*Hansard*, 17 November 1964, cols 362–73; 390–3), but Sir Frank Soskice, the new Home Secretary, concentrated on the practical problems of immigration control. He drew attention to evasion of the present controls and agreed there should be more elaborate and long-term legislation. He concluded: 'I close with this remark so that there can be no doubt about the government's view. The government are firmly convinced that an effective control is indispensible. That we accept, and have always accepted, although we couple it with the feeling that the Commonwealth must be brought in. We must have an effective control whatever we have' (*Hansard*, 17 November 1964, col. 290).

THE CREATION OF A BIPARTISAN CONSENSUS

The Cabinet had clearly decided to organise the issue out of party politics and achieve some form of bipartisan agreement with the opposition so that the impending election could be fought on the more secure and traditional grounds of economics and class (Katznelson, 1973). Richard Crossman, a leading Cabinet minister, provides a good example of the dramatic change in the Labour leadership's view from the period of Gaitskell's speech on the second reading of the Commonwealth Immigrants Bill to the position after Smethwick. On the first occasion he wrote, 'I am proud the Labour party is leading the fight against the Government's immigration Bill. We oppose it as a shameful piece of colour bar legislation (*TV Times*, 19 January 1962). On the second occasion he wrote, 'Ever since the Smethwick election it has been quite clear that immigration can be the greatest potential vote loser for the Labour party if we are seen to be permitting a flood of immigrants to come in and blight the central areas of our cities' (Crossman, 1975, pp. 149–50).

The urgency of achieving a bipartisan consensus was greatly increased by Gordon-Walker's further defeat at the Leyton by-election on 21 January 1965. This reduced the government's majority to only three and further increased the likelihood of an early election. It was a damaging blow to the morale of the new government that its Foreign Secretary should lose the safe seat specially chosen for him to return to the House of Commons. Also, while the race issue was hardly raised in the by-election campaign, in a poll organised by Mark Abrams after the dramatic result, many of the Leyton electors interviewed thought that the race issue was the major factor contributing to Gordon-Walker's further defeat. Fears had been raised by several Labour speakers in the debate on 17 November that the Conservative candidate in Leyton was going to run a racialist campaign (e.g. Michael Foot, *Hansard*, 17 December 1964, col. 367), but Central Office made sure the issue was not used in the campaign. (For a discussion of the impact of race in the by-election see Teear, 1966). The by-election had a further unfortunate effect in that the transfer of Reginald Sorenson to the House of Lords to create the vacancy for Gordon-Walker meant that another outspoken defender of Commonwealth citizens' rights was lost to the Commons.

There were also signs that the Conservative Party was rapidly moving to a position of advocating tougher and more stringent controls. This was the implication of Sir Alec's speech in Hampstead on 3 February and also of his replacement of Edward Boyle by Peter Thorneycroft as party spokesman on race and immigration later that month. Cyril Osborne, successful yet again in the ballot for Private Members' Bills, announced yet another Bill to control immigration, proposing to ban all immigrants except those whose parents or grandparents were born in the UK. Such a Bill would have been anathema to Edward Boyle. Thorneycroft persuaded Osborne to modify the provisions of his Bill which was then, ominously, supported by Sir Alec and many members of the Shadow Cabinet.

On 4 February, less than a fortnight after the Leyton by-election and the day after Sir Alec's call for tougher controls, Sir Frank Soskice specified the measures the government intended to take to increase control of immigration. He announced to the House that he was tightening the immigration regulations governing the entry of dependent relatives. He also sought powers to deport illegal immigrants as, he argued, evasion of the immigration rules was taking place on a large scale (*Hansard*, 4 February 1965, cols 1284–5).

After a series of meetings in a Cabinet committee set up to discuss immigration policy (Wilson, 1971, p. 119; Crossman, 1975, pp. 149–50), Harold Wilson made a major statement on immigration policy to the House on 9 March. He announced the appointment of Maurice Foley, Under-Secretary of State at the Department of Economic Affairs, as minister in charge of government policy for co-ordinating action to encourage assimilation and better community relations, especially in the big cities. He also announced that the government would fulfil its pledge to introduce a Bill forbidding racial discrimination and would legislate to provide penalties against incitement to racial hatred. There would also be a fresh examination of the machinery of control because of the problem of evasion. Finally a high-level mission would be sent to discuss the problems of control with the relevant Commonwealth governments. On 23 March the government announced that Lord Mountbatten would head this mission (*Hansard*, 9 March 1965, cols 249–50; Wilson, 1971, p. 121). The Mountbatten mission was dispatched to redeem the manifesto pledge to negotiate immigration controls with the Commonwealth sending countries and, as the Conservatives had predicted, it was an ignominious failure. Not only was Mountbatten to return empty-handed from his tour, but he was not even allowed to visit Pakistan, one of the major sending countries.

At home, the government pressed ahead with its strenuous efforts to establish a bipartisan consensus which came to fruition the following month when Thorneycroft initiated a major debate on immigration. The debate was marked by a wide measure of conciliation and agreement between the government and the opposition. Most speakers on both sides agreed on a dual policy of strict controls and positive measures to assist the integration of those immigrants already settled in Britain. Nigel Fisher, expressing this new mood, said, 'I myself am a believer in the bipartisan approach to the problem. I think that as far as possible it should be taken out of party politics' (*Hansard*, 23 March 1965, col. 385). All the Labour MPs who spoke in the debate endorsed this view and the Home Secretary, summing up, said, 'There has been disclosed in the course of the debate a very great degree of unanimity on the broad aspects of the problem with which we are faced. The government accepts that there must be – simply because of the scale of possible immigration – effective control of numbers' (*Hansard*, 23 March 1965, col. 443).

Having achieved success in its strategy of creating a bipartisan consensus on immigration, the Labour government then proceeded to build on this in the sphere of race relations. In April it published its Race Relations Bill and vigorous efforts were made to get opposition agreement to it. The Campaign Against Racial Discrimination, which included some influential Labour lawyers in its leadership, lobbied intensively for conciliation rather than criminal penalties for breaches of the Act (Rose *et al.*, 1969). Conciliation was accepted by the opposition as a reasonable principle and after a narrow majority on second reading, Soskice withdrew the contentious sections of the Bill, substituting conciliation for criminal penalties and establishing the Race Relations Board to supervise the conciliation process through local committees. The Bill prohibited any restriction on the transfers of tenancies imposed because of race and outlawed racial discrimination in public places. It extended the Public Order Act to increase penalties for incitement to racial hatred. The Bill was too restrictive as far as the left wing of the Labour Party was concerned and was disliked in principle by the right of the Tory Party. However, by accepting conciliation, Soskice had made the Bill acceptable to most MPs of all parties and obtained opposition support for the principle of outlawing racial discrimination (Hindell, 1965, pp. 390–405). The Bill duly became law in November 1965.

THE 1965 WHITE PAPER

The determination of the government to consolidate the bipartisan policy on immigration grew as it became apparent that anti-immigrant feeling was growing in various parts of the country, notably the West Midlands, the West Riding of Yorkshire and the Home Counties (Crossman, 1975, pp. 270–1). This determination bore fruit on 2 August 1965 when the White Paper *Immigration from the Commonwealth* was published. This set out the government's future policy on Commonwealth immigration which was presented as a dual strategy. First there were to be strict controls on entry, supposedly to match Britain's capacity to absorb immigrants, but in reality to appease public opinion and outflank the Conservative move to gain political popularity by promoting tougher contols. Secondly, there would be positive policies to aid integration. The White Paper announced a level of controls which was extremely harsh, especially in a period of labour shortage. The number of vouchers to be issued to Commonwealth citizens would be limited to 8,500 of which 1,000 would be reserved for Malta. Category C vouchers for those with no job to come to and no special skills would be discontinued. In fact none had been issued by the Labour government, as applications for categories A and B had taken up all the available places. There was no discussion of controls on Irish or alien immigration as the clear intention of the White Paper was to impose strict controls on New Commonwealth immigration. As Crossman puts it once again with amazing frankness in his *Diaries*:

> This has been one of the most difficult and unpleasant jobs the government has had to do. We have become illiberal and lowered the quotas at a time when we have an acute shortage of labour. No wonder all the weekend liberal papers have been bitterly attacking us. Nevertheless I am convinced that if we hadn't done this we would have been faced with certain electoral defeat in the West Midlands and the South East. Politically fear of immigration is the most powerful undertow today. (1975, p. 299)

The White Paper also proposed extending the Home Secretary's powers of deportation to remove illegal immigrants and additional health checks on intending immigrants. *The Economist* (7 August 1965) described the proposals as a Black Paper which would strain both liberal consciences and the economy. In contrast to these restrictive provisions, the positive proposals were meagre. No special provisions for immigrants in housing or employment were proposed, though some assistance was proposed in the area of education. The major positive proposal was the intention to establish a new National Committee for Commonwealth Immigrants which would co-ordinate the work of local voluntary liaison committees whose main aim would be to work for a climate of tolerance and to combat racial prejudice. In September the Prime Minister announced that the Archbishop of Canterbury had agreed to chair the new Committee. The appointment of the leading churchman in Britain to chair the National Committee for Commonwealth Immigrants was yet further evidence of the government's determination to take the issue out of the political arena.

The White Paper marked the end of the role of the Commonwealth as an important factor in domestic British politics. The Mountbatten mission was a last obeisance to the Commonwealth ideal, though it had been undertaken mainly to fulfil the manifesto pledge and promises in Parliament. The failure of the mission was further evidence of the decline of the Commonwealth ideal as a viable principle of British policy and increased the likelihood that from then on purely national considerations would determine both foreign and domestic policy priorities.

The political response to the White Paper was what the government had hoped for. Public opinion polls indicated that some 88 per cent were in favour of the proposals and only 5 per cent were against (Social Surveys, 1965). The opposition welcomed the White Paper and even the TUC agreed to support it (Miles and Phizacklea, 1977b). Within the Labour Party there was considerable anxiety and concern at the restrictions, and forty-one MPs signed an appeal for the withdrawal of the White Paper. An emergency resolution was moved at the annual conference urging the government 'to withdraw the White Paper on *Immigration from the Commonwealth*, believing this to be the expression of a surrender, however disguised, to the currents of illiberal opinion. Conference further requests the Government not to introduce legislation along the lines of this reactionary White Paper' (Labour Party, *Annual Conference Report*, 1965, p. 212).

The conference debate was short and acrimonious. It was notable for a provocative speech by Bob Mellish, who warned of the most grievous racial disturbances if blacks were given preference in public housing allocation. He argued that racial tensions were just under the surface at the moment. In spite of the opposition from the floor that his speech provoked, the emergency resolution was easily defeated on a card vote: the result was 4,736,000 against, and 1,581,000 for the emergency resolution (Labour Party, *Annual Conference Report*, p. 220). The government's tough approach had carried the day, presumably with the overwhelming support of the affiliated trade union delegations. However, partly in response to criticisms made at the conference, the government decided to set up a committee of inquiry into immigration procedures under Sir Roy Wilson.

ROY JENKINS AS HOME SECRETARY

In December Sir Frank Soskice retired because of ill health. He had presided over Labour's bipartisan strategy on race and immigration and had supported tough controls on immigration and weak race relations legislation in order to get agreement with the opposition. He was replaced by Roy Jenkins, who brought a wholly new approach to race and immigration questions. Jenkins was determined to be remembered as a liberal, reforming Home Secretary who had shifted the focus of the immigration debate away from controls and towards integration. He was determined to encourage the integration of New Commonwealth immigrants and to foster policies which would avoid the racial problems that had developed in many major American cities.

Jenkins's first move was to appoint Mark Bonham-Carter as chairman of the new Race Relations Board with the promise that he could come back after a year and ask for increased powers for the Board. (Rose *et al.*, 1969, give a very full account of Roy Jenkins's period as Home Secretary.) He knew that nothing could be done to strengthen the Race Relations Act before the General Election was over and the government was freed from the pressures of parliamentary defeat, public opinion polls and an impending election. This also meant that positive legislation would have to come early in the next Parliament, providing Labour won, otherwise electoral constraints would again come into play. Maurice Foley, the government co-ordinator of race relations matters, was moved from the Department of Economic Affairs to join Jenkins at the Home Office. Foley was widely regarded as having done a good job as co-ordinator of race relations policy within the constraints of overall government policy.

The General Election was held in March 1966 and Labour was returned with an overall majority of 100 seats. The tough measures and statements of the Labour government, as exemplified by the 1965 White Paper, combined with Edward Heath's refusal to allow Conservative candidates to exploit the race issue, resulted in immigration not being an issue in the election campaign. The polls taken by Gallup in the Midlands found that most respondents considered there was little to choose between either of the major parties on the issue and national opinion polls found that only one person in twelve ranked immigration as the most important issue facing the country. There was enormous relief in the Labour Party as the seats lost on the race issue in 1964 were recaptured in 1966. Brian Walden, who held Birmingham All Saints for Labour, expressed this relief when he claimed 'We have buried the race issue' (Foot, 1969, p. 65). It was noticeable that in many areas a substantial improvement in immigrant registration and turnout had taken place which appears to have helped Labour in areas of immigrant settlement (Layton-Henry, 1978a; Studlar, 1978).

The electoral victory cleared the way for a more positive approach by Jenkins, who retained his position as Home Secretary. Publicly he set out the way ahead in a major speech to a meeting of voluntary liaison committees of the National Council for Commonwealth Immigrants. It was in this speech that he gave his famous and oft-quoted definition of the goal of integration 'not as a flattening process of assimilation but as equal opportunity, accompanied by cultural diversity in an atmosphere of mutual tolerance' (Jenkins, 1967, pp. 267–73). He emphasised the positive contribution of immigrants to Britain and warned of the 'vast trouble we shall be building up for ourselves if the talents of the second generation are wasted and their expectations disappointed'. He claimed to be open-minded about strengthening the Race Relations Act and stressed the need to carry public opinion and the major vested interests such as the TUC and the CBI. Privately Jenkins argued that independent evidence of racial discrimination was needed if the Cabinet and public opinion were to be convinced of the need for stronger anti-discrimination legislation. He stimulated the Race Relations Board and the National Committee of Commonwealth Immigrants to commission jointly two studies: one by Political and Economic Planning (PEP) on discrimination in Britain and the other by a group led by Professor Harry Street on the experience of anti-discrimination legislation abroad, particularly in the USA (Lapping, 1970, p. 116). Jenkins was particularly concerned that unless strong government action were taken Britain might experience the racial violence that had occurred in America. He warned of this again in a speech to the Institute of Race Relations in October when he promised to re-examine the Race Relations Act when the evidence of its working was collected. In the meantime he was convinced that controls should be maintained: 'Certainly the precise level should not be as high as to create a strong and widespread resistance to civilised immigration policies. But also it cannot be so low that it creates a profound sense of injustice and alienation in the immigrant community itself' (Jenkins, 1967).

In April 1967 the PEP report on racial discrimination was published and this was followed in October by the Street report on anti-discrimination legislation (PEP, 1967, Street *et al.*, 1967). The PEP report revealed much higher levels of discrimination than had previously been thought to exist and there were widespread demands, particularly in the press, for urgent action. The Street report argued that voluntary conciliation was not effective and that legal sanctions were necessary for anti-discrimination legislation to be effective. It was well known that the TUC was strongly opposed to the extension of anti-discrimination legislation into the area of employment. However, Jenkins persuaded the Cabinet of the need for a stronger race relations Bill and in May announced the government's intention to introduce new legislation.

During this period when Jenkins was persuading the Cabinet of the need for new legislation, events began to move against positive action. The Labour Party was experiencing a period of considerable unpopularity, losing control of the Greater London Council in April 1967 and doing badly in the local government elections in May. The summer saw landings of small numbers of illegal Asian immigrants on beaches in south-east England and these were given considerable publicity in the press. There was also a rise in Asian immigration from Kenya. These Asians were British passport holders, not covered by Commonwealth immigration controls, who had retained their British citizenship on Kenyan independence. The Kenyan government was determined to give preference in employment to Kenyan citizens and as a result Asians who had retained British citizenship were losing their jobs and were being forced to close their businesses. As a result of these measures small but growing numbers were coming to Britain, and a campaign was initiated by Duncan Sandys and Enoch Powell to control this new source of immigration. Press and public attention thus began to shift away from the problem of racial discrimination and back to the question of immigration control.

On the positive side the NEC working party report on race relations came out strongly in favour of extending legislation to cover employment and housing, but ominously the TUC representative on the working party refused the sign the report (Rose *et al.*, 1969, p. 545). The Labour Party conference in the autumn unanimously passed a resolution in favour of extending the Race Relations Act to employment, housing, insurance and other services. It also called on the government to provide more aid for education and housing in areas with large immigrant populations (Labour Party, *Annual Conference Report*, 1967, p. 312). The report of Sir Roy Wilson was also published in the autumn and contained proposals for the revision of admission procedures for Commonwealth citizens and aliens and a right of appeal against refusal of entry. These recommendations were implemented. At the annual Expiring Laws Continuation Bill in November, which was to be Jenkins's last speech as Home Secretary in this Parliament, he and Quintin Hogg still appeared agreed that the bipartisan consensus was worth continuing and that government and opposition could agree on constructive solutions to the problem of evasions of controls and the implementation of the Wilson recommendations (*Hansard*, 15 November 1967, cols 441–75). However, the debate showed mounting evidence of Tory dissent. At the end of November Jenkins was moved to the Treasury and Callaghan became Home Secretary with the major task of piloting Jenkins's Race Relations Bill through Parliament. However, Callaghan's first measure as Home Secretary was, inauspiciously, to be a new Commonwealth Immigrants Bill.

THE KENYAN ASIAN CRISIS

The stimulus to this further measure of control was the campaign led by Sandys and Powell to pressurise the government to halt the growing influx of British Asians from Kenya, a campaign which reached a climax in February 1968. There were major speeches from Sandys on the 8th and from Powell on the 9th. On the 12th Sandys tabled a motion calling on the government to take immediate action and this was signed by a number of prominent backbenchers including William Deedes and Sir David Renton. On the 18th the government showed signs of panic by dispatching Malcolm MacDonald to Kenya for discussions with the Kenyan government, which predictably refused to ease its policy against non-citizens. Once again the growing campaign for control and signs of government vacillation caused panic among the intended victims of the campaign and Kenyan Asians with British citizenship rushed to come to Britain before restrictions were imposed. In the last two weeks of February some 10,000 came to Britain, fuelling the press campaign and creating a further excuse for legislation. On 20 February Sandys tabled another motion requesting legislation and ninety Conservative MPs signed it. More surprisingly fifteen Labour MPs signed an amendment agreeing some kind of legislation was necessary (Steel, 1969). On the 22nd the Cabinet met and decided to impose a quota on the number of British Asians allowed to enter Britain from Kenya each year. Once again Crossman is vividly illuminating about this decision. He wrote:

> A few years ago everyone there would have regarded the denial of entry to British nationals with British passports as the most appalling violation of our deepest principles. Now they were quite happy reading aloud their departmental briefs in favour of doing just that. Mainly because I am an MP for a constituency in the Midlands, where racialism is a powerful force, I was on the side of Jim Callaghan. (Crossman, 1977, p. 679)

The Bill was introduced on 27 February and rushed through all its stages in three days. The major provision was that unconditional rights of entry to the UK were restricted to those with close ties to the UK by birth, naturalisation or descent. This was the first immigration control measure to include the 'grandfather clause' which gave preferential treatment to those with a British parent or grandparent. While the leading government and opposition spokesmen denied the Bill was racial it was clearly designed to restrict the entry of British citizens without close ties to the UK, the vast majority of whom were non-white.

In the House the Liberals led the opposition to the Bill which was also opposed by some Conservative and Labour members, notably Iain

Macleod who, as Colonial Secretary, had guided Kenya to independence. Outside the House the Bill was widely condemned by the voluntary organisations concerned with race relations, the quality press and the churches. *The Times* (1 March 1968) thundered: 'The Labour Party now has a new ideology. It does not any longer profess to believe in the equality of man. It does not even believe in the equality of British citizens. It believes in the equality of white British citizens.' Auberon Waugh, writing in the *Spectator* (1 March 1968), described the Act as 'one of the most immoral pieces of legislation to have emerged from any British Parliament'. Nevertheless, because of the support of both government and opposition it achieved a majority on second reading of 310 (372 to 62). In the Lords the Archbishop of Canterbury, still chairman of the National Committee for Commonwealth Immigrants, condemned the Bill.

This Bill was the logical outcome of the policy of appeasement that the Labour government had adopted in order to achieve a bipartisan consensus with the Conservatives. They were so afraid of the electoral consequences of appearing weaker than the Conservatives on immigration controls that in both 1965 and 1968 they had introduced measures which it is unlikely that even the Conservatives, if they had been in government, would have dared to introduce. The inherent weakness of this strategy of appeasement by a party or government on the political left is that their opponents know they have a winning issue which can be raised at any time in the knowledge that the left will immediately retreat and concede the case in the hope of saving votes. The strategy gives the right a permanent trump card and also allows the battle to be fought on their terms: it is a recipe of disaster for the left. All the effort and work that Jenkins and his friends had invested in creating a climate of opinion favourable to a stronger Race Relations Act, and their efforts to move the debate from immigration controls to integration, particularly of the second generation, were undermined precipitously by the government's capitulation to the campaign of Sandys and Powell. This capitulation was a disastrous betrayal of principle and exposed the vulnerability of the government on this issue. The result was a racially discriminatory Bill which devalued British citizenship by creating two classes of citizens: one subject to immigration controls and the other not. It was a clear breach of faith with people who had kept British citizenship for their own protection in a situation where they felt insecure, and they were betrayed at the hour of their greatest need. Moreover the Kenyan Asians were relatively well-qualified and well-educated people with a good command of English who, if they had been white, could have expected a warm welcome. The Act finally buried the ideals of *Civis Britannicus sum* and showed that Britain wished to rid herself of the obligations of Empire and Commonwealth. Both the government and the opposition emerged without credit from the Act. The government was responsible for the Bill but the opposition had not opposed it despite the fact that it was a Conservative administration which had given the undertaking in the first place (Macleod, 1 March 1968). The worst consequences, though, were still to come. The Bill had raised the salience of the immigration issue, it had shown the fear and power it evoked in leading politicians and the popular support it could generate, and it gave every incentive to unscrupulous politicians who were prepared to exploit the issue for personal or political advantage to do so.

THE RACE RELATIONS BILL, 1968

The government had created the worst possible climate for the passage of the Race Relations Bill which Callaghan was now even more committed to since he had linked it with the passage of the recent Commonwealth Immigrants Act as part of a fair and balanced policy which involved tough immigration controls but positive measures towards immigrants settled in Britain. The new Bill would establish in this country equality of treatment in the very sensitive areas of housing and jobs (*Hansard*, 27 February 1968, col. 1242). However, elated by their success over the Kenyan Asians, Powell and Sandys began a new campaign to sabotage the Race Relations Bill.

The Conservatives were deeply divided on how to respond to the new race relations legislation as they too were committed to the dual policy of tough controls combined with equality of treatment for black British citizens. The Bill, therefore, had supporters on the liberal wing of the party, including some support in the Shadow Cabinet, but the majority of backbench and constituency opinion was opposed to the Bill. The compromise agreed by the opposition was to support a reasoned amendment approving the principles of the Bill but opposing the measures themselves. This hypocritical stand did little to conceal Tory divisions and on balance was a victory for the Bill's opponents.

THE 'RIVER OF BLOOD' SPEECH

Two days before the Race Relations Bill was introduced there occurred perhaps the most cataclysmic event in the remorseless process by which the race issue has been politicised. This was the apocalyptical speech made by Powell in Birmingham which made him the focal expression of anti-immigration resentment in the country and a major challenger to the party leadership, as his speech had not had official approval (*Hansard*, 23 April 1968, cols 74–5). Powell used reported incidents and conversations to raise fears of immigrant invasion and takeover of streets and areas, fears of harassment of old people and even fears of prosecution under the new Race Relations Bill. He warned about the future of Britain if immigration was allowed to continue. 'We must be mad, literally mad, as a nation, to be permitting the annual inflow of some 50,000 dependants who are for the most part the material of the future growth of the immigrant descended population. It is like watching a nation busily engaged in heaping up its own funeral pyre.' The most dramatic and well-remembered part of his speech came at the end when he attacked the forthcoming Race Relations Bill. He said:

> For these dangerous and divisive elements the legislation proposed in the Race Relations Bill is the very pabulum they need to flourish. Here is the means of showing that the immigrant communities can organise to consolidate their members to agitate and campaign against their fellow citizens, and to overawe and dominate the rest with legal weapons which the ignorant and the ill-informed have provided. As I look ahead, I am filled with foreboding. Like the Roman, I seem to see 'the River Tiber foaming with much blood'. (Powell, 1969c)

Powell's speech obtained tremendous publicity and appeared to generate enormous popular support. It made him the best-known and most popular member of the opposition overnight and even a serious challenger for the position of leader of the party. The popular support for Powell could be measured in the polls, the deluge of favourable letters he received (Spearman, 1968) and the public demonstrations of support. It was clear that Powell's views and Powell himself commanded much wider support in the Conservative constituency associations and the electorate as a whole than they did in the Shadow Cabinet, but Powell had become a factor that Heath could not ignore in spite of his immediate dismissal of Powell from the Shadow Cabinet. Quintin Hogg was particularly furious with Powell not only because of the content of his speech but because he had trespassed without permission on his area of Shadow Cabinet responsibility. This was unacceptable behaviour from a Shadow Cabinet colleague. There is no doubt that Hogg would have resigned as Shadow Spokesman on Home Affairs if Heath had not sacked Powell. But Powell's speech tapped the widespread popular frustration with the bipartisan approach to immigration and race relations issues which had existed since 1965 (Schoen, 1977, pp. 34–44). There was considerable dissatisfaction with the anti-discrimination legislation which many people did not understand and did not support. Many felt it gave black immigrants a privileged position.

Powell's 'river of blood' speech enraged the government which saw its carefully constructed policy based on a bipartisan consensus

destroyed overnight. The government became even more determined
to press ahead with its Race Relations Bill. The Bill had three major
provisions: first, a declaration that discrimination was unlawful on
grounds of race, colour, ethnic group or nationality; secondly, a
process of conciliation; and thirdly, enforcement provisions. Discrimination was made unlawful in any place to which the public had
access: in accommodation in hotels and boarding houses, in banking,
insurance, loans, credit and finance facilities, in education, instruction
or training, in facilities for entertainment, recreation or refreshment, in
facilities for travel and transport, and in the services of any business,
trade or profession. Exclusion from trade unions, employers' and trade
organisations and discrimination in the sale or rent of housing and
premises were also made unlawful, as was advertising which indicated
an intent to discriminate. These provisions were made binding on the
Crown which made government departments answerable to the Race
Relations Board (*Hansard*, 23 April 1968, cols 53–67; Race Relations
Act, 1968). The Race Relations Board was expanded to cope with the
wider scope of the Act although employment complaints were to go first
to the Ministry of Labour. The Act also abolished the National
Committee for Commonwealth Immigrants and in its place established
a Community Relations Commission to emphasise that Britain was now
a multi-racial society and the primary goal was the integration of black
British citizens, increasing numbers of whom were British born
(*Hansard*, 23 April 1968, col. 63). The Home Secretary also announced
an urban programme to provide an additional £20–25 million to assist
urban areas facing acute social problems.

The government made some minor concessions in committee to
those who felt the Bill went too far and this was enough to persuade the
opposition not to oppose the Bill on its third reading. Nevertheless
forty-five Conservative MPs rebelled against the official opposition
decision and voted against the third reading. The Bill became law in
November 1968.

Despite its success in enacting the Race Relations Act the initiative
on race and immigration matters had passed decisively away from the
government to Powell. On 5 May Harold Wilson had made a major
speech attacking Powell but it had nothing like the public impact that
Powell's speech had had. Edward Heath, the Conservative leader, who
had sacked Powell from the Shadow Cabinet, felt obliged to announce a
toughening of Conservative Party policy in September when he said
that Commonwealth immigrants should only enter Britain under the
same conditions as aliens and that dependants should also be subject to
controls.

In September the annual Labour Party conference was notable for
another fierce attack by Wilson on Powell and for the passing of a
resolution requesting more financial aid for inner-city areas and

reaffirming Labour's principles of racial and religious equality. It called for a national policy for immigration based not on colour but on the social and economic needs of the country; the amendment of the Race Relations Act by excluding any clauses permitting racial discrimination in industry; and a massive programme of education to counteract racial prejudice in all its aspects. In particular it urged the Department of Education and Science to undertake a campaign to guide teachers in counteracting racial prejudice in schools (Labour Party, *Annual Conference Report*, 1968, p. 283). The government avoided criticism for the Commonwealth Immigrants Act because of the more recent Race Relations Act.

Between the conference and the General Election of 1970 the Labour government initiated two further positive developments. The Immigration Appeals Act, implementing the recommendations of the Wilson committee, became law in 1969 and in the following year the Alien (Appeals) Order gave similar rights to foreign nationals. However, in the main the government was on the defensive, desperately trying to hold the bipartisan consensus against the continuing onslaughts of Enoch Powell and his friends, with Edward Heath trailing behind Powell but gradually moving the Conservative policy on immigration towards tougher and tougher controls. The electoral effect on the Labour Party of the demolishing of the bipartisan consensus on immigration and race could be seen in the General Election of 1970 as having lived up to the worst forebodings of Labour politicians. This will be considered in the next chapter.

CONCLUSION

It is impossible to agree with Brian Lapping (1970, p. 109) that 'one of the few areas where the final judgement of history on the 1964–70 Labour government seems likely to be strongly favourable is its handling of race relations'. In fact Rex's (1968) judgement that Labour's policy was catastrophic seems much more accurate. It is clear that the strategy adopted by the Labour government in the aftermath of Smethwick and Leyton was one of appeasement, a determination to organise race out of party politics and to establish a bipartisan accord with the opposition. This strategy could only work with the co-operation of the Conservative Party leadership and for a time it did work with the consent of Heath and Hogg. The cost was the adoption by Labour of tough immigration controls and the introduction of weak race relations legislation which emphasised conciliation rather than legal sanctions. The consensus, however, was broken by Sandys and Powell in 1968, and Labour's policy of appeasement, highlighted by the betrayal of British Asians in Kenya, failed to work as Powell moved ferociously on to the offensive with the rank and file of the Conservative Party and most of the electorate largely in support. The policy of appeasement led to concession after concession by the Labour government which encouraged right-wing Conservatives to believe that they had a winning issue which commanded widespread popular support and which could be used against the Labour government. They were thus encouraged to strengthen their demands until finally it led to the powerful exploitation of the issue by a major Conservative outsider, Enoch Powell.

CHAPTER 6

Right-Wing Crescendo: Powell and the Heath Government

The bipartisan consensus, so carefully fostered by the Labour government, was destroyed by the success of Powell's campaign against Kenyan Asian immigration and by the impact of his Birmingham speech. This destruction was not immediately noticeable because Powell was so much at odds with the leadership of his own party, but the popularity of his campaign was striking. Polls completed after his Birmingham speech showed that between 60 and 75 per cent of the electorate were in sympathy with Powell and disapproved of Heath's sacking of Powell from the Shadow Cabinet (Studlar, 1974a). Powell also had a considerable impact on the rank and file of the Conservative Party and as a result of his speech eighty resolutions on immigration were submitted by constituency parties for debate at the annual party conference in 1968, where Powell received a standing ovation for a speech advocating tighter controls. 'We deceive ourselves', he said, 'if we imagine, whatever steps are taken to limit further immigration, that this country will still not be facing a prospect which is unacceptable' (Conservative Central Office *Annual Conference Report* 1968, p. 67). Quintin Hogg, however, had no difficulty in defending the Shadow Cabinet's position and also received a standing ovation from the conference delegates. A carefully selected, innocuous resolution on immigration was passed. Heath had, of course, already begun to move his party's policy on immigration towards tougher controls with his September speech.

Powell, however, returned to the offensive with another ferocious speech at Eastbourne in November. He warned of the dangerous gap that had developed between the overwhelming majority of the people throughout the country on the one side, and on the other a tiny minority with almost a monopoly hold upon the channels of communication who seemed determined not to know the facts and not to face the realities. He predicted a minimum immigrant population of 4.5 million by the year 2000 and advocated large-scale voluntary, but organised, financed and subsidised repatriation. He even advocated the establishment of a Ministry of Repatriation in this speech which was delivered before the Greater London Rotarians (Powell, 1969b, pp. 298–314). He concluded: 'The West Indian or Indian does not, by being born in England, become an Englishman. In law he becomes a United Kingdom citizen by birth; in fact he is a West Indian or Asian still.'

Powell's campaign on immigration and particularly his emotive speeches and the tremendous media publicity they generated, raised the salience of race and immigration issues enormously. They legitimised the expression of gut prejudices and racial hostility which most people thought embarrassing, immoral and even illegal to voice, given popular confusion over the Race Relations Act and the incitement to racial hatred provisions of the Public Order Act. In Powell, popular hostility and prejudice against black immigrants found a national political leader, highly respected for his ability and oratory, willing to raise issues and articulate fears that the major parties had preferred to keep off the agenda of national politics.

The Eastbourne speech was widely condemned in the press and by leading politicians of all parties who felt that this time Powell had gone too far, well beyond the bounds of acceptable conduct. Heath described Powell's speech as 'character assassination of one racial group' and added, 'that way lies tyranny'. He also said that the Conservative Party would never accept a total ban on coloured immigration (Foot, 1969, p. 121; Schoen, 1977, p. 41). However, Powell's popular support remained considerable. In December the Conservative Political Centre carried out a survey of its 412 constituency groups and found that 327 wanted all immigration stopped indefinitely and a further 55 favoured strictly limited immigration of dependants combined with a five-year ban on new immigration. Party officials and leaders were horrified by these results (Walker, 1977, p. 111).

In January Heath made a major speech on Conservative immigration policy which marked a continuation of the party's slide to tougher controls. He argued that Commonwealth immigrants, like aliens, should have no automatic right to permanent residence. They should be allowed into Britain only for a specific job, in a specific place and for a specific time. Their permit to stay would have to be renewed annually and work permits would have to be renewed every time they changed jobs. There would be no absolute right to bring in relatives, however close. The decision on entitlement to enter should be made in the country of origin and not on arrival in Britain (*Observer*, 26 January 1969). These proposals would give the British government complete control over immigration and, if implemented, would put Commonwealth immigrants on a 'guestworker' footing, completely under the control of the immigration authorities. While these proposals represented the ultimate in a tough immigration control policy they would, of course, no longer satisfy Powell who had moved on from immigration controls as a solution to racial problems to the idea of voluntary repatriation. However, Powell's views on repatriation had no support whatsoever in the Shadow Cabinet or among the vast majority of the parliamentary Conservative Party. They did, however, command an alarming degree of popular support (Schoen, 1977, pp. 42–50).

The campaign mounted by Enoch Powell had forced the Conservative Party leadership to abandon totally the ideal of Commonwealth citizenship to which it had been so firmly committed only ten years previously, and to adopt policies which meant complete governmental control over all sources of immigration. Many aspects of these new policies appeared to contradict the fundamental beliefs of many prominent liberal and Christian Tories in the party, including some like Quintin Hogg who acceded to them (Hailsham, 1975). But every compromise was not enough to satisfy Powell and his supporters and only seemed to spur them on to make more outrageous demands.

Powell continued his campaign in 1969 with two speeches in June and July urging repatriation. At the party conference, where he spoke on the economy, there was only a small majority in favour of a resolution which stated that Conservative Party policy was the only policy likely to be successful in controlling immigration; and the narrowness of the vote has been credited to Powell's influence in the constituency associations (Schoen, 1977, p. 47). But by the time the General Election was announced in May, Powell was totally at variance with Heath and the Conservative leadership, and on more issues than immigration. His views, although enormously influential on party policy, were in conflict with official policy on many major issues, particularly the EEC to which Heath was personally deeply committed. Heath had publicly stated that there would be no place for Powell in the Conservative government if they won the election (*The Times*, 24 January 1970).

THE GENERAL ELECTION OF 1970

Conservative Party leaders did not exploit the race issue in the General Election despite the fact that opinion polls suggested that the Conservative move towards tougher controls was preferred by most electors and that the issue was generally considered to be the fourth most important in the campaign. Immigration was mentioned by only 26 per cent of Conservative candidates in their election addresses and was almost completely ignored by Labour candidates, only 2 per cent of whom mentioned the issue (Butler and Pinto-Duschinsky, 1971). The reticence on the Conservative side was largely due to central disapproval of exploiting the issue. In fact Crossman even suggested that there was a tacit understanding between the parties not to raise the issue in the campaign (Deakin and Bourne, 1970, p. 205). The Conservative manifesto reflected Mr Heath's more recent policy statements. It reaffirmed the commitment to existing Commonwealth immigrants that they could bring in their wives and young children but confirmed Conservative intentions to end further large-scale immigration by ensuring that work permits in the future would not carry the right of permanent settlement for the holder or his dependants and that they would normally only be issued for twelve months.

The most extraordinary feature of the 1970 election campaign was the role of Powell who, though a Conservative candidate, acted as though he was a political force in his own right. His election address, issued early in the campaign, was treated by the press as a manifesto and on the issues of immigration and entry into the EEC was directly at variance with party policy and a challenge to Heath and the Shadow Cabinet. On immigration he demanded a complete halt to new immigration, a new citizenship law to distinguish UK citizens from everyone else, and voluntary repatriation. Otherwise the immigration problem could bring a 'threat of division, violence and bloodshed of American dimensions' (Schoen, 1977, pp. 51–2). It was widely believed that if the Tories lost the election, as was expected, Powell would attempt to gain the leadership for himself.

The election campaign began quietly with Conservative leaders attempting to ignore Powell. However, on 3 June Benn dramatically attacked Powell, accusing him of 'raising the flag of racialism over Wolverhampton – a flag which was beginning to look suspiciously like the one that fluttered over Dachau and Belsen' (Wood, 1970). Benn's attack received enormous publicity and made Powell the centre of attention once again. Benn's extravagant rhetoric enabled Heath to condemn Benn's language while disassociating himself from Powell's views on immigration. On 11 June Powell himself dropped a bombshell when he returned to an old theme of his, accusing the authorities of misleading the public about the numbers of immigrants coming into the country to the point 'where one begins to wonder if the Foreign Office was the only Department of State into which enemies of this country were infiltrated' (Schoen, 1977, p. 53). This speech was widely criticised but Heath refused to disown Powell as a Conservative candidate and contented himself with saying 'I will never use actions or words or support actions which exploit or intensify divisions within our society' (Butler and Pinto-Duschinsky, 1971, p. 163). The violence of the language used by Benn against Powell distracted attention from the hostility which existed between Heath and Powell. The latter realised that he would have no chance of serving in a Conservative administration under Heath but, hoping to succeed him after the likely defeat, he called on his supporters to vote Conservative.

The unexpected Conservative victory at the General Election, when the Conservatives gained 77 seats and had a comfortable overall majority of 43, greatly strengthened Heath's position as leader and led to Powell's increasing isolation in the party and finally to his departure to the Ulster Unionists. Paradoxically Powell may have been a major factor contributing to the Conservative victory and therefore to his own political downfall. The very high swings to the Conservative Party in parts of the West Midlands suggested that Powell's campaign had an important local effect in Birmingham and parts of the Black Country. In Birmingham in seats with few immigrant voters the swings to the Conservative Party were well above the regional average for the West Midlands which was 5.3 per cent: for example Perry Barr had a swing of 6.8 per cent, Stetchford 7.1 per cent, Yardley 6.5 per cent, Hall Green 6.2 per cent and Northfield 8.6 per cent. In Black Country seats close to Powell's own seat of Wolverhampton South-West the swings were: Wolverhampton North-East 9.1 per cent, Cannock 10.7 per cent, Dudley 9.2 per cent, Brierley Hill 9.1 per cent, and in his own seat of Wolverhampton South-West, 8.3 per cent (Layton-Henry, 1978a). Walker (1977, pp. 111–12) shows that Powell's support was highest in the West Midlands.

The possible impact of Powell on the 1970 General Election has led to a number of academic studies of the role of immigration in influencing the result. It appears clear that Powell's campaign associated the Conservative Party with opposition to immigration in the perceptions of the general public, as Table 6.1 illustrates.

At the time of the General Election of 1966 a majority of the electorate could perceive no difference in the position of the major parties on immigration control, but by the General Election of 1970 a majority saw the Conservative Party as being the toughest. It was

Table 6.1   *Perceived Position of the Parties on Control of Immigration*

Which party is more likely to keep immigrants out?

	Autumn 1964 %	Spring 1966 %	Summer 1969 %	Summer 1970 %
Conservative	26	26	50	57
Labour	19	13	6	4
No difference	41	53	36	33
Don't know	14	8	8	6

Source: Butler and Stokes, 1974, p. 306.

Powell's campaign which had made the difference. The analyses of Studlar (1978) and Miller (1980) of the impact of immigration on the election result, while coming to different conclusions about the size of its impact, both agree that there was a national effect which contributed very substantially to the Conservative victory. Schoen (1977, ch. 3) is also convinced it was decisive.

Another factor also noted in analyses of the General Election was the small but growing significance of the black vote. It appears that among the black community Powell's campaign had helped Labour by mobilising black voters and securing their support despite Labour's tough policy on immigration controls and the restrictions imposed on Kenyan Asians. The registration and turnout of black voters was reported to be much higher than in previous elections though this was partly due to the dramatic growth in the black population which was only later revealed by the results of the 1971 census. In constituencies with high proportions of black voters the swings to the Conservatives were greatly reduced which suggests that the mobilisation of black voters for Labour reduced the national swing to the Tories among the rest of the electorate (Deakin and Bourne, 1970; Butler and Pinto-Duschinsky, 1971; Layton-Henry, 1978a). Another indication of Powell's impact in raising the salience of the race issue was the defeat at Clapham of Dr David Pitt, the first West Indian to contest a winnable seat for either of the major parties. The swing against him was 10.8 per cent, more than double the average swing against Labour in South London.

It now seems certain that Powell made a major contribution to the decisive victory of his great political rival, Edward Heath. Naturally Heath claimed the credit for the electoral victory of the party of which he was the leader. Heath's appointment as Prime Minister dashed any hopes Powell had for advancement in the Conservative Party and the new Conservative administration was dominated by Heath's supporters, and of course excluded Powell.

THE HEATH ADMINISTRATION AND THE
UGANDAN ASIANS CRISIS

The new Conservative administration proceeded to fulfil its policy commitments on immigration by introducing the Immigration Act of 1971, which came into force on 1 January 1973. The main provisions of the Act were that employment vouchers would be replaced by work permits which would not carry the right of permanent residence or the right of entry for dependants, and secondly that patrials, that is, people with close connections with the United Kingdom through birth or descent, would be free from all controls. There were also provisions to strengthen the powers to prevent illegal immigration and finally voluntary repatriation was to receive some financial assistance (Immigration Act, HMSO 1971).

Powell continued his campaign on immigration in 1971 with speeches which brought increasing condemnation upon him from the press and other politicians. His continued accusations of deliberate fraud in the presentation of immigration statistics and his warnings of racial civil war made him appear to be more and more a fomenter of racial strife rather than a credible politician and prophet of the future. In Parliament his actions in committee on the Immigration Bill helped to get the patriality clause restricted to anyone who had British nationality at the time of their birth. He also continued to infuriate Heath by his continued attacks on the government's economic policy and particularly Heath's espousal of British entry into the EEC which Heath successfully negotiated, Britain becoming a member of the Community on 1 January 1973.

The hope of the Conservative leadership that the Immigration Act of 1971 would finally end the immigration debate and defuse the race issue was brutally shattered on 4 August 1972 when General Idi Amin, President of Uganda, announced the expulsion of all Asians from his country. Most of the 50,000 Asians in Uganda were British passport holders, though a small minority were Ugandan citizens, and many were of uncertain citizenship. As most were British citizens it was clear that Britain was primarily responsible for them.

The announcement that Britain might receive some 50,000 Asian immigrants from Uganda all at once was greeted with shock and horror in the media and by some politicians, particularly Powell, who claimed that Britain was not responsible for the Asians in East Africa and they should be returned to India or Pakistan. There was considerable lobbying of MPs and the Home Office, which received very substantial mail on the issue. Some local authorities like Leicester were reluctant to receive any more Asian immigrants (Humphrey and Ward, 1974, p. 31). However, the government decided that Britain would have to accept them and established a Ugandan Resettlement Board to assist their reception, dispersal and integration. Strenuous diplomatic efforts were made to get other countries to assist by admitting some of these Asians, particularly the stateless ones, and substantial numbers were accepted by India, Canada and other countries. Britain finally accepted 27,000.

The Ugandan Asian crisis received considerable publicity in the media and was a major boost to anti-immigrant organisations both within the Conservative Party, like the Monday Club, and further to the right, like the National Front. The Monday Club, a right-wing group formed to oppose decolonisation in Africa, started a 'Halt Immigration Now' campaign. The Monday Club had a growing membership at this time and was at the peak of its influence. It claimed 2,000 members of its national organisation including thirty-four MPs and fifty-five university groups, and an inflated estimate of 6,000 members in its regional organisation (Walker, 1977, p. 118). The Club was very hostile to many of Heath's policies and was increasingly obsessed with immigration, where it was very sympathetic to Powell's views. The National Front, an ultra-right-wing party, exploited the issue for all it was worth and particularly the fact that it was a Conservative government which had reneged on its electoral promises and betrayed the country by accepting the Ugandan Asians. The Front hoped to exploit this opportunity of presenting itself as the major anti-immigrant party on the right and for a time it was successful. The Ugandan Asian crisis enabled it to begin a period of growth and electoral advance which was not decisively rebutted until the General Election of 1979.

The crisis in the Conservative Party reached its climax at the annual party conference in October when the leadership was presented with a major challenge. A motion on immigration was voted on to the agenda by conference delegates and moved by Powell in his capacity as President of the Hackney South and Shoreditch constituency association whose motion had been successful in the ballot. (It is usual practice at Conservative Party conferences for space on the agenda to be left open for one motion to be selected for debate by representatives in a secret ballot.) The motion was similar to the one passed in 1969 and declared 'that this conference is convinced that the Conservative Party's declared policy on immigration is the only solution likely to be successful and should be implemented by this Government at the earliest opportunity' (Conservative Central Office, *Annual Conference Report*, 1972, p. 72). Unfortunately for the Conservative leadership Powell made it clear that his interpretation of Conservative policy was that New Commonwealth immigration should be ended, even reversed by voluntary repatriation, and that as there was in his view no legal obligation to accept the Ugandan Asians they should be included under this policy. He warned that the electorate would not forgive a party which left its promises unfulfilled (Conservative Central Office, *Annual Conference Report*, 1972).

However, the Young Conservatives and the Federation of Conservative Students, both under progressive leadership at this time, came to the rescue of the party leadership. They mobilised their generous conference representation behind an anti-Powellite resolution. David Hunt, the National Chairman of the Young Conservatives, moved an amendment to Powell's motion, deleting all the words after 'successful' and inserting 'and congratulates the Government on its swift action to accept responsibility for the Asian refugees from Uganda'. The Young Conservatives' amendment was carried and the amended resolution won by 1,721 votes to 736, a majority of 985. It was a rare but substantial victory for liberal conservatism which must have delighted the party leader. But the defeat infuriated many Conservative right-wingers who felt it was the result of a Young Conservative and Conservative Students' coup. This view was expressed, in an interview, by Anthony Reed-Herbert, who resigned from the Conservative Party after this conference and joined the National Front.

The anger felt by many right-wing Conservatives with government policy on immigration led to increasing co-operation between members of the Monday Club and the National Front, and it appeared that this was not only due to common sympathies but also to National Front infiltration of some branches. At the Monday Club rally on 16 September in Central Hall, Westminister, there was ample evidence of National Front participation. Also during the Uxbridge by-election in December the West Middlesex branch of the Monday Club was dissolved for endorsing the National Front candidate. There also appeared to be support by members of the North Kent branch of the Monday Club for the anti-Common Market candidate at the Sutton and Cheam by-election which the Tories lost to the Liberals (Humphrey and Ward, 1974, pp. 129–31; Walker, 1977, p. 128). These activities helped to discredit the Monday Club as an influential group within the Conservative Party and most of its prominent members quickly resigned. The Club then became increasingly involved in an internal struggle over its leadership which was to leave it a spent force by 1974.

Shortly after the annual conference, the government announced new immigration rules further restricting the entry rights of Commonwealth citizens, a further concession to Powellite feeling in the party. They also provided for freer access for EEC citizens (*The Times*, 23 November 1972). These rules provoked a major rebellion of Conservative MPs when they were presented to Parliament and they were defeated by 35 votes (Norton, 1976). In January 1973 revised immigration rules were introduced limiting entry to those with a parent or grandparent born in Britain. All others had to have work permits. These new rules were partly designed to prevent possible recurrences of the Kenyan and Ugandan Asian crises. They mollified those Conservative MPs who had rebelled over the first introduction of the rules because they would have endangered free entry of white Commonwealth citizens from Canada, Australia and New Zealand.

After this further success in influencing government policy Powell concentrated largely on other policy areas for the remainder of the Heath administration's period in office. He disputed with his party's leadership over economic policy, Ulster and membership of the EEC, which latter policy was to lead to his final break with the Conservative Party in the run up to the General Election of February 1974. However, he continued to press for a new Nationality Bill, arguing that much of the controversy over immigration was due to the lack of a clear legal dividing line between Commonwealth and British citizens. This was yet another policy proposal of Powell's which was to be taken up by both the major parties as a means of resolving the immigration problem by turning it into a matter of citizenship. Rarely in British political history can a single politician, excluded from the leadership of a major party, have played such a major role in policy formation and political events.

LABOUR IN OPPOSITION 1970–74

The unexpected electoral defeat was a major blow to the Labour Party but it provided an opportunity for considered reflection on the failures of its race relations and immigration policies. The initial reaction to defeat was to blame Powellism and this was reflected in many of the speeches at the annual conference and even in the motion on racialism and discrimination which stated that 'this conference condemns discrimination on the grounds of race, creed or colour. It is concerned that the pernicious and reactionary ideology of Powellism has, with the help of the Tory Party and press, gained a hold with many electors who have been frightened into support through not having enough facts to counter the argument . . .' (Labour Party, *Annual Conference Report*, 1970, p. 205).

The considered response came from the National Executive Committee's study group on immigration which in March 1972 produced an opposition Green Paper on *Citizenship, Immigration and Integration* (Labour Party, 1972). This document was the first detailed examination of race relations and immigration policy ever produced by the Labour Party. It provided a careful examination of the development of immigration policy and outlined how it considered immigration and race relations policy should be developed in the future. The study group argued that it was possible to devise a coherent and acceptable immigration policy which was not based on the colour or race of the prospective migrant; that a discriminatory policy makes integration more difficult and contributes to racial hostility; and that the notion that increasingly severe restrictions on coloured immigration would play a major part in reducing racial hostility had proved to be false, since each move towards stricter controls had led to a demand for even narrower exclusiveness or for a complete ban on coloured immigration. The report called for a major review of the citizenship laws as it argued that a logical immigration policy must be based on a logical concept of citizenship. Since 1962 colonial citizenship had had much of the positive content, such as free access to the mother country, removed. The report argued that a government inquiry should be appointed to examine all aspects of the citizenship of the United Kingdom and colonies. It needed to be decided, for example, whether to retain colonial citizenship or abandon it and allow the remaining colonies to enact their own citizenship provisions. British citizens of overseas origins with no colonial, dual or other citizenship should be allowed free entry to the United Kingdom on the same basis as other UK citizens. The report also demanded that free movement within the EEC should be extended to all citizens of the UK and not be restricted to the narrow concept of UK national as presently defined in the Treaty of Accession. Immigration controls, once the citizenship laws had been redefined, would only apply to non-citizens and this would be the logical basis of a non-discriminatory policy (Labour Party, 1972, pp. 31–6).

On integration the report called for more aid to inner-city areas on the basis of social need generally and not primarily for the welfare of immigrants. Also since the proportion of immigrants among the black population was declining and the proportion of British-born black citizens was rising, the study groups recommended that responsibility for integration policies, including the responsibility for the Community Relations Commission and the Urban Aid programme, should be transferred from the Home Office to the Department of Health and Social Security, this being the department most concerned with overall social policy. The Home Office would retain responsibility for the enforcement provisions of the Race Relations Act and the Race Relations Board. The debate within the Labour movement which the Green Paper was meant to provoke was largely pre-empted by the Ugandan Asian crisis but even so the careful work of the study group was to provide the basis for the policy statements on immigration in *Labour's Programme 1973* (Labour Party, 1973) and the Labour party *Manifesto* in 1974.

In Parliament the Labour opposition was in a more embarrassing position in developing its response to Conservative immigration policy as it was saddled with the legacy of its tough immigration policy of 1965–70. The blatantly racist aspects of the patriality clauses of the Immigration Act of 1971 were clearly foreshadowed in Labour's own Commonwealth Immigrants Act of 1968. The opposition's strategy in opposing the 1971 Act was largely based on stressing the need for a review of the citizenship laws in order to resolve the anomalies of immigration legislation.

The Ugandan Asian crisis in 1972 also provoked comparisons with the Kenyan Asian crisis in 1968 and the relatively positive response of the Heath administration compared well with the negative treatment of the Kenyan Asians by the previous Labour government. This was particularly so as the Heath government had substantially increased the number of vouchers available for Kenyan Asians (*Hansard*, 26 May 1971, cols 380–5).

Outside Parliament both the TUC and the NEC made positive

statements accepting Britain's obligations to the victims of Amin's expulsion order. The Home Policy and International committees of the NEC issued a joint statement saying that

> the Labour Party fully accepts this country's moral and legal obligations towards the Asian UK citizens and passport holders who are being expelled from Uganda . . . we therefore welcome the decision of the Government to accept their responsibilities to receive the UK citizens from Uganda and we will give our support to measures introduced by them which will positively assist the resettlement and integration of those expelled. (Labour Party, *Annual Conference Report*, 1972, pp. 383–4).

The 1972 annual Labour Party conference endorsed the NEC statement and condemned the actions of President Amin (pp. 153–8).

In November the opposition, with the help of a diverse coalition of dissident Tory MPs, successfully opposed the introduction of the immigration rules on the grounds that they overrode the rights of many immigrants, but this unexpected success was reversed by the government in January when revised rules were accepted by Parliament. In June 1973 the opposition tried to introduce a debate on the position of illegal immigrants. They pressed for an amnesty for illegal immigrants who came between 1968 and the passage of the 1971 Immigration Act and who were unable to be prosecuted if they had been here for more than six months under the old immigration rules. The new rules removed this right retrospectively. The opposition's request was rejected by the government but was later implemented when Roy Jenkins once again became Home Secretary in 1974.

CHAPTER 7

The National Front

No political system is without its dissenters and fanatics and this has been true for Britain as for any other political system despite her reputation as a stable parliamentary democracy with an emphasis on moderation and consensus. The focus of attention as far as political dissent is concerned has generally been on the left, with concern about communist activity in the trade unions and Marxist infiltration in the Labour Party and among students. This often leads to a relative neglect of the activities of the extreme right (Clutterbuck, 1978). However, rightism, as Parsons (1969, pp. 82–97) has argued for America, is deeply rooted in the social structure and dynamics of our society, and this is certainly true for Britain where much of it finds expression in the Conservative Party which has been the most successful party, electorally, this century. However, fringe groups on the far right have shown themselves capable of exploiting popular grievances and occasionally, in particular areas, have posed an electoral threat to the established parties. In isolated instances the extreme right has been able to gain the support of sizeable minorities of electors, for example in Leicester in 1976 when the National Front contested all sixteen wards and gained 16.6 per cent of the vote. In Deptford in one ward in 1976 the National Party and the National Front between them shared 44 per cent of the vote. In Blackburn in 1976 the National Party captured two district council seats from Labour. This may have been partly due to an absence of Conservative Party opposition as only one Conservative candidate contested the six seats involved.[1] In 1973 at the West Bromwich by-election the National Front gained 16 per cent of the vote. While these results are sporadic and ephemeral, they far outstrip the electoral achievements of the far left. Generally parties on the extreme right have tended to be electorally more popular than parties on the extreme left, although neither of the political extremes has achieved more than a derisory share of the national popular vote, as Table 7.1 shows. On occasion these extreme groups have been able to make more impact in other contexts, such as by leading industrial action or instigating political demonstrations.

Table 7.1 shows the comparative success of the National Front and

Table 7.1   *The Comparative Electoral Success of the National Front and the Communist Party in General Elections 1970–79*

	Seats contested	Votes gained	Average share of votes per seat	Average % of vote in each seat contested
1970				
NF	10	11,449	1,145	3·6
CP	58	36,969	637	1·1
Feb. 1974				
NF	54	75,875	1,405	3·3
CP	44	32,743	744	1·7
Oct. 1974				
NF	90	113,844	1,265	3·1
CP	29	17,426	601	1·5
1979				
NF	303	191,719	633	1·4
CP	38	16,858	444	0·9

Source: Times Guides to the House of Commons, 1970–79.

the Communist Party in British general elections from 1970 to 1979. What is remarkable is the stability of the average share of the vote per seat until 1979, when there is a significant decline. The decline in the National Front average vote in 1979 was partly due to the tremendous increase in seats contested but also to real loss of support.

IMMIGRATION AND THE FAR RIGHT

Immigration seems to have been a crucial factor stimulating the emergence of extreme right-wing groups in Britain. In 1902 the British Brothers League was formed to oppose Jewish immigration into Britain (Benewick, 1972, pp. 27–39). The League concentrated its activities in the East End of London to which came the large majority of Jewish immigrants fleeing from the pogroms in Tsarist Russia. Between the two world wars the major movement on the extreme right was the British Union of Fascists founded by Oswald Mosley in 1932. Like the British Brothers League it concentrated its activities in the East End of London where something of an anti-semitic, chauvinistic tradition seems to have been established. Certainly support for extreme right-wing movements continues to be more marked in the East End than elsewhere. The British Union of Fascists copied the militaristic style and discipline of the Italian and German Fascists and their cult of the charismatic leader. However, they failed to attract much support despite all their efforts to provoke violence in order to gain publicity and members. Their main achievement was to stimulate the passing of the Public Order Act in 1936 after the 'Battle of Cable Street'. The movement fizzled out with the onset of the Second World War and Mosley and other leading Fascists were interned when war was declared.

Immediately after the war Mosley tried to revive his Union Movement and there was a flurry of marches and activities organised by his New Union Movement, especially in 1948 and 1949, but his efforts failed to generate much support. A disheartened Mosley went into voluntary exile in 1951.

Then in 1954 a new right-wing movement, the League of Empire Loyalists, was founded by A. K. Chesterton. This was a ginger group to the right of the Conservative Party. Its members were appalled at Conservative acceptance of the decline of Empire, independence for India and eventual independence for the remaining colonies. The League favoured a continuation of the Empire, especially in Africa, where they strongly supported the white settlers. They were opposed to coloured immigration into Britain which they felt would lead to the 'mongrelisation' of the British race. Many of the League's leaders, including Chesterton, believed in the myth of a world-wide Jewish conspiracy. They longed for a return to the age of British imperialism when Britain's authority in the world was paramount (Thayer, 1965). The League specialised in political stunts, especially disrupting Conservative Party meetings, and its members were particularly hostile to Harold Macmillan after his 'winds of change' speech. In 1958 the League claimed 3,000 members but their disruptive tactics at the annual Conservative Party conference that year aroused considerable disapproval among Conservative leaders who began actively to discourage membership of the League. The League then went into steep decline which was accelerated by the Conservative electoral victory in 1959, so that by 1961 the League claimed only 300 members (Walker, 1977). Even before its peak in 1958 some members of the League had left to form more aggressively militant movements such as Colin Jordan's White Defence League and John Bean's National Labour Party. This tendency for groups on the extreme right to fragment, re-form and split again has been a constant factor and one which shows no sign of diminishing. It also occurs on the far left, though not, perhaps, to the same extent.

The race riots in 1958 in Nottingham, but more especially those in Notting Hill, presented the extreme right with a new issue to exploit, namely the growing public hostility to coloured immigration. The White Defence League and the National Labour Party immediately became active in Notting Hill in order to exploit the racial tension and recruit members. Oswald Mosley also saw the riots as an opportunity to rebuild his Union Movement and he returned to England to contest

North Kensington in the General Election of 1959. However, Mosley gained only 8.1 per cent of the vote and lost his deposit. This was the first time he had lost a deposit in a general election and he was incredulous and bitterly disappointed by his poor performance. He even attempted to challenge the result of the election (Butler and Rose, 1960, p. 185).

In 1960 the White Defence League and the National Labour Party merged to form the British National Party. This organisation involved many leading rightists, some of whom were to become leading members of the National Front. Andrew Fountaine, the president of the British National Party, was a Norfolk landowner who had been adopted as Conservative parliamentary candidate for Chorley in 1949 but was refused official endorsement after an anti-semitic speech at the annual party conference. He stood as an independent conservative in the 1950 Election, without official Conservative opposition, and nearly won the seat (Walker, 1977, pp. 34–5). Colin Jordan, John Bean and John Tyndall were other prominent members of the new party. The British National Party was in favour of repatriating coloured immigrants, preserving the British race and freeing Britain from the domination of international Jewish financiers. In 1962 Colin Jordan withdrew from the British National Party to form the National Socialist Movement which was even more openly Nazi in its sympathies (Walker, 1977, p. 41). John Tyndall and Martin Webster, soon to be the most well-known leaders of the National Front, left the British National Party with Jordan. Two years later they split off from the National Socialist Movement to form their own party, the Greater Britain Movement.

As has already been argued in Chapter 3, the passage of the Immigration Control Act in 1962 raised the salience of New Commonwealth immigration but at the same time did not assuage public concern. In the following year the Southall Residents Association was formed to protest at the continuing influx of Asians into the borough and the rising numbers of Asian children in the schools. The British National Party decided to exploit the fears of local residents who were opposed to the changing nature of their area and were particularly worried about property values and education. Many residents felt that the politicians of the major parties were unwilling to respond to their anxieties. For example, in October 1963 Sir Edward Boyle addressed a meeting of 400 Southall parents where he made it clear that the government was opposed to establishing separate immigrant schools (Foot, 1965, p. 142). In the local elections of 1963 members of the Southall Residents Association supported two British National Party candidates in Hamborough and Glebe wards where they achieved 27.5 per cent and 13.5 per cent of the votes. In the 1964 General Election, in an attempt to build on this effort, the British National Party put up

John Bean as its parliamentary candidate and he gained 3,410 votes, 9.1 per cent of the poll. His vote was larger than the majority of the winning Labour candidate, George Pargiter, who was returned for Labour with a majority of 1,897 (*Times Guide to the House of Commons*, 1964; Walker, 1977, p. 41). While the ability of the extreme right to achieve relatively good polls has tended to be sporadic and ephemeral, their importance should not be overlooked as it showed that quite large numbers of electors who felt their fears and anxieties were not being acted upon by established politicians were, on occasion, prepared to support extremist candidates at least on this issue. The Smethwick victory of Peter Griffiths in this election showed how popular concern over immigration could have a major political impact and Griffiths himself justified his campaign by arguing that unless strong popular feelings were represented by mainstream politicians the result might be a turn to violence and extremism (Griffiths, 1966, p. 154). However, between 1964 and 1966 the Labour government acted vigorously to introduce tough immigration controls and with the co-operation of the Tory leadership to reduce the salience of the issue and make it subject to a bipartisan consensus. They were successful in reducing public concern and the issue played no part in the 1966 General Election. Candidates of the extreme right did badly and even Peter Griffiths was easily defeated.

THE FORMATION OF THE NATIONAL FRONT

However, after their 1966 débâcle groups on the extreme right began to move towards unity and as the result of a union between the League of Empire Loyalists and the British National Party, the National Front was founded. Several other groups and individuals were also involved. John Tyndall dissolved his Greater Britain Movement and urged all the members to join the National Front. The English National Party also joined as did some branches of the Anglo-Rhodesian Society and members of the Racial Preservation Society (Hanna, 1974, p. 49).

The first year of the National Front was taken up by a controversy over whether John Tyndall and members of his Greater Britain Movement should be allowed to join. They had originally been excluded because of their association with fascism and militarism but they were eventually absorbed into the new movement. Soon after this problem was resolved the extreme right received a tremendous boost with Powell's campaign against the Kenyan Asians and his 'river of blood' speech of April 1968 which brought the immigration issue once more into the forefront of public consciousness. The National Front welcomed Powell's speech and Chesterton told *The Times*, 'What Mr Powell has said does not vary in any way from our view', though John

Tyndall reminded the National Front members, 'Let us not forget who uttered the warning long, long ago' (Foot, 1969, pp. 126–7).

Powell's campaign brought direct benefits to the National Front. It gave tremendous publicity to the race issue which was their major *raison d'être*, it legitimised consideration and support for policies like repatriation which had hitherto been considered not only extreme but also illegitimate, and it consequently stimulated recruitment. Paul Foot was told by a leading National Front official that at this time in Huddersfield 'We held a march in support of what Powell had said and we signed eight people up as members of the branch that afternoon. Powell's speeches gave our membership and morale a tremendous boost. Before Powell spoke, we were getting only cranks and perverts. After his speeches we started to attract in a secret sort of way the right-wing members of the Tory organisations.' In Huddersfield the impetus was maintained and in the local elections in May 1969 the National Front candidates averaged 8 per cent of the vote in the wards where they stood. In May 1970 in Huddersfield the National Front contested thirteen out of fifteen wards and won 10.5 per cent of the vote (Walker, 1977, pp. 90–1). But this momentum was not maintained in the General Election of June 1970 when the National Front put up ten candidates and these averaged only 3.5 per cent of the vote in the seats they contested. There were two major reasons for this electoral setback suffered by the National Front. First, it is apparent that the National Front vote tends to be rather stable in absolute terms and more committed than that of other parties so that the higher turnouts in general elections compared with local elections or by-elections substantially reduces the National Front share of the poll (Steed, 1978). Secondly, in the 1970 General Election the focus of anti-immigrant attention was on Enoch Powell who called on his supporters to vote Conservative, and it is clear from Chapter 6 that much of the potential support for the National Front was diverted by Powell to the Conservative Party.

In a number of ways the National Front and the Conservative Party are in direct competition for activists and voters. The National Front claims much of the same political ground as the Conservatives. It claims to be a patriotic party and uses the Union Jack as its major symbol; it supports the Ulster Unionists against the IRA; it is anti-communist; it is anti-Common Market as this undermines British sovereignty; it favours capital punishment and tough penalties for criminal offenders; and it is opposed to coloured immigration and in favour of the repatriation of coloured immigrants (Walker, 1977; Fielding, 1981). All of these policies would find favour with many Conservatives, especially those on the right wing of the party. It is not surprising then that the National Front has tended to attract numbers of disillusioned Conservatives and to be most successful when the Conservative Party is unpopular.

Conversely, when Conservative popularity is high the extreme right tends to be less successful.

A further problem for the National Front leadership is that members and supporters are attracted predominantly by the National Front's stand on immigration and for this reason this is the issue which dominates National Front campaigns and publicity. The fascist sympathies of many National Front leaders, their past involvement in militaristic fascist groups and their belief in the international conspiracy of world Jewry are tenets which do not have mass appeal and are therefore hidden from the mass membership and the wider public to which the party appeals for members and support. Billig distinguishes between the more respectable surface ideology which is the public face of the National Front and the depth ideology which sustains the convictions and enthusiasm of the inner circle. Public references to this depth ideology of anti-semitism and fascism are made in oblique and ambiguous ways so that those who wish to ignore these uncongenial meanings can comfortably do so (Billig, 1978, pp. 137–8).

Another dilemma facing the leaders of extreme right-wing parties including the National Front is the relationship between electoral politics and street politics. On the one hand, participation in electoral politics provides purposeful activity for full-time members and conveys an image of a respectable, legitimate and democratic political party. It confers prestige on full-time activists who understand the technical details of electoral law and running a campaign, but some success is necessary to maintain enthusiasm and attract new members. On the other hand, aspects of street politics such as marches, demonstrations, heckling opponents and disrupting their meetings provide immediate satisfaction for those involved, attract publicity and make fewer demands upon the limited ideological and administrative resources of lukewarm members, particularly young people on the edge of the movement attracted by the violence and excitement of confrontation. Scott (1975, pp. 230–1) argues that there may be an inverse relationship between electoral politics and street politics, but for a small fringe party like the National Front the two may be surprisingly complementary. The publicity generated by violent clashes with opponents may rebound to the National Front's advantage as appeared to happen after the Lewisham march and the meetings held during the Ladywood by-election in August 1977. The publicity generated by these clashes appears to have increased the National Front's share of the poll and much of the blame for the violence was placed by the press on the extreme left-wing opponents of the National Front (Layton-Henry and Taylor, 1977/8, pp. 130–42; Troyna, 1982, pp. 259–78). There is no doubt that street politics and violence have been important elements in the armoury of the National Front (Fielding, 1981, pp. 157–91) and this is fully in accord with the fascist traditions espoused by the inner core of its leadership and approved of by many ordinary members as well (Billig, 1978).

After the electoral setback of the 1970 General Election there was increasing dissatisfaction with Chesterton's leadership and he was forced to resign. John O'Brien, an ex-Conservative Party member who had drifted into extreme right-wing politics after Powell's speech in April 1968, succeeded Chesterton as chairman. O'Brien encouraged close links with Powellite groups, the Immigration Control Association and branches of the Monday Club, some of which were infiltrated by National Front members (Walker, 1977, pp. 108–32). This strategy of building up the National Front as a respectable right-wing party and recruiting members from right–wing Tory groups was thrown into jeopardy by growing evidence of Tyndall's and Webster's links with European neo-Nazi parties. O'Brien attempted to expel Tyndall and Webster from the National Frorrt but failed and in 1972 it was Tyndall who became the new chairman of the National Front after O'Brien had left to join the National Independence Party.

TYNDALL AND THE RISE OF THE NATIONAL FRONT

Shortly after Tyndall became chairman, the National Front's greatest recruiting sergeant, President Idi Amin, announced the explusion of Asians from Uganda. The Ugandan Asians crisis and the enormous publicity it generated gave the National Front a considerable boost. Anxieties were raised concerning a massive immigration of Asians to particular areas like Southall and Leicester. Moreover, once Heath announced, against Powell's advice, that the government would honour its obligations and accept the British passport-holders from Uganda, then those opposed to Asian immigration could not look to the Conservative Party to represent their wishes. The defeat of Powell and his supporters at the annual party conference further infuriated many right-wing Conservatives who felt the defeat was the result of a Young Conservative coup. Many right-wingers left to join the National Front and many who remained were more willing to co-operate with the extreme right. At the. Uxbridge by-election in December the West Middlesex branch of the Monday Club supported the National Front candidate who gained 2,960 votes, 8.2 per cent of the poll. The branch was dissolved, as was the Essex branch of the Monday Club in June 1973, because of its close links with the National Front (Walker, 1977). In July Roy Painter, the Conservative parliamentary candidate for Tottenham, defected to the National Front.

The Ugandan Asian crisis stimulated a period of rapid growth for the National Front which one observer claimed raised its membership to a peak of 14,000 in 1973 (Nugent and King, 1977, p. 175). In July 1973 the National Front claimed that it had thirty-two branches and eighty groups (Hanna, 1974, p. 49) which suggests that the above membership claim was exaggerated; nevertheless the National Front was expanding rapidly. It achieved a spectacular success, for a fringe party, in the West Bromwich by-election of May 1973 when its candidate, Martin Webster, gained 4,789 votes, 16 per cent of the poll. This was the first and only occasion when the National Front gained over 12.5 per cent of the vote in a parliamentary election and thereby saved its deposit. The public refusal of Enoch Powell to support the Conservative candidate because of his liberal views on immigration and his support for British membership of the EEC may have helped the National Front. The low poll certainly raised the National Front's proportion of the vote. In the non-metropolitan district elections in June the National Front ran forty-seven candidates, ten of whom achieved between 20 and 26 per cent of the vote: five in Blackburn, three in Leicester and one each in Nottingham and Staines. The National Front candidate was placed higher than the Conservative in six Leicester wards and in one ward in Staines. These results were rather better than the April and May local election results held before the by-election, though these did included occasional good results for the National Front (Hanna, 1974, p. 52; Taylor, 1982). However, the National Front proved unable to sustain these encouraging results as memories of the Ugandan Asians crisis faded. In a by-election in Hove in November the National Front gained 1,409 votes, only 3 per cent of the poll, which was a great disappointment after the West Bromwich result. At Hove most of the anti-government protest vote appears to have gone to the Liberals who came second to the Conservatives with 37.7 per cent of the poll. At West Bromwich the Liberals did not stand and this was probably another important factor helping the National Front in that by-election (Husbands, 1975, pp. 403–5).

The success of the National Front in the two years following Amin's expulsion of the Ugandan Asians was to result in two major problems. First, there was a large influx of new members which included some with considerable political experience like Roy Painter and John Kingsley Read. This influx was to provide an alternative leadership and power base within the National Front, which was to result in a challenge to the leadership of Tyndall and Webster. Most of these new members had not previously been involved in extreme right-wing politics. Secondly, the more success and publicity the National Front achieved, the more opposition it generated from a wide variety of sources, for example from extreme left-wing groups, the trade unions, Jewish organisations, immigrant groups, the major parties and the media. In September 1974 there was a hostile television programme on ITV which included interviews with Tyndall and O'Brien. Tyndall was closely questioned about his racialist policies and their implications, and O'Brien made accusations about the neo-Nazi affiliations of Tyndall and Webster. The programme appalled the leaders of the new wave of recruits to the National Front and they were just able to mobilise enough support on the directorate to vote Tyndall out of the leadership. John Kingsley Read, who had been a leading Conservative in Blackburn before joining the National Front, replaced Tyndall as chairman. His success, however, was to be shortlived (Walker, 1977, pp. 148–9).

In the General Election of February 1974 the National Front fielded fifty-four candidates, all of whom lost their deposits. Only thirteen achieved more than 4 per cent of the vote in their contests and the best result was in West Bromwich West, where George Bowen gained 3,107 votes, 7.8 per cent of the poll. These results were bitterly disappointing to the National Front, as they appeared to represent a substantial decline from the local and by-election results of the previous year.

THE RESPONSE FROM THE LEFT

However, the growing activity of the National Front and its increased numbers of candidates did not go unnoticed on the left. On 15 June the National Front had organised a march to be followed by a meeting at Conway Hall to protest against government immigration policy. The National Front had held meetings in this hall over the previous four years and in October 1973 a meeting had been picketed by left-wing demonstrators. Liberation, the successor organisation to the Movement for Colonial Freedom, decided to organise a counter-demonstration against the National Front. It also booked a room for a meeting in Conway Hall on 15 June and informed the police that it wished to march along the same route as the National Front. Meanwhile the leaders of Liberation invited other left-wing groups to support its counter-demonstration. The police insisted that the marches should use separate routes and on the day 923 police were on duty to keep the 900 National Front marchers and the 1,000 Liberation supporters apart. Some members of the Liberation march were determined to orchestrate a violent confrontation with the National Front marchers and, according to Lord Justice Scarman, they mounted 'a deliberate, determined and sustained attack' on the police lines separating the marches: 'It was unexpected, unprovoked and viciously violent' (Clutterbuck, 1978, pp. 152–67; see also Scarman, 1975). In the ensuing violence Kevin Gately, a student, died and a police inspector was fatally injured. In the subsequent analyses of the disturbances supporters of the International Marxist Group were largely blamed, though there was some criticism of the police as well.

Many members of the far left believed it was an affront to democracy that members of a fascist party should be allowed to march, to publicise their policies and to give the impression that they were members of a legitimate political movement. Both the extreme left and the extreme right were opposed to the established party system and were appealing to the same constituency. Tyndall had told the Essex Monday Club that the National Front wished 'to win over millions of working-class voters to a patriotic and non-leftist movement' (Walker, 1977, p. 173). As the National Front grew bolder in its campaigns and more provocative in organising marches in immigrant areas to encourage intimidation and a violent response, its left-wing opponents mobilised in kind. The pattern of the National Front marching protected by the police and being harassed by its left-wing opponents was to become more and more intense over the next few years. It was also to raise the question of whether the right of freedom of speech, freedom of assembly and other attributes of a parliamentary democracy should be accorded to a party which was racist and militaristic. The left felt that the incitement to racial hatred provisions of the Public Order Act should be enforced against the National Front whose marches should be banned. The National Front favoured such marches as they achieved publicity for itself and provoked its opponents into violence with the police who were protecting the National Front's democratic right to march. The result was often bad publicity for the left and relatively good publicity for the National Front. In marches held in August in Leicester and in September in London the National Front had to march with heavy police protection from left-wing counter-demonstrators who greatly outnumbered the National Front marchers. The left increasingly proved that it could organise far more people for its public demonstrations than the National Front.

THE GENERAL ELECTION OF OCTOBER 1974

The National Front nominated ninety candidates in the General Election held in October 1974. It thus gained television and radio broadcasting time. However, the Labour Party was so concerned at the efforts of the National Front to break into the party system that Labour candidates were forbidden to appear on public platforms or on radio or television programmes with National Front candidates. Under the broadcasting rules of equal access for the candidates of the major parties this prevented the National Front from appearing on any programmes in addition to those it was legally entitled to by virtue of its number of candidatures. The results of the Election for the National Front Candidates were mixed. All ninety deposits were lost at a cost to the party of £13,500, but some moderately good results were achieved, particularly in London. In thirteen London seats the National Front gained over 4.5 per cent of the vote with a best performance in a general election contest of 9.4 per cent in Hackney South. Outside London the party's results were very poor with only four candidates achieving over 4.5 per cent of the vote – in Leicester East and West, Wolverhampton South-East and West Bromwich West. The success in the London seats appeared to be largely due to the National Front capitalising on the legacy of support for the far right in the East End of London and on an anti-black protest vote in a number of constituencies (Taylor, 1982, pp. 36–43).

After the General Election the battle between Tyndall and Kingsley Read was joined in earnest. Read was the leader of the relatively recent wave of recruits, many of whom were ex-Conservatives and who were suspicious of Tyndall and his supporters with their past involvement in neo-Nazi groups. In October the ruling body of the National Front, the directorate, was elected for the first time by a ballot of all the members and the result was a body finely balanced between the two sides. Tyndall was demoted from chairman to vice-chairman and Read was elected chairman. However, Read did not have enough support to assert his authority and expel Tyndall. Almost the whole of 1975 was taken up with this internal power struggle and in October, in a crucial vote, the directorate decided to take no further action against Tyndall. Read's subsequent attempt to expel Tyndall was overturned by the courts and Read and his supporters left to form the National Party. This split left Tyndall with the National Front name and premises and his own journal 'Spearhead', which was to prove an invaluable asset in the battle for membership. When the dust had settled the National Party had taken only twenty-nine branches or groups and 2,000 members; 101 branches and 8,000 members had stayed with Tyndall (Walker, 1977).

THE MALAWI ASIANS CRISIS

The bruised and introverted movements on the far right were soon galvanised into a frenzy of activity by a new immigration scare in May 1976. Early that year small numbers of Asians from Malawi began arriving in Britain as the result of restrictive measures taken against them by the Malawi government. These Asians were UK passport holders entitled to come to Britain under the quotas established for non-patrials in 1968. Some of these migrants were temporarily housed by West Sussex Council in a four-star hotel and this provoked an eruption of hostile headlines and stories, particularly in the popular press. The *Sun* headline on 4 May was, 'Scandal of £600 a week immigrants', which was followed by 'New Flood of Asians in Britain' (*Daily Mirror*) and 'We Want More Money Say the £600 a Week Asians' (*Daily Express*). Eagerly the National Front and the National Party leapt at this new opportunity and organised demonstrations at the airports and in Downing Street. These media events took place two days before local elections outside London and the extreme right had a string of good results. In Leicester, where the National Front fought all sixteen wards, it averaged 16.6 per cent of the vote with a highest share of 27.5 per cent. In Sandwell (West Bromwich) the National Front contested eleven wards and averaged 17.6 per cent. In Bradford, where the National Front had organised a march through immigrant areas the previous month and provoked young Asians into attacking the police escort, the party achieved 10.9 per cent with a highest share of 21.3 per cent. In Wolverhampton the National Front gained 20.7 per cent in one ward and an average of 9.2 per cent in the eight wards it contested. In Blackburn, the local stronghold of Kingsley Read, the National Party won two seats and their eight candidates achieved an average of nearly 40 per cent of the vote. These were the best results, and elsewhere the National Front performance was patchy (there were no local elections in London that year) but they showed how powerfully the media could inflame popular prejudices over coloured immigration and how, when these prejudices were aroused, quite large minorities of the electorate were prepared to vote for extreme right-wing candidates. Taylor (1982, pp. 45–8) argues that the presence of a large settled Asian community to which the new Malawi Asian settlers might come seems to have stimulated National Front voting in areas like Leicester and Bradford.

223352

THE LABOUR PARTY'S RESPONSE

These local election results, particularly the National Party's victories in Blackburn where Barbara Castle, a prominent member of Labour's NEC, was MP, shocked Labour Party leaders. It was clear that large numbers of hitherto Labour voters had supported the extreme right and that this challenge was no longer confined to London and the Midlands but had penetrated the northern heartlands of the party. The national agent was sent on a tour of northern constituencies and Transport House officials drew up a list of twenty-one constituencies where National Front candidates might allow the constituency to fall to the Conservatives (Walker, 1977, p. 200; Layton-Henry, 1978a).

The NEC decided to launch a campaign against racialism in September jointly with the TUC. The aim was mainly to educate Labour Party members and trade unionists about the evils of racialism and the anti-working class implications of the policies of the National Front and other right-wing groups. Many members of the Labour Party hoped that this marked the end of the leadership's previous policy of appeasing racism and a turn to a more positive offensive. An amnesty announced by Roy Jenkins for illegal immigrants caught retrospectively by the 1971 immigration legislation, his relaxation of the immigration rules, the introduction of a tough new Race Relations Bill and criminal penalties for incitement to racial hatred also suggested that the Labour government as well as the NEC was committed to a new positive approach to race relations issues and that the continuous process of capitulating to racist pressures was at an end.

Local committees against racism and fascism were formed or re-established after the 1976 elections in most towns and cities with large black populations. Local trades councils, trade union branches, student organisations, Labour Party branches and far left groups were involved as well as immigrant organisations. The Labour Party conference passed a resolution calling for a campaign against racialism and advising all Labour councils to ban the use of council property by the National Front and the National Party. It appealed to all constituency parties to support fully the formation of local anti-fascist and anti-racist committees (Labour Party, *Annual Conference Report*, 1976).

CONTINUING MOMENTUM

In the early summer of 1976 a number of events occurred which provided an eager press with sensationalist stories on immigration and race. These provided an unfortunate backcloth to the government's Race Relations Bill. In May Enoch Powell released details of the confidential Hawley Report on Asian immigration which alleged widespread fraud and evasion of immigration controls. Once again Powell warned of impending violence if coloured immigration were allowed to continue. The same month Robert Relf, a man long involved in extreme right politics, went on hunger strike after being jailed for contempt of court after refusing to remove a notice from outside his Leamington house which advertised it as being for sale to English people only. He had been prosecuted and convicted under the Race Relations Act 1968, but had refused to comply with the judgement of the court. After seven weeks of court appearances, protests and demonstrations during his hunger strike he was released by the judge who felt his martyrdom had continued long enough. However, he had refused to apologise for his actions, had gained considerable publicity and had become a hero of the extreme right. Also, even more seriously, in May there were a number of apparently racial murders. In Southall on 19 May an 18-year-old Sikh, Gurdip Singh Jagger, was stabbed to death and Kingsley Read was reported to have responded by saying 'One down – a million to go'. There were violent demonstrations in Southall by the Asian community in response to the murder, and Read was unsuccessfully prosecuted under the incitement to racial hatred provisions of the Public Order Act. The Asian community generally was becoming increasingly concerned by the growing activities of the National Front and the National Party and the incidence of racial attacks on Asian people and property.

In June the National Front and the National Party shared 44.5 per cent of the vote in a local council by-election in Deptford, though Labour won the seat. The National Front also gained 6 per cent and 6.6 per cent of the vote in parliamentary by-elections in Rotherham and Thurrock. However, later in the year the National Front's results were mixed, with a 'success' in the Walsall North by-election of 7.3 per cent when the Liberals were pushed into fourth place; and a dismal failure at Newcastle Central where the National Front gained 1.8 per cent and was beaten into fifth place by a far left candidate.

During 1977 the National Front made considerable efforts to maintain its momentum and to present itself as a major respectable party challenging for power. In three by-elections in March the National Front stood in all contests, gaining 3.8 per cent in Ashfield and 5.2 per cent in the City of London and Westminster South; but in Stetchford, Birmingham, it shocked its opponents by achieving 8.2 per cent of the vote and pushing the Liberals into fourth place. In local elections in May the National Front achieved rather poor results outside London but in the Greater London Council elections the National Front contested ninety-one of the ninety-two seats; it won 120,000 votes, gaining 5 per cent or less of the poll in fifteen seats, 5–10 per cent in fourteen seats, and over 10 per cent in three seats. Its best three were 17.8 per cent in Tower Hamlets, 13.9 per cent in Hackney and 12.5 per cent in Newham (Taylor, 1982). Steed (1978) has argued that this apparently good performance in London appeared better than it actually was due to the low turnouts in local elections combined with the stable commitment of hard-core National Front supporters and that the results were not a dramatic advance but more a reflection of traditional support for the extreme right, particularly in its heartlands in the East End.

In order to maintain its momentum the National Front planned a series of marches and organised a youth movement to show it was serious about establishing itself as a major party. Its attempts to attract young people caused consternation among teachers' organisations and its political opponents (Taylor, 1978). In August a combination of factors resulted in an explosion of publicity for the National Front. First, the National Front had organised a march in Lewisham, an area of immigrant settlement in London, on 13 August. The Socialist Workers Party, which had been recruiting well among black people, determined to stop the National Front march and drive the National Front off the streets in order to show its militancy and gain further recruits (Clutterbuck, 1978). Then on 28 August there was a by-election in the Ladywood constituency of Birmingham which probably had the largest proportion of black voters of any constituency in the country (Layton-Henry and Taylor, 1977/8).

A counter-march to the National Front's march was organised by the All Lewisham Campaign Against Racialism and Fascism. This was a broadly based body with representatives from trade unions, churches and political parties and this march passed off peacefully. However, the National Front march was attacked by members of the Socialist Workers Party and once again there occurred the spectacle of ordered ranks of National Front marchers, protected by ordered ranks of policemen, being attacked by large numbers of left-wing demonstrators. As with the Red Lion Square demonstrations, the press blamed the far left for the violence. The far left felt this violence was justified. A representative of the Socialist Workers Party said, 'We want to make it absolutely clear to the police that we are not going to allow the Nazis to walk the streets of this country. We shall do everything to stop them' (Clutterbuck, 1978, pp. 217–18). The Socialist Workers Party attacks on the police at Lewisham brought universal condemnation in the press which felt the far left was playing into the hands of the National Front. *The Sunday Times* had an article under the headline 'How the left-wingers win new recruits for the National Front' (21 August 1977) and George Gale in the *Daily Express* argued that fascism had become the prerogative of the far left and that 'The National Front is not committed to violence or to the overthrow of parliamentary institutions. And the great majority of its supporters and members are not fascists. They do not start the fighting and they do not attack the police' (15 August 1977). The National Front was well pleased with the publicity which led to recruits and offers of help in the by-election in Ladywood, to which battleground attention then turned. The far left mobilised its forces on 15 August to prevent the National Front from holding an election meeting, and once again Socialist Workers Party supporters attacked the 400 police on duty to allow the forty National Front supporters to hold their election meeting. Kim Gordon, the Socialist Workers Party, candidate, is reported to have said: 'Our intention is to frighten people from joining the National Front. We want to intimidate them. I can understand black youngsters carrying weapons. They are not afraid. They are just more militant' (Clutterbuck, 1978, p. 219; see also Layton-Henry and Taylor, 1977).

The result of the by-election gave the National Front third place with 888 votes and 5.7 per cent of the poll. The Labour candidate won easily in this safe Labour seat despite problems early in the campaign. The Socialist Workers Party candidate gained only 152 votes, 1 per cent of the poll, but an Asian Socialist Unity candidate gained 534 votes, 3.4 per cent, which probably reflected Asian concern at the role of the National Front in the campaign and expressed a protest from Asians at aspects of the local Labour Party (Layton-Henry and Taylor, 1977/8). Despite the publicity and attention the National Front received it only increased its vote by 137 over its General Election performance of February 1974 when it received 751 votes, 2.9 per cent of the poll. The success of the National Front was once again based on differential turnout and publicity and did not represent a significant electoral advance. They were also helped in Ladywood by a very poor Liberal campaign.

THE BEGINNINGS OF DECLINE

The results of the violence at Lewisham and Ladywood were twofold. First, the police became more aware of the scale of the threat to law and order posed by National Front marches and counter-demonstrations by the left. Large numbers of policemen had been injured in these two confrontations and chief constables became more willing to ban National Front marches under the Public Order Act. Attempts were made to ban a National Front march in Manchester in October and when this failed considerable efforts were made to keep the venue secret and avoid a confrontation. In February 1978 the Metropolitan Police Commissioner banned all marches and demonstrations in London for two months to prevent clashes at two by-elections in Ilford and Lambeth. Secondly, the various groups which opposed the National Front were stimulated into a major attempt to co-ordinate their efforts and in November the Anti-Nazi League was launched with the support of prominent figures from sport, the universities and the acting profession as well as trade unions, the Labour Party and far left groups. In December the more moderate Joint Committee Against Racialism was launched with the support of the major parties, immigrant organisations, the British Council of Churches, the Board of Deputies of British Jews and the National Union of Students. A further manifestation of the counter-attack on the National Front was the highly controversial party political broadcast by the Labour Party on 8 December which was totally devoted to attacking the National Front. It was followed by another joint Labour/TUC campaign against the National Front, which was to involve the wide distribution of a leaflet entitled 'The National Front is a Nazi Front' and included the phrases 'Yesterday – the Jews; today – coloured people; tomorrow – you' (Taylor, 1982, pp. 138–9).

This counter-offensive against the National Front was massive, but a potentially more damaging blow was to follow shortly. The Conservative Party had, after the General Election of 1974, become more aware of the electoral importance of black voters and between 1974 and 1976 had taken a number of positive initiatives, but the Malawi Asian crisis had stimulated a massive 140 resolutions on immigration at the annual party conference in October 1976. Mrs Thatcher decided that the party should harden its attitude and Mr Whitelaw promised the conference that the party would develop a policy which was clearly designed to work towards an end to 'immigration as we have seen it in the postwar years' (Layton-Henry, 1980a, p. 67). In early 1978 Mrs Thatcher reinforced this hardening of Conservative immigration policy in her interview with Gordon Burns on the *World in Action* programme on 30 January. In this interview she stated that 'People are really rather afraid that this country might be rather swamped by people with a different culture', and 'We do have to hold out the prospect of an end to immigration except, of course, for compassionate cases'. She went on to argue that although she would not make immigration a major issue in the general election which was expected shortly, she felt that for major parties to neglect people's fears about immigration would only drive them to support the National Front. When Burns asked 'So, some of the support that the National Front has been attracting in recent by-elections you would hope to bring back behind the Tory party?' she replied, 'Oh, very much back, certainly, but I think that the National Front has, in fact, attracted more people from Labour voters than from us. But never be afraid to tackle something which people are worried about. We are not in politics to ignore people's worries; we are in politics to deal with them.' (Granada Television, *World in Action* 30 January 1978).

Mrs Thatcher's remarks were widely condemned as pandering to popular prejudices and even as 'giving aid and comfort to the National Front' (*The Sunday Times*, 26 February 1978). They had certainly once again raised the salience of the race issue and brought about a surge in popular support for the Conservative opposition even though Mrs Thatcher had difficulty in indicating where further cuts of a compassionate kind could be made in Britain's already tough immigration policy. But as the National Front had been most successful in recruiting members and winning support when the salience of the race issue was combined with neglect by the major parties, particularly the Conservative Party, of popular anxieties, Mrs Thatcher's initiative was potentially even more damaging to the National Front than the efforts of its opponents on the left. At the Ilford North by-election the next month the Conservatives easily captured the seat from Labour and Mrs Thatcher's initiative seems to have been an important factor. The National Front gained 4.7 per cent of the vote at this by-election and in the Lambeth Central by-election held in an area of major immigrant settlement in March, Labour held the seat while the National Front took 6.2 per cent of the vote.

Opposition to the National Front continued at a high level throughout 1978 with teachers' organisations taking a strong stand against National Front activity in the schools, a carnival against racism organised by the Anti-Nazi League in April, and action by local authorities to ban the use of facilities by the National Front. Stronger police action over marches and demonstrations deprived the National Front of the publicity accruing from violent confrontations with their opponents. In the local elections in May the National Front performed less well than in the previous year and did very badly in a by-election in Manchester, Moss Side in July, where it had hoped to exploit once again the existence of a substantial immigrant settlement.

The leaders of the National Front had decided to put all their resources into a major display of strength at the long-anticipated General Election, promising its members to field 300 candidates and to gain its legitimate right to the television and radio facilities that went with this. The National Front was also entitled to free postal delivery of literature in each constituency where it put up a candidate. When the election was announced in March 1979 the National Front was able to field an unprecedented 303 candidates. The Anti-Nazi League mobilised its supporters to oppose the National Front wherever it held election meetings and major clashes took place in Leicester and Southall. In Southall on 23 April the Anti-Nazi League and the local Asian community mobilised in thousands to prevent a National Front meeting. It was estimated that 10,000 people joined the anti-National Front demonstration, which was in major contrast to the mere fifty supporters the National Front was able to achieve for its meeting. Clashes took place between the police and demonstrators as the protests intensified and arrests were made. Blair Peach, a New Zealand teacher, was killed during these clashes and the Special Patrol Group of the Metropolitan Police was blamed by the demonstrators. Peach's death became a *cause célèbre* and the Anti-Nazi League mobilised a massive demonstration of support at his funeral on 28 April. The role of the police in Southall became a major issue of civil liberties and subject to both official and unofficial inquiries by distinguished investigators. (The results of official inquiries into the evidence at Southall and the death of Blair Peach were not published but the Director of Public Prosecutions decided that there was insufficient evidence to charge anybody with murder. The jury at his inquest agreed a verdict of death by misadventure. The unofficial inquiry – *Southall 23 April 1979* – was published by the National Council for Civil Liberties in 1980.)

DEFEAT AND COLLAPSE

The General Election results were a total disaster for the National Front. It won only 0.6 per cent of the total vote compared with 0.4 per cent in October 1974 despite its massive increase in candidates from ninety to 303. Its share of the vote in each constituency fell from 3.1 per cent in October 1974 to 1.4 per cent in 1979 (see Table 7.1 on p. 88).

Even in its East End strongholds of Tower Hamlets, Newham and Hackney the National Front achieved an average of only 5.2 per cent of the vote. In the Leicester area it gained only 2.4 per cent and in its West Midlands bastions of Wolverhampton, West Bromwich, Walsall and Dudley, only 2.5 per cent. These areas include almost all the forty-nine seats where the National Front achieved over 2 per cent of the poll (Taylor, 1982). It seems clear that the major reason for the electoral reverse was Mrs Thatcher's public identification of the Conservative Party with a tough line on immigration. The massive swings to the Conservatives in the ten constituencies stretching from Islington Central through the East End to Dagenham, which averaged 14.2 per cent, were areas where the National Front had achieved some of its highest support and it appears to have lost much of it to the Conservatives. The defeat was devastating to the leadership of the National Front which had placed so much of its prestige and so much of the movement's resources on fighting the election. The bill for lost deposits alone had come to £45,450 and the free publicity available on television and radio as party political broadcasts had not paid off in terms of votes and recruits. Moreover the massive mobilisation of the left through the Anti-Nazi League had shown the National Front that it was unlikely ever to achieve its goal of becoming a respectable and accepted political party. The leaders of the National Front were forced to reconsider their whole strategy as dissatisfaction mounted in the movement. John Tyndall attempted to strengthen his leadership by constitutional reforms but this was rejected by the membership and he was unable to prevent fragmentation and disintegration. In November Andrew Fountaine and his supporters formed the National Front Constitutional Movement and the leaders of the powerful Leicester branch also left the National Front and established the British Democratic Party. Tyndall, unable to assert his authority, resigned in January 1980 and formed the New National Front. The collapse and disintegration of the National Front ended speculation about the possible rise of the National Front as a fourth English party representing English chauvinism and nationalism. It also undermined the momentum of the Anti-Nazi League though this was also disintegrating under internal divisions (Taylor, 1982). However, the fragmentation of the far right and its loss of support has not ended the activity of the far right but appears to have diverted it away from electoral politics and more towards sporadic violence and racial attacks against black people.

NOTES TO CHAPTER 7

1 Blackburn District Council Elections, May 1976:

St Judes Ward		*St Thomas Ward*	
J. Frankman (NP)	1,588	J. Kingsley Read (NP)	1,106
F. Gorton (Lab)	1,478	Rev. J. E. Watson (Lab)	1,090
E. W. Gorton (Lab)	1,446	T. Ellis (Lab)	1,071
R. T. Foreman (Lab)	1,435	M. A. Madigan (Lab)	874
J. Doran (NP)	1,365	E. Adamson (NP)	802
K. Bolton (Con)	1,056	M. A. McNamee (Lib)	777
		J. Dickinson (Lib)	686
		A. Dean (Lib)	615

CHAPTER 8

The Politics of Racial Attacks

Britain is widely regarded and has regarded itself as a tolerant and fair-minded country which has always been remarkably free of political violence and extremism. There are numerous references to this tolerance and fair-mindedness by political leaders: for example, in a speech on the Race Relations Bill (1976) Mr Winston Churchill said, 'Would the Home Secretary at the same time pay tribute to the wonderful way in which the British people have accepted, for the greater part, the very substantial influx of alien culture and alien race into their midst without open conflict or racial prejudice?' In reply Mr Jenkins said 'Yes, I would' (*Hansard*, 4 March 1976, cols 1550–1). Differences between individuals and groups are not deeply felt and are assumed to be capable of resolution by compromise through accepted political, legal or economic institutional processes which are widely accepted as legitimate (Almond and Verba, 1963; Birch, 1967; Rose, 1974). Insurrection, violence and disorder are unacceptable means of expressing political dissent and there is widespread opposition to and condemnation of those who attempt to go outside accepted procedures and processes. There is considerable opposition, for example, to the use of strikes as a political weapon. This tradition of continuity and peaceful political change is symbolised by the absence of a separate and specialised riot police (though some would argue that the Special Patrol Group of the Metropolitan Police now performs such a function) and the tradition of an unarmed police force which commands widespread respect and support among the population which it is expected to serve rather than coerce.

But this picture of tranquillity and non-violence has been over-drawn, particularly by political scientists impressed by the continuity of British political institutions and the evolutionary nature of political change, especially since the middle of the nineteenth century. There are numerous examples of riots, agitation and disorders in recent British history. The power and violence of the London mob was always a factor which eighteenth- and nineteenth-century politicians had to take into account. To give an early example, Lord George Gordon's petition against Catholic relief in 1780 was supported by a mob of 50,000 and provoked five days of rioting in the capital. When the troops were called out to suppress the riots 285 rioters were killed and 173 were wounded before order was restored. In the early nineteenth century there were the Rebecca riots in south-west Wales and also the Last Labourers' revolt of 1830 and the Bristol riots of 1831. Concern about violence and disorder assisted the passage of the 1832 Reform Act and there were severe disturbances in Birmingham, Nottingham, Bristol, London and elsewhere before the Act was passed. The nationwide Chartist agitation of the 1840s and 1860s involved considerable agitation and disorder. In the 1860s there was also considerable concern about Fenian terrorism and many anti-Irish riots in both England and Scotland (Richter, 1981). The incidence of riots and disorder continued in the latter half of the nineteenth century and Richter (1964) has categorised some 452 riotous disturbances between 1865 and 1914. The twentieth century has also seen a number of similar disorders, though the incidence of these has been far less and more sporadic than those of the nineteenth century. The early twentieth century witnessed the anti-Jewish agitation in the East End of London, the Tonypandy massacre in 1911 and the Glasgow riots of 1919, which occurred in the same year as the widespread racial disturbances which took place in South Wales, Liverpool, London and Manchester. The 1930s saw the fascist agitation provoked by Mosley and his Union Movement once again centred on the East End of London.

Immigration has historically been one of the more important social phenomena provoking riots and violence. Immigrants are often perceived as alien intruders, illegitimate competitors for scarce resources such as accommodation, jobs and welfare benefits. Social tension may also be increased, particularly among young men, by competition for sexual and marriage partners. Large-scale immigration, especially if it occurs over a short period, is likely to result in considerable resentment and hostility as particular areas become the focus of immigrant settlement and local people find their neighbourhoods rapidly changing with new people, new languages and new customs. The resulting social strain and antagonism may provoke an extreme response from those who feel threatened by the influx of outsiders, particularly if the area is losing status and there is fear that property values may fall.

In Britain there has been a long history of resentment and antagonism towards foreign settlers which goes back to mediaeval times and beyond (Kiernan, 1978). This has continued to be the case even though succeeding waves of immigrants and refugees have been integrated and assimilated so successfully that their children have considered themselves 'True-Born Englishmen' and, as Defoe satirically put it,

> Proudly they learn all men to condemn
> And all their race are true-born Englishmen

Dutch, Walloons, Flemmings, Irishmen and Scots,
Vaudois and Valtelins and Hugenots.

In the nineteenth century the major migration to Britain came from
Ireland and it provoked considerable resentment, particularly in
Scotland where Irish immigration had proportionately a much greater
impact than it did in England. In 1861 some 3 per cent of the English
population had been born in Ireland, but in Scotland the proportion
was more than double this at 6.7 per cent. Riots between Scots and
Irish were common, particularly in the west of Scotland, and in
Glasgow there was an annual demonstration against Irish immigrants
which included the sport of 'Hunting the Barney' in which the mob
would beat up an Irishman (Foot, 1965, pp. 80–1). Jewish immigration
between 1880 and the First World War also led to resentment, and a
campaign for control focused on the East End of London where most of
the immigrants settled. In 1901 the British Brothers League, a militant
anti-Jewish organisation, was formed by the Conservative MP for
Stepney, Major Evans Gordon, who played a leading role in the
anti-immigrant agitation. As a result of this agitation the Conservative
government passed the Aliens Act of 1905 which gave the Home
Secretary powers to refuse entry to those who could not support
themselves and their dependants, to those whose infirmities were likely
to lead them to become a charge on the rates and also to some known
criminals. The principle of political asylum in Britain, however, was
reaffirmed and the Liberal government elected in 1906 was able to use
reports of violence against Jews in Russia to nullify the effects of the
Act, although they did not repeal it. The later attempts by Mosley and
his Union Movement to stir up anti-semitism in the East End of
London in the 1930s was relatively unsuccessful and the intitial
hostility to these immigrants gradually died away as had happened to
previous waves of migrants before. The descendants of the Irish and
the Jews and even of later waves of migrants like the Poles, Italians and
Cypriots are following the Dutch, Walloons and Hugenots. As Defoe
wrote,

Fate jumbled them together, God knows how;
Whate'er they were, they're true-born English now.

HOSTILITY TO COLOURED IMMIGRANTS

During the First World War small settlements of coloured people were
established in such seaports as Liverpool, Cardiff, Manchester, South
Shields and the East End of London. These communities were
established by colonial seamen. After the war considerable hostility and

resentment developed as black seamen and workers were sacked to make way for demobilised white soldiers seeking work and as unemployed whites objected to the very presence of blacks competing for jobs. Antagonism was no doubt increased by racial prejudice and racial stereotypes disseminated from the experience of imperialism, and feelings of Anglo-Saxon superiority towards black colonial peoples. The black settlers were doubly disadvantaged despite being British subjects as they were not native British and were therefore treated as foreigners by local residents and, being black, suffered from racial discrimination and prejudice. In 1919 race riots took place in Liverpool, Cardiff, Barry, Newport, London and Manchester (May and Cohen, 1974). These riots left a legacy of bitterness and resentment which caused the black communities to withdraw as much as possible into their own enclaves and little integration took place. These colonial communities were confined to the most depressed parts of the towns and in Liverpool and Cardiff in particular their districts were little better than coloured ghettos (Ministry of Labour, 1948). The depression and consequent high levels of unemployment between the wars provided no incentive for further immigration of colonial workers and these port settlements remained small. During the war a considerable improvement in relations between the black and white communities took place even though the numbers of black workers substantially increased. The special conditions of war when every pair of hands was needed to save the country from defeat and then work for victory caused racial prejudice to be suppressed and encouraged a better climate of racial tolerance.

The beginning of New Commonwealth immigration to Britain after the war provoked little manifest indications of hostility though discrimination against black immigrants in the provision of accommodation and employment was widespread (Glass, 1960). There were occasional incidents when special police action was required to restore order between blacks and whites. In Liverpool there was rioting from 31 July to 2 August 1948 and another race riot in Deptford on 18 July 1949. There was a series of attacks on an industrial hostel housing Indian workers near Birmingham from 6–8 August 1949. However, these appeared to be isolated incidents and New Commonwealth immigrants generally appeared to be absorbed into the expanding British economy without difficulty.

The race riots in 1958 in Nottingham and Notting Hill shattered the complacency about black immigration and gave a decisive boost to the campaign for immigration control. However, the severe sentences passed on some of the white perpetrators of the attacks on black people and the widespread condemnation of the riots prevented any recurrence. Tension and fear of similar outbreaks remained high for some time, especially in Notting Hill where right-wing groups were attempting to exploit the situation. The murder of Kelso Cochrane, a young West Indian carpenter stabbed to death by a gang of white youths in May 1959, added to the tension but the failure of Mosley to capitalise on the racial situation in North Kensington in the General Election of October 1959 brought widespread relief.

In the 1960s there began to be widespread reports of 'Paki-bashing' in the press. These were sporadic, unprovoked attacks on Asians, usually by white youths. Pearson (1976) describes one such outbreak in Accrington in the summer of 1964 and attempts to relate it to other forms of violent working-class behaviour in times of stress, such as machine-breaking in the early nineteenth century. The more immediate causes were competition for jobs and girls. The underlying cause, he argues, was the economic insecurity of the cotton towns for which the Pakistani migrant worker became a convenient scapegoat and thus an object of attack. The incidence of 'Paki-bashing' reached a peak in the period 1969–70 in the heightened racial tension following Powell's speeches and it took place in widely dispersed locations over the whole country. *Race Today* (Institute of Race Relations, 1969–71) gives numerous examples from all over the country of racial attacks and fights, some resulting in death.

RACIAL VIOLENCE IN THE 1970s

In the late 1970s and early 1980s there was further public and political concern relating to the widespread and fairly systematic attacks that had been taking place against members of the ethnic minorities in Britain. In 1978 the Bethnal Green and Stepney Trades Council published a report listing over a hundred separate incidents of racial attacks in Tower Hamlets between 1976 and August 1978. These included two murders and numerous serious assaults resulting in physical injury. The report concluded that racial abuse and attack were no longer rare and unexpected events but a constant factor of everyday life for Bengalis living in the East End of London. This report was the first to suggest that large-scale harassment and physical assaults were being perpetrated against members of the Bengali community and stated that 'there now exists in the East End a barrage of harassment, insult and intimidation, week in, week out, which fundamentally determines how the immigrant community lives and works, and how the Bengali people think and act' (Bethnal Green and Stepney Trades Council, 1978, pp. 2–3).

The growing incidence of racial attacks, it was argued, had undermined Bengali confidence in the police. Many complainants felt their complaints were not followed up and they were sometimes advised to take out private prosecutions against their assailants which they were naturally extremely reluctant to do. Some victims complained that they were themselves treated by the police as if they were guilty of an offence by complaining, often being asked to produce passports to prove they were not illegal immigrants. The report alleged that Asian victims of attacks were more likely to be arrested by the police than their white assailants, especially if they had reacted to provocation and in defending themselves had became involved in an affray. The arrest of two Bengali youths in such an incident led to a protest demonstration and sit-down by some 3,000 people outside Bethnal Green Police Station on 17 July 1978. A number of strikes and demonstrations occurred in the Brick Lane area in the summer of 1978 after the murder of Altab Ali on 4 May. Disillusionment with the police had caused Bengalis to give up complaining and to tolerate attacks as a fact of life which they could do little to prevent except by retreating further into their own ghetto for the protection and security provided by living close to members of their own community.

A crucial question which the Trades Council and later the Commission for Racial Equality (1979) wished to examine was the role of the far right, especially the National Front, in encouraging and organising racial attacks. The National Front at this time was very active in Tower Hamlets and encouraged racial hostility and incited racial hatred at street corner meetings, during marches and in printed propaganda. However, its direct involvement in racial attacks was hard to prove, as most racial attacks appeared to be the work of 'apolitical' white youths. The local community leaders had no doubts about the role of the National Front. One respondent stated that 'The National Front organise street corner meetings. These meetings are used for hate campaigns against the Bengalis . . . they use all sorts of ploys to incite the local whites against us. They tell shopkeepers that Bengalis are taking over their businesses.' Another said, 'The National Front keeps on coming to Brick Lane, apparently to sell their papers which are highly offensive anyway . . . but they take the opportunity to hurl abuses and insults on the Bengalis. The adult Bengalis ignore these insults but the youths react . . . Brick Lane has become a flashpoint of racial violence' (Commission for Racial Equality, 1979). The CRE study found the attitudes of young Asians towards the police to be very negative, that they were resentful about being stopped and searched, and that they accused the police of giving protection to the National Front and clamping down on Asians.

The murder of Akhtar Ali Baig on 17 July 1980 focused national attention on racist attacks and led to two protest demonstrations in East Ham over the murder and alleged lack of police protection for Asians in the borough (Runnymede Trust Bulletin, September 1980, p. 4). On 21 February 1981 a 17-year-old skinhead, Paul Mullery, was convicted of Baig's murder at the Old Bailey. The motive was said by the prosecution to be pure race hatred (*Guardian*, 13 February 1981).

On 18 January 1981, the fire at a West Indian party in Deptford underlined the fears, insecurity and frustration of the black community, of which racial attacks are partly the cause. The fire caused the deaths of thirteen young people and injured a further twenty-nine. Many members of the minority community were convinced that the fire and deaths were the result of a racial attack, despite the failure of the authorities to discover the cause. Even if the fire did start accidentally, in an area where National Front activity was relatively high and given the regular occurrence of racist attacks, it is not surprising that anguished parents and relatives should suspect arson. The fears and anger of the minority community were expressed on 2 March 1981, when over 6,000 people joined in a march organised by the New Cross Massacre Action Committee.

In February 1981 the all-party Joint Committee Against Racialism (JCAR) presented to the Home Secretary a dossier of over 1,000 racial attacks and requested a meeting to discuss what they argued was an increasing degree of violence being inflicted upon the persons and property of members of the ethnic minorities in Britain. The Home Secretary, William Whitelaw, was impressed by the detailed evidence collected by the JCAR on individual cases and specific incidents and was concerned by the contention that the frequency of racial attacks was increasing and that this was not entirely attributable to sporadic incidents of hooliganism but was the result of organised attempts at intimidation by extreme right-wing movements. The JCAR also reported that the police response to the problem was variable, but generally inadequate, and they suggested that specialised police units should be set up to investigate and monitor the incidence of racial harassment and violence. In response to the JCAR's approach and also to the Deptford fire, the Home Secretary agreed to set up a Home Office inquiry into racial attacks and the activities of the racist organisations alleged to be responsible, and also to consider the suggestion that specialised police units be set up. During the months before the meeting with the JCAR the Home Secretary had also been lobbied on the subject of racist attacks and harassment by the CRE, the Board of Deputies of British Jews, and ethnic minority organisations (Home Office, 1981b).

But even as the inquiry got under way the fears, frustration and alienation of young blacks were brutally exposed by the riots which occurred in Brixton in April and which were followed by similar disturbances in Liverpool in August, and elsewhere on a smaller scale.

These events dominated the headlines for a few weeks, but a constant, remaining problem is that a number of factors combine to create considerable tension in inner-city areas. The preliminary results of the 1981 census showed clearly the continuing movement of people out of the major urban centres, leaving behind inner-city areas increasingly composed of immigrant families and poor, often elderly, whites. Both these groups living in inner-city areas feel frustrated and alienated by their situation and environment. The white residents, especially the elderly, are demoralised and alienated by urban decay and the decline in status of their neighbourhood. They are frustrated by their inability to leave. The changing social composition of the area in which they live is an added cause of resentment. The expanding black community increases their feeling of status loss and decline in self-esteem and, as the once-pleasant area in which they were brought up becomes a slum, they blame their new black neighbours for the change (Rex and Tomlinson, 1979; Phizacklea and Miles, 1981; Ratcliffe, 1981). Their insecurity is also increased by fears of criminal attack and physical assault. These fears naturally increase with age and infirmity and there is no doubt that unemployment has contributed to crime. Naturally, elderly white residents feel vulnerable and look to the police for protection and vigorous action to stamp out crime.

Immigrant communities are also frustrated by their environment, poor housing and fear of racial harassment and discrimination. The high level of unemployment among young blacks is a major source of concern as it contributes to poor relations with the police. The communities are concerned at the failure of the police to take decisive action against such attacks, and at the failure of the law to act strongly against the spread of racist literature and other forms of incitement to racial hatred. They contrast this with the willingness of the police to concentrate resources on stamping out crime in areas of immigrant settlement, of which the now notorious 'Swamp 81' in Brixton is the best-known example (Scarman, 1981). These factors all combine to produce an explosive mixture in inner-city areas. Unemployment is, of course, both a cause and an exacerbating factor as immigrants are a convenient scapegoat and focus for the resentment and frustration of unemployed white youths and one which racist organisations like the National Front and the British Movement are only too willing to exploit.

During the spring and summer of 1981 continuing evidence of violence and harrassment against members of the ethnic minorities was widely reported in the media. On 10 April a black youth was murdered in Swindon in what was described by the local press as a race riot (*Swindon Evening Advertiser*, 13 April 1981). On 18 April a 20-year-old student, Satnum Singh Gill, was stabbed in Coventry city centre in a fight with skinheads. A 16-year-old youth was later charged with murder. A series of further incidents followed, including another murder, the petrol bombing of a Sikh temple, and arson at the India and Commonwealth Club, as well as numerous attacks on individual Asians and threats to shopkeepers. A march against racial attacks organised by the Coventry Committee Against Racism prompted further violence involving skinheads who appear to have been encouraged to attack marchers by two members of the British Movement and by Robert Relf, a well-known anti-immigrant campaigner in the Midlands (Taylor, 1981, p. 200). On 2 July in Walthamstow an arson attack on an Asian house led to the death of Mrs Barene Khan and her three children. Questions were raised in Parliament concerning the incidence of racial attacks, and in October 1981 Leon Brittan reported to Parliament that in 1975 there had been 2,690 cases of assault, robbery and other violent theft on victims of Afro-Caribbean or Asian appearance. In 1977 there had been 3,492 such incidents, in 1978 3,686, and in 1979 3,827 (*Hansard*, 31 October 1981, cols 380–1).

As it is only the worst incidents which gain national publicity, and since these are often geographically disparate, increasing efforts to collect systematic evidence were made in 1981 by a number of groups. For example, Dr Zaki Khan, General Secretary of the Union of Pakistani Organisations, presented William Whitelaw with a report showing that racist attacks had grown from an average of twenty to twenty-five a week in 1980 to fifty to sixty a week in 1981 (*Observer*, 14 June 1981); Ealing Community Relations Council compiled a report, *Racialist Activity in Ealing* (1981); and the police, partly responding to the Home Office Inquiry, for which thirteen police areas provided the data, compiled statistics. In a written submission to the Home Affairs Select Committee, the Metropolitan Police reported an increase in racial incidents from 177 in 1980 to 727 in 1981. The most important systematic report, *Racial Attacks*, was published by the Home Office in November (1981b).

THE HOME OFFICE REPORT

The Home Office Report defined a racial attack as 'an incident or alleged offence by a person or persons of one racial group against a person or persons or property of another racial group, where there are clear indications of a racial motive'. The Home Office study team carried out a survey of inter-racial incidents in thirteen police areas over a two-month period, from mid-May to mid-July. The thirteen areas included the major areas of immigrant settlement, and were: Bedfordshire, Greater Manchester, Kent, Lancashire, Leicestershire, Merseyside, the Metropolitan Police District, South Wales, Sussex, Thames Valley, Warwickshire, West Midlands and West Yorkshire. Information was collected on 2,630 racial incidents involving 2,851 victims. In 10 per cent of the incidents reported there was strong evidence of a racial motive as both the police and the victim agreed this was the case. In a further 15 per cent of cases there was some evidence of a racial motive with either the police or the victim believing this to be so. In 52 per cent of the incidents there was clear evidence of a non-racial motive and in the remaining cases the evidence was unclear. There was a high degree of agreement on the classification of incidents by the victims and the police. The report argued that racial attacks constituted only a very small proportion of recorded crime (less than 0.25 per cent) though if only offences of violence against the person and property were considered, this rose to 3 per cent. Moreover, it admitted that reported incidents represented only a small proportion of all such incidents. Even so, the Home Office estimated that some 7,000 racially motivated incidents would be reported in the UK in 1982, and that this estimate was likely to be on the low side (Home Office, 1981b, pp. 7–14).

The incidence of cases in which members of the ethnic minorities were the victims was much higher than for white people. The rate for Asians was fifty times higher than for white people, and for blacks it was thirty-six times higher. The report argued that there was evidence that the incidence of racial attacks was rising and that there had been a substantial increase in the past year. The JCAR's view that gangs of white youths were often involved was confirmed. Jostlings in the street, abusive remarks, broken windows and slogans daubed on walls are among the less serious kinds of racial harassment which many members of the ethnic minorities (especially Asians) experience, sometimes repeatedly. The fact that these are interwoven with far more serious, racially motivated, attacks such as murders, physical assaults and gang attacks on homes at night makes for considerable fear and insecurity among members of the ethnic minorities. The Home Office study team stated in their report that:

It was clear to us that the Asian community widely believes that it is the object of a campaign of unremitting racial harassment which it fears will grow in the future. In many places we were told that Asian families were too frightened to leave their homes at night or to visit shopping centres at weekends where gangs of skinheads congregate. Even in places where few racial incidents have occurred, the awareness of what is happening in other parts of the country induces a widespread apprehension that the climate locally is likely to deteriorate and that more serious incidents are likely in the future. In some places there was a sense of uncomplaining acceptance among some Asians of manifestations of racial violence. The problem was thought to be so widespread that they regarded it as little more than an unwelcome feature of contemporary British life. (Home Office, 1981b, p. 16)

THE ROLE OF THE ULTRA RIGHT

A major weakness in the Home Office Report was its inadequate coverage of the role of extremist organisations in instigating and encouraging racial violence and harassment. The report accepted the police view that the direct involvement of the extreme right in organising racial violence is hard to prove, as many of the attacks are carried out by young men influenced by racist propaganda but not formally involved with any particular right-wing group. However, there is considerable evidence that the extreme right does attempt to promote violence by its actions as well as indirectly through its propaganda and language. Fielding (1981, ch. 8) discusses the relationship between the National Front and violence, and certain other right-wing groups are known to have been involved in paramilitary activities; Column 88 and members of the British Movement have been convicted for illegal possession of firearms (Runnymede Trust Bulletin, March 1981, pp. 4–5). Violence is functional for the extreme right as it provides it with publicity and new recruits. It is particularly valuable if it can provoke violence in its left-wing opponents who may then be blamed by the media, and the far right thus appears respectable in comparison. In the 1970s, the main far right organisation – the National Front – achieved some modest electoral support in a few areas and was able to use these results to gain publicity, new members and a degree of respectability. Some of the leaders of the National Front even came to believe that the ballot box might be a means of achieving political gains for the movement. However, there remained a considerable emphasis on street politics in the form of marches, demonstrations and inflammatory propaganda. Scott (1975, pp. 214–38) has suggested that there may be an inverse relationship between electoral success and street politics and that, while committed members are prepared to engage in electoral activity with little hope of success, peripheral members, especially the young, are more attracted by the excitement of direct action which is provided by such activities as provocative marches in areas of immigrant settlement, demonstrations and disrupting or breaking up opponents' meetings. Fielding (1981, pp. 157–91) has shown clearly how violence is an important element in the make-up of the National Front and Billig (1978) has shown how violent individuals are attracted to National Front membership.

A further dimension of the inverse relationship between electoral activity and street politics is shown by the increasing emphasis on the latter as the former has diminished in importance. The total failure of the National Front in the General Election of 1979, after the hopes of many members had been raised by the leadership, resulted in the disintegration of the National Front and growing support for the more violently orientated British Movement. *Searchlight* (June, 1982) found that the number of people associated with ultra right-wing groups who have been convicted of violent crimes rose from fourteen in 1980 to forty in 1981. These crimes ranged from murder to causing actual bodily harm and in each case those involved were members of the National Front or the British Movement or admitted, in court, their sympathies with either organisation (*Guardian*, 5 January 1981). While ultra right-wing organisations may condemn specific acts of violence and disown members who are convicted of criminal acts, there is no doubt that they foster a climate of violence, approve certain forms of violence and attract members for whom physical action is a major return of participation in the movement. In some cases it is hard to believe that the organisations are not fully aware of, and do not condone, the activities of their members. For example, in January 1981 Roderick Roberts, said to have been the quartermaster of the British Movement in the West Midlands, was jailed by Birmingham Crown Court for seven years on conviction of arson, ten charges of possession of firearms and ammunition, and conspiracy to incite racial hatred. He was said by the judge to have wanted to provoke racial violence and then use his cache of weapons to escalate such violence (Runnymede Trust Bulletin, March 1981, p. 5). A thorough investigation of the activities of extreme right-wing groups would probably reveal substantial involvement in illegal activities.

It is clear that in the period of postwar migration black people have been subjected to a substantial amount of racial harassment and violence, though it is difficult to estimate the extent. Such crimes are hard to define and distinguish from other crimes and many such incidents are unreported. Some of these attacks represent the fruits of deliberate efforts by the far right to exploit racism and to scapegoat the ethnic minorities in an attempt to deny them their right to live and work in peace and security and to be accepted as full British citizens. Other attacks seem to be based on deep racial prejudice and hostility to people belonging to strange or different groups. In both cases it appears that the intention is to make life so insecure that black and brown citizens will be forced to leave particular housing estates, areas or even the country. There have been a number of reports of harassment on local authority estates, for example *Racial Harassment on Local Authority Housing Estates* (Commission for Racial Equality, 1981). Sivanandan (1978) gives a more general analysis. At the very least fear of harassment and attack may restrict the opportunities of blacks and Asians to live and work wherever they wish. Furthermore, if racial attacks are not vigorously suppressed, members of the minorities may be provoked into organising self-defence groups or to retaliate in kind against the provocative actions of the far right and other perpetrators of racial attacks. Both of these responses would undermine still further the fragile relations between the police and the ethnic minorities.

In June 1982 twelve young Asians in Bradford were found not guilty of charges of conspiracy and making petrol bombs with intent to endanger life and property after thirty-eight petrol bombs had been found on waste ground in the city. The defendants did not deny making the petrol bombs but argued that they did so in self-defence against expected racial attacks and that the Asian community could not rely on police protection against such attacks. This was reported by Pierce in the *Guardian* (21 June 1982) under the headline 'Revealed: A British Community Living in Terror', and also by the Runnymede Trust (August 1982, pp. 1–2). Such a verdict suggests that police relations with the ethnic minorities are already seriously strained by the widespread belief in both Asian and black communities that the police could do more to prevent racial attacks and to prosecute the perpetrators more vigorously. The Home Office Report found that there was a tendency on the part of the police to underestimate the significance of racialist incidents and activities for those threatened and there was also concern over the conviction rate for these crimes.

The incidence of racial attacks is of major concern not only because it is morally repugnant but also because of its political implications. It is crucially important for black and brown citizens to feel that they do receive equal protection under the law; otherwise their confidence in, and respect for, the law itself will be undermined. The rule of law and its enforcers, the police, are important symbols of the state's authority and its legitimacy. The police are visible mediators between the citizen and the wider structure of authority, and if the police lose the confidence of part of the community then the authority and legitimacy of the state is eroded as well.

The security and confidence of the ethnic minorities in Britain are also undermined by attacks from some politicians and groups which advocate policies of repatriation and make constant references to them as an 'alien wedge' in British society, warning of violence and civil war to come. Prominent among such groups is the Monday Club (see Chapter 6, pp. 81–3, Proctor and Pinniger, 1981), while Enoch Powell is the most prominent politician advocating such policies and expressing such views, for example in his speech to Ashton-Under-Lyme Young Conservatives on 28 March 1981, (*Sunday Times*, 29 March 1981), or in the House of Commons on 3 June 1981 and 16 July 1981 (*Hansard*, 1981). These pronouncements foster the very dangers of which they claim to warn. They encourage and rationalise activities like racial attacks and contribute to alienation among members of the ethnic minorities.

Political attacks and racial violence keep race relations and immigration issues most salient for black citizens, thus hindering the emergence of class-related issues and political integration. Fear of racial attacks and harassment may result in residential segregation continuing at a higher level than might otherwise be the case and may legitimise self-defence groups which would lead to further friction with the police. Feelings of alienation and conflict with the police might provide a rationalisation for crime, hostile outbursts and riots among the young, as occurred in Bristol, Toxteth and Brixton, which would inevitably lead to increased hostility between the ethnic minorities and the majority community.

A loss of legitimacy for the police, the courts and major political institutions among members of the minority could result in increased support for these institutions among the majority if they felt their institutions were being criticised, attacked and even flouted by members of the ethnic minorities. Such a consequence might strengthen the legitimacy of those institutions in the short run, although it would be disastrous for community relations. In the longer term the erosion of support among a large and growing minority could only have an undermining effect on these institutions.

There is some evidence that the government and Parliament are aware of dangers and have been taking some action to suppress racist attacks and to prosecute flagrant attempts to incite racial hatred. Evidence of such concern was shown by the Home Secretary's initiation of the Home Office Inquiry, and by speeches by politicians condemning racist attacks, for example by Timothy Raison on 18 April 1982 in Leicester, and on 14 September 1982 in Coventry. Furthermore, in January 1982 the editor of the Young National Front magazine *Bulldog* was found guilty of incitement to racial hatred and was given a six-month jail sentence (*Searchlight*, February 1982). However, major efforts are needed to ensure that the minorities feel protected from racial harassment and attacks and feel confident of their future in their new society.

CHAPTER 9

Race Relations Legislation and Institutions

Successive British governments, as has already been argued, were well aware of the problems of prejudice and discrimination that coloured immigrants from the New Commonwealth were likely to face in Britain. The small coloured communities which became established in a few seaport towns during the First World War had been subject to considerable discrimination and hostility and both politicians and civil servants felt that the post-Second World War immigrants would face similar problems, especially in their search for accommodation and jobs. At first some assistance was given to the new migrants. Officials from the Colonial Office, for example, met the *Empire Windrush* in June 1948 and helped the West Indian immigrants to find accommodation and employment. Similar help was given to the passengers of subsequent immigrant ships, but as West Indian immigration grew the resources of the Colonial Office became overstretched and this assistance to new migrants was discontinued in 1954. Given the widespread awareness of the difficulties facing New Commonwealth immigrants and the need for additional workers in the labour-hungry economy it is surprising that successive Conservative governments between 1951 and 1964 failed to consider that there was any need for positive measures to assist the settlement, acceptance and integration of these new citizen settlers. Consideration was given only to the need to reduce the flow by means of controls.

RACE RELATIONS LEGISLATION: EARLY INITIATIVES

In the 1950s the main initiatives of a positive nature in Parliament were a series of Private Members' Bills presented by MPs such as Reginald Sorensen and Fenner Brockway to outlaw racial discrimination. As early as 17 November 1950 Sorensen introduced a Colour Bar Bill 'to make illegal any discrimination to the detriment of any person on the basis of colour or race' (*Hansard*, 7 November 1950, col. 2044). It would have applied to discrimination in hotels, cafés, restaurants, theatres, cinemas, dance halls, inns and public houses. Offenders would have been subject to summary prosecution and criminal penalties. If found guilty they would have been fined. The Bill failed to be considered for a second reading for lack of parliamentary time.

Shortly after the failure of the Sorenson Bill, the NEC of the Labour Party considered whether to commit the party to anti-discrimination legislation. It consulted an academic expert on race relations, Dr Kenneth Little, who advised that there was a good case for the enactment of colour bar legislation to stir the national conscience and create a new standard of public behaviour in relation to coloured people. However, Sir Lynn Ungoed-Thomas, the Labour Party's legal adviser, was sceptical of the value of such legislation and the matter was dropped (Hindell, 1965; Kushnick, 1971).

On 1 May 1953 the Commons debated a motion tabled by Fenner Brockway demanding the condemnation and immediate abolition by legislation of the colour bar in British territories overseas. This motion was opposed by a substantial minority of Conservative backbenchers who tabled an amendment that the colour bar should be condemned and eliminated progressively, but not by legislation (*Hansard*, 1 May 1953, cols 2505–95). In 1956 Brockway turned his attention from colonial affairs to racial discrimination in Britain and introduced his first Private Member's Bill to outlaw racial discrimination in places of public entertainment, housing agreements and employment. Such discrimination would be punishable by fines, damages and, if appropriate, refusal or loss of licence or registration. The Bill was strongly opposed by two Conservative backbenchers, Ronald Bell and Bernard Braine, who were successful in getting the Bill talked out (*Hansard*, 10 May 1957, cols 1425–38; 24 May 1957, cols 1602–8). Brockway was to introduce a further eight such Bills in the period up to 1964 but all failed to reach the statute book. They did however gain increasing support, especially after the 1958 riots when a small number of Conservative and Liberal MPs added their support, but Brockway was not able to persuade the government to support his Bill. Spokesmen for the Conservative governments were unconvinced that anti-discrimination legislation was necessary or that it was the best way of preventing discrimination and prejudice in individuals' private dealings with black people. Some government spokesmen argued that anti-discrimination legislation might increase discrimination by giving the subject publicity and in addition cause popular resentment by restricting freedom of speech and action. It was also argued that such legislation might be difficult to enforce. The education of public opinion through the good example of responsible bodies and individuals was frequently given as the best method of improving individual behaviour, for example by the Earl of Perth, Minister of State for Colonial Affairs (House of Lords Debates,

19 November 1958, cols 681–2), Lord Chesham (House of Lords Debates, 19 November 1958, cols 717–20) and Mr R. Butler, the Home Secretary (*Hansard*, 4 June 1959, col. 371 and 7 December 1959, cols 170–8).

On the Labour side it was the 1958 riots which precipitated the development of party policy. The riots persuaded the NEC to oppose immigration controls and to support anti-discrimination legislation. The NEC statement after the riots included the following commitment:

> Although we believe that the fundamental and long-term solution of this problem is educational, nonetheless there are public manifestations of racial prejudice so serious that they must be dealt with by legislation. (Labour Party, 1958, p. 4)

In 1962 the Labour Party reaffirmed its commitment to legislation to outlaw discrimination with the publication of *The Integration of Immigrants: A Guide to Action*, and this commitment was included in the party's general election manifesto of 1964.

The NEC asked the Shadow Cabinet and the Society of Labour Lawyers to draft proposals for legislation. A small Shadow Cabinet committee under Sir Frank Soskice recommended amending the Public Order Act of 1936 to cover incitement to racial hatred by making it illegal to publish defamatory libel against an individual or group with the intention of provoking hatred or disorder. The penalties were to be severe, namely three years' imprisonment or a fine of £10,000, but all prosecutions would have to be referred first to the Attorney General to prevent trivial or factious proceedings (Hindell, 1965; Kushnick, 1971). The committee set up by the Society of Labour Lawyers, under Professor Andrew Martin, wanted a strong Bill which would outlaw both incitement to racial hatred and racial discrimination in all public places. They felt that government should be seen to be giving a lead in this area and so wanted public employment agencies and local authority housing to be covered by future legislation. The committee noted the American practice of attempting to combat racial discrimination by administrative action and also the American emphasis on conciliation procedures. Both of these ideas were later to be taken up enthusiastically by members of the Martin committee and were to be incorporated in the 1965 Race Relations Act.

The election of the Labour government in October 1964 was marred by the impact of the Smethwick result and the government's tiny majority. The new Labour Cabinet was determined to organise the race issue out of the arena of party political conflict by seeking a bipartisan consensus with the Conservatives; on the other hand, they could not be seen to capitulate on both immigration controls and anti-discrimination legislation. Some of the Labour lawyers who had been members of the

Martin committee advising the NEC were determined that the new government should fulfil its manifesto promise to introduce a Race Relations Bill. They mounted an intense lobbying campaign led by a Labour barrister, Anthony Lester. They had become convinced from American experience (Jowell, 1965) that a statutory commission should be established, whose first priority should be conciliation, and that legal enforcement of anti-discrimination law with commercial penalties should only be a last resort. They wanted legislation with a strong declaratory effect but were worried that strong penalties would lead to popular resentment and could undermine enforcement if juries proved reluctant to convict and as a result the police became reluctant to prosecute. Lester and his supporters were involved in the Campaign Against Racial Discrimination and the Institute of Race Relations as well as the Society of Labour Lawyers; and they convinced these organisations of the value of their proposals and gained their lobbying support. They contacted MPs, particularly those associated with the British Caribbean Association, and stimulated favourable press comment (Hindell, 1965).

THE RACE RELATIONS BILL, 1965

When the Home Secretary, Sir Frank Soskice, published the Race Relations Bill on 7 April 1965 it appeared that he had not been won over to conciliation. Discrimination in hotels, public houses, restaurants, theatres, cinemas, public transport and any place maintained by a public authority was to be a criminal offence punishable by fines of up to £100. Prosecution was only to be undertaken with the authority of the Director of Public Prosecutions. Incitement to racial hatred in speech or written material was made a criminal offence punishable by a fine. of up to £1,000 or two years' imprisonment or both, and the scope of the Public Order Act was extended so that it would be illegal to publish threatening or insulting material with the intent to provoke a breach of the peace.

Between the publication of the Bill and the debate on the second reading on 3 May the Home Secretary was persuaded to drop criminal sanctions and accept conciliation. This was partly in response to the advocates within his own party but also in order to secure the bipartisan consensus with the Conservatives that was developing on race and immigration matters. The Conservatives were divided on how to respond to the Race Relations Bill. On immigration control their stance was hardening and Edward Boyle was replaced as opposition spokesman on home affairs by Peter Thorneycroft at the end of February to reflect this change. But the government was rapidly toughening its position too and a great deal of cross-bench unanimity was evident in the immigration debate held on 23 March (*Hansard*, 23 March 1965, cols 334–453). The right wing of the Conservative Party wanted total opposition to the Race Relations Bill, but after two meetings of the Conservative Home Affairs Committee the opposition front bench decided on a compromise motion which deplored discrimination on racial or religious grounds but opposed the Bill for introducing criminal sanctions into an area more appropriate for conciliation. It also warned of the dangers to the principle of free speech inherent in the provisions to make incitement to racial hatred a criminal offence (*Hansard*, 3 May 1965, col. 943). The Home Secretary was thus in the position of proposing a Bill he had already decided to amend radically and was being attacked on much of the ground he was going to concede. However, Soskice and the government were pleased and relieved that the opposition had accepted in principle the broad objectives of anti-discrimination legislation (*Hansard*, 3 May 1965, col. 928).

The Home Secretary amended his Bill after the second reading. Criminal penalties were dropped for discrimination in public places and civil remedies were introduced instead. A statutory agency, the Race Relations Board, was to be created under the Act to appoint and supervise the work of local conciliation committees which would investigate complaints of discrimination and where appropriate use their best endeavours to secure a settlement between the parties and the law. If conciliation failed the local committees could report to the Race Relations Board which could then refer the case to the Attorney General who could take out an injunction. Anyone ignoring such an injunction would risk imprisonment or fines for contempt of court. By making the Bill so much weaker and limited in scope the Home Secretary had made it more acceptable to the Conservatives and he had to rely on Conservative support at the committee stage to carry his own amendments as a majority of the Labour members on the committee wished to strengthen the Bill. On the third reading the Conservative opposition accepted the Bill and did not oppose its passage. Soskice could thus claim to have succeeded in committing the Conservatives to the principle of anti-discrimination legislation and to have fulfilled the manifesto pledge even though the Bill itself was symbolic and declaratory and too weak to have an impact through enforcement. Soskice, however, appeared to believe that enactment would be enough. 'It would be an ugly day in this country', he said, 'if we had to come back to Parliament to extend the scope of this legislation which is designed to prevent friction from developing between different communities in this country' (*Hansard*, 16 July 1965, col. 1056).

The first Wilson administration made two other moves towards the development of a positive race relations policy. First, in March 1965 Maurice Foley, a junior minister at the Department of Economic

Affairs, was given wide-ranging responsibility for co-ordinating government policy in regard to integration and race relations policy. His work, however, was hampered by the government's determination to concentrate its efforts on immigration control. Secondly, in August 1965 the highly restrictionist element of the government's White Paper was partially balanced by an emphasis on integration measures and the establishment of the National Committee for Commonwealth Immigrants (NCCI).

THE NATIONAL COMMITTEE FOR COMMONWEALTH IMMIGRANTS

The NCCI replaced a non-statutory body, the Commonwealth Immigrants Advisory Council (CIAC), which had been established under the 1962 Commonwealth Immigrants Act to advise the Home Secretary. The CIAC has published four reports, two on housing, one on education and one on the problems of immigrant school leavers. It had also co-ordinated the efforts of local groups which were promoting race relations work in their areas. These latter became known as Voluntary Liaison Committees. The new NCCI was required to promote and co-ordinate on a national basis efforts directed towards the integration of Commonwealth immigrants into the community. In particular it was to promote and co-ordinate the activities of local Voluntary Liaison Committees and to advise them on their work; where necessary to assist in the recruitment and training of suitable men or women to serve these committees as full-time officials; to provide a central information service; to organise conferences, arrange training courses and stimulate research; and to advise on those questions which were referred to them by government or which they considered should be brought to the attention of government (National Committee for Commonwealth Immigrants, 1967, p. 24). In November 1965 the Prime Minister announced that the Archbishop of Canterbury had agreed to serve as chairman of the NCCI. This appointment was clearly intended to emphasise the importance the government attached to the NCCI and also its non-partisan nature.

The NCCI consisted of individuals invited by the government of the day and it quickly became a focus for experts on race relations who worked on its various panels on such topics as housing, education and employment. They were also involved in organising conferences and advising local groups. The NCCI, like subsequent race relations institutions, has been criticised for diverting the attention of able and energetic black professionals from creating a black political movement which could have mobilised New Commonwealth immigrants to force the government to be more responsive to their needs and interests. Some observers saw the Campaign Against Racial Discrimination as a potential black civil rights movement though at this time it was an élitist organisation of black and white liberal professionals with little mass support. However, the formation of the NCCI did divert the energies and commitment of some black professionals from the Campaign Against Racial Discrimination which, for example, lost both its chairman and vice-chairman to the NCCI (Heineman, 1972).

Mullard (1973) scathingly argues that the NCCI was the liberal face of a reactionary immigration policy. This is exactly what Labour's dual strategy was intended to be. In fact many politicians argued that a tough policy on immigration control was a necessary precondition for good race relations within Britain, and that the native white population needed to have its fears reassured by effective controls before positive steps towards integration could be taken. Black radicals, of course, have wanted race relations bodies to be political, combating racism, campaigning for political goals and opposing government policies when they are racially discriminatory. However, government agencies are not vehicles for independent militant action and radicals who expect them to be so are inevitably disappointed. The moderate liberal professionals co-opted on to the national council of the NCCI were conciliators, cautious in their approach and unwilling to take too militant a line for fear of provoking a white reaction or failing to gain the support of timid politicians.

The local committees of the NCCI were also hamstrung. They did not have the freedom to engage in political campaigning as many of the committed blacks and whites who joined them wished. The constitutions of the local Liaison Committees laid down that they had to be as widely representative of local interests as possible: no group which wished to join could be refused, so churches, parties, social welfare groups and immigrant organisations were all encouraged to participate. Of particular importance for Liaison Committees was their relationship with local authorities, which were in a position to dominate local committees and to control their funds. According to the 1965 White Paper and the NCCI interpretation of it, local authorities had to provide a contribution to local groups which matched the NCCI grant. Unless the local authority did this the NCCI would not provide money for the salary of a full-time officer. This meant that local authorities had considerable influence. They could decide whether they wanted a local liaison group, how much support to give it and whether to dictate to the group what kinds of activities it should undertake. As the withdrawal of local authority funds meant the loss of NCCI funding too there existed a major constraint on the local committees and their full-time officers who could only offend local politicians at their peril.

Katznelson (1973) argues that at the local level the establishment of Voluntary Liaison Committees succeeded in creating buffer institutions which were officially sponsored and sanctioned. Immigrant demands were filtered through these organisations. The Liaison Committees formed a local political arena where blacks and whites could meet in an atmosphere of non-party good will. Instead of blacks participating directly in the political process through organisations under their own control and thereby representing their own interests, they were linked to the local and national polity through non-party political mediating committees which were guaranteed to be quiet, respectable and well behaved. They could thus be ignored with impunity (Hill and Issacharoff, 1971; Katznelson, 1973). These government-sponsored organisations did provide some access to local and national politicians and officials and some hope of public funds and grants which might otherwise be difficult to achieve, as at this time during the 1960s the ethnic minorities had relatively little electoral muscle. They also offered some status and legitimacy to those members of the minority communities who participated and wished to be recognised as leading members of their communities. They did, of course, assume a degree of co-operation and responsibility from those who participated and thus offered some official integration in exchange for moderation.

In November 1965 Sir Frank Soskice resigned as Home Secretary for reasons of ill health and was replaced by Roy Jenkins. This was an important change as Jenkins was firmly committed to the view that legislation had a vital role to play in combating racial discrimination and was in favour of strengthening the legislation and extending its scope once political considerations made this possible. Jenkins appointed Mark Bonham-Carter as the first chairman of the Race Relations Board, which was established by the Race Relations Act, readily agreeing to his condition that he should be allowed to put the case, after a year, for the extension of the scope of the Act and a revision of the Board's powers (Rose *et al.*, 1969, p. 520). In January 1966 Maurice Foley was moved to the Home Office from the Department of Economic Affairs and was to prove a powerful ally supporting Jenkins's campaign for new legislation to extend and strengthen the Race Relations Act. His move also confirmed that the Home Office would take charge of both immigration control and race relations matters, which some observers found a worrying development (Deakin, 1968b).

THE RACE RELATIONS BOARD

The Race Relations Board was established in February 1966 to secure compliance with the provisions of Section 1 of the Race Relations Act which made it unlawful to practise racial discrimination in specified places of public resort. The Board consisted of the chairman, Mark Bonham-Carter, and two other members, Sir Leary Constantine and Alderman B. S. Langton. It was the Board's duty to establish local conciliation committees which would receive and consider complaints of unlawful discrimination. These committees, but not the Board, were empowered to investigate complaints, achieve a settlement between the parties and receive where appropriate assurances of future behaviour.

The strategy the Board adopted was *festina lente*. It established five conciliation committees in its first year and joined with the NCCI to sponsor the research into racial discriminaton to be undertaken by the independent research body Political and Economic Planning. It also sponsored the research under Professor Street into anti-discrimination legislation overseas. It was hoped that these research projects would provide evidence to support the strengthening of the Act.

The Board quickly found considerable problems in its attempts to implement the Act. Most places of public resort, for example shops, appeared to be excluded from the Act and it was unclear whether religious groups like Sikhs and Jews were included. Gypsies were another group whose members complained of discrimination but whose status under the Act was unclear. The Board also found that most of the complaints it received were outside its jurisdiction. In its first year it received 327 complaints of which 238 (73 per cent) were outside its scope (Race Relations Board, 1967, para. 16). In its second year, out of 690 complaints, 574 (83 per cent) were found to be outside the Board's jurisdiction (Race Relations Board, 1968, para. 15). Most of the complaints outside the scope of the Act concerned employment and housing although in the second year there was a substantial increase in complaints against the police (Race Relations Board, 1968, para. 24). There were also considerable problems of enforcement and the Board had no power to compel those alleged to have committed acts of discrimination to co-operate with its officers or attend its hearings. In some cases they simply refused to co-operate.

The Board thus faced considerable problems from its inception. It had been created under a weak Act, highly restricted in scope, with minimal powers of enforcement. The Act was intended to have a declaratory effect and was not designed to suppress acts of racial discrimination by legal sanctions but to encourage people to do what was right by conciliation. It thus provided little effective protection for victims of discrimination. Moreover the Board was created at a time when the Labour government was determined to defuse the race issue and the Board could expect little political support for vigorous action while the government had such a precarious majority. The Board thus proceeded cautiously, pursuing only clear cases of discrimination and asking for only nominal damages. It wished to get the new law established and accepted, and then to press for its extension. The lack of political support was apparent in the reluctance of the Attorney General to pursue the tiny number of cases referred to him by the Board for possible prosecution (Race Relations Board, 1968, paras 16–17).

The impression that the government was toughening its attitude towards the ethnic minorities was reinforced by the results of cases prosecuted by the Attorney General under the incitement to racial hatred provisions of the Race Relations Act. It was invoked in a weak case against a white youth who had attached a racist tract to an MP's door and his conviction was quashed on appeal (Lester and Bindman, 1972, p. 367). In a more serious case Colin Jordan, leader of the National Socialist Movement, was convicted in January 1967 and received eighteen months' imprisonment and in May that year a follower of Jordan was found guilty of inciting two youths to distribute racialist leaflets and was sentenced to six months' imprisonment by magistrates at Leek (Lester and Bindman, 1972, pp. 368–9). However, the cases which attracted the most attention were both prosecutions against black people. In November 1967 Michael Abdul Malik, also known as Michael X, was sentenced to twelve months' imprisonment for using insulting words to stir up racial hatred at a Black Power meeting in Reading, and in the same month four members of the Universal Coloured People's Association were also prosecuted for using words to stir up hatred against white people at Speakers' Corner, Hyde Park. They were found guilty and fined. In March 1968 four members of the Racial Preservation Society were prosecuted for distributing a broadsheet opposing race mixing and advocating repatriation. They were acquitted of incitement of racial hatred (Lester and Bindman, 1972, pp. 369–71). In April Enoch Powell made his 'river of blood' speech and the Attorney General turned down suggestions that he should be prosecuted.

It was against this unhelpful political background that the Board was struggling to implement the Race Relations Act. The first annual report from the Board concluded by recommending that the Act be extended to cover housing, employment, financial facilities and places of public resort not covered already by the Act. It also recommended that the considerable ambiguities in the Bill should be eliminated and emphasised the importance of legislation, arguing that:

(i)   a law is an unequivocal declaration of public policy;
(ii)   a law gives support to those who do not wish to discriminate, but who feel compelled to do so by social pressures;
(iii) a law gives protection and redress to minority groups;
(iv) a law thus provides for the peaceful and orderly adjustment of grievances and release of tensions;
(v)   a law reduces prejudice by discouraging the behaviour in which prejudice finds expression. (Race Relations Board, 1967, paras 65–6)

However, a law without strong public or political support which is weakly enforced and for which the penalties are negligible is unlikely to fulfil the legislative aims outlined by the Board. It will rapidly become disregarded and ignored. Its very existence will add to the frustrations and sense of grievance of those who attempt to gain its protection. They will find the procedures a waste of time and effort and even if successful the derisory compensation will add to feelings of humiliation that they have already experienced (Mullard, 1973, pp. 75–88).

However, almost overnight the climate of opinion on racial discrimination was changed by the publication of the report on racial discrimination carried out by Political and Economic Planning. This report was published in April 1967 and gave powerful support to Jenkins's campaign to strengthen the Race Relations Act (PEP, 1967). It provided the first systematic evidence on the extent of racial discrimination in Britain and was based on a series of situational tests using black and white actors. These actors posed as applicants for jobs or accommodation, claiming identical qualifications or housing needs. In some cases black applicants claimed higher qualifications than their white counterparts. The results of the study suggested very high levels of discrimination in employment and housing with West Indians experiencing the highest levels, no matter how good their qualifications or command of English (Daniel, 1968). It seemed likely that second generation black Britons would experience just as much discrimination as their parents and there were widespread calls in the press and elsewhere for stronger legislation. *The Times*, *The Guardian* and *The Economist* demanded tough action and even the *Daily Telegraph* called for urgent remedial measures (Lapping, 1970). In July the Home Secretary responded by announcing his acceptance of the Race Relations Board's call for new legislation. His advocacy of stronger legislation had been greatly reinforced by the Political and Economic Planning findings and the Cabinet agreed to support new legislation, which was announced in the Queen's Speech in October. Also in October the Street Committee on Anti-Discrimination Legislation published their report which included detailed proposals for strengthening the 1965 Act (Street, *et al*, 1967). The report was well received in the national press and its recommendations were carefully studied by the Home Office officials responsible for the new legislation. The wind seemed set fair for a new comprehensive Bill (Lester and Bindman, 1972, pp. 98–105; p. 132).

The following month Roy Jenkins was moved from the Home Office to the Treasury. Jenkins had shown strong and skilful determination in promoting the extension of legislation to housing and employment despite the opposition of the CBI and the TUC. He had encouraged the Race Relations Board and the NCCI to sponsor the reports into racial discrimination and race relations legislation and had worked hard to create a favourable climate for the new Bill by speeches and persuasion.

His departure from the Home Office meant that the new Home Secretary, James Callaghan, would be responsible for the legislation that Jenkins had worked so hard to achieve (Rose *et al.*, 1969, pp. 511–50).

The favourable climate of opinion which the Political and Economic Planning report and Jenkins's campaign had engendered for the Race Relations Bill was quickly destroyed when the government capitulated to the Sandys–Powell campaign to control the entry of British Asians from Kenya. The first major legislative act of the new Home Secretary was therefore not the new Race Relations Bill but the restrictive Commonwealth Immigrants Act (1968) which made holders of UK passports subject to immigration controls unless they had a parent or grandparent born or naturalised in the UK or who had become a citizen by virtue of adoption or registration in the UK. This Bill was rushed through Parliament in three days in February. The government's weakness in response to this anti-immigrant campaign did not augur well for their commitment to positive race relations policies. It showed that they were prepared to go to extreme lengths to maintain, for electoral purposes, the position of being just as tough on immigration controls as the most right-wing Conservatives and that this was a very high priority (Crossman, 1977, p. 679). This rapid and complete capitulation to the Sandys–Powell campaign was an invitation and encouragement to the anti-immigrant lobby to raise their demands even higher, which Powell did, to dramatic effect, a few weeks later when he shattered what remained of the bipartisan consensus with his 'river of blood' speech on 20 April, just three days before the Race Relations Bill was due to receive its second reading.

THE RACE RELATIONS BILL 1968

The new Race Relations Bill was published on 9 April. It made it unlawful to discriminate on grounds of colour, race, ethnic or national origins, in employment, housing and the provision of commercial and other services. The publication or display of discriminatory notices or advertisements was also banned. The Bill gave a reconstituted and expanded Race Relations Board the duty to secure compliance with its provisions by investigating complaints of racial discrimination, instituting conciliation procedures and, if these failed, by legal proceedings. However, as in the earlier Act, considerable emphasis was placed on conciliation procedures, and legal proceedings were seen as a last resort. The Bill also created the Community Relations Commission to promote 'harmonious community relations' and to act in an advisory capacity on behalf of the Home Secretary, performing as a statutory body the duties and functions previously carried out by the NCCI.

Introducing the second reading debate the Home Secretary said:

This is a time for responsibility, for leadership and, if I may say so, nobility. My starting point is that a society is most healthy and most free from tension when it is based on the simple principle that every citizen within its boundaries shares equally in the same freedoms, the same responsibilities, the same opportunities and the same benefits . . . none of us can shrink from the challenge of racialism . . . what this Bill is concerned with is equal rights, equal responsibilities and equal opportunities and it is therefore a Bill for the whole nation and not just minority groups. Its purpose is to protect society as a whole against actions which will lead to social disruption and to prevent the emergence of a class of second-class citizens. (*Hansard*, 23 April 1968, cols 53–5)

These sentiments sounded less than noble after the indefensible Commonwealth Immigrants Act passed in February. However, after such a flagrantly discriminatory Act Labour leaders were under considerable pressure to balance their negative immigration policy with a positive Act for internal race relations. The Hattersley formula was thus pursued as a justification, namely 'Integration without control is impossible but control without integration is indefensible' (*Hansard*, 23 March 1965, cols 378–85). The government therefore pursued its Race Relations Bill which became law in October 1968.

The reconstituted Race Relations Board was much happier with the new legislation, particularly its wider scope. There were, however, still some loopholes such as the allowance of discrimination in order to maintain a racial balance (Race Relations Act, 1968, section 8 [2]) and some important areas which remained outside the scope of the legislation, notably complaints against the police (Race Relations Board, 1970, p. 5). The first report of the new Board did express concern at a complaints-based procedure, arguing that the number of complaints could well be limited because victims might not realise they had been discriminated against; they might accept it and not complain to the Board and, moreover, as there was often little financial loss, they might be deterred by the low level of compensation. The report noted that the number of complainants was linked to the siting of the Board's offices.

The operations of the Race Relations Board failed to live up to its early legislative promise. Despite the widespread evidence of discrimination, the number of complaints the Board received was relatively small and in a high proportion of these the Board formed the opinion that discrimination had not occurred. Between 1 April 1969 and 31 March 1970 the Board investigated 982 complaints and formed an opinion of no discrimination in 734 cases (75 per cent) (Race Relations Board, 1970, para. 42). In the 248 cases where the Board did form an opinion of discrimination, over half (143) concerned advertisements, an area of the Act where violations could easily be proved, and the Board was successful in eliminating this form of discrimination. In other areas such as employment and housing it was much harder to prove that discrimination had taken place and the high proportion of complaints where the Board formed an opinion of no discrimination was a continuing feature of its annual reports. The problems of proof also made the Board extremely reluctant to take cases to court and great efforts were made to achieve results by conciliation. By 31 March 1972 the Board had investigated 2,967 cases, of which it had taken court action in only seven cases. Even when it went to court the Board usually asked for only nominal damages. In its first successful case in April 1970 the Board asked for and received damages of five shillings (Lapping, 1970, p. 126; Hiro, 1973, p. 221). Not surprisingly, the number of complaints the Board received remained at a low level.

Table 9.1   *Complaints Received by the Race Relations Board 1969–75*

1969–70	1,549	1972	913*
1970–71	1,024	1973	885
1971–72	917*	1974	1,068
		1975	1,227

* In 1972 the Board changed its annual basis of calculation from 1 April–31 March to the calendar year. There is therefore a three-month overlap in these figures.
Source: Annual Reports of the Race Relations Board, 1969–75.

The impact of the Board was thus minimal given the high levels of discrimination which were known to exist. It gradually became clear that the Board needed far stronger powers to make a major impact, including subpoena power and discretion to initiate strategic investigations.

THE COMMUNITY RELATIONS COMMISSION

The Community Relations Commission (CRC) was established on 26 November 1968 under the chairmanship of Frank Cousins. Unlike its predecessor the NCCI, it was a statutory body accountable to the Home Secretary and in financial matters to the Treasury. Its terms of reference were rather vague, namely 'to encourage the establishment of harmonious community relations and to co-ordinate on a national basis the measures adopted for that purpose by others and to advise the Secretary of State' (Race Relations Act, 1968, s. 25). The CRC saw its functions as being to combat racial prejudice by persuasion and education, by positive measures to promote understanding and by explaining and interpreting the cultures and backgrounds of the different ethnic groups to the host community and vice versa (CRC, 1970, p. 5).

In practice the Commission gave a high priority to expanding the network of Voluntary Liaison Committees, which were renamed Community Relations Councils, and to supplying them with professional staff. In 1967 there were forty-seven local Community Relations Councils with full-time officers. This rose to seventy-five in 1971, with fifty-eight full-time officers, and by 1975 had reached eighty-five Community Relations Councils with 144 Community Relations Officers (CROs) and assistant CROs. The Community Relations Councils were under similar constraints as the earlier local Liaison Committees. Substantial participation by local authorities and voluntary organisations was a precondition for grant aid from the Commission and there was, on occasion, intense conflict between campaigning activists at the local level who felt they were representing the members of the ethnic minorities in their communities and the cautious, non-partisan approach of the national officers of the Commission (Mullard, 1973).

The CRC continued with the NCCI's expert advisory panels on employment, education, housing, children, information and training. These provided information and training to a wide range of professionals such as teachers, social workers, trade union officers, police, local government officers, immigration officers and magistrates.

However, it is always hard to measure the national impact of this kind of promotional and educational work and the CRC constantly felt that its work was undermined by the fact that successive governments continually linked progressive community relations initiatives with increased restrictions on immigration. The promotion of harmonious race relations was almost impossible against a background of public and political opinion which was hostile to New Commonwealth immigration.

By the mid-1970s the optimism and hopes surrounding the Race Relations Act of 1968 and its statutory institutions had been dissipated. Both the Race Relations Board and the CRC were arguing that existing legislation was insufficient to tackle racial discrimination and that the work of the Board and the Commission lacked credibility among members of the black communities. Extensive surveys by Political and Economic Planning between 1974 and 1976 (summarised by Smith, 1977) confirmed that discrimination in the areas of rented accommodation and employment remained high and that the problems of disadvantage suffered by the ethnic minorities also added greatly to their general social deprivation. The Select Committee on Race and Immigration, established in 1968, had also criticised the government for failing to devise effective race relations policies and recommended a clear demonstrable government commitment to equal rights, the provision of greater resources and the strengthening of race relations administration, including a Minister of Equal Rights attached to the Home Office. It also recommended the merging of the Race Relations Board and the CRC in a report published in 1975 (House of Commons, 1975), one of a number of valuable reports on a variety of topics connected with immigration and race relations. (In 1979 it was merged into the Home Affairs Committee and is now its Sub-committee on Race Relations and Immigration.) The government issued its own White Paper on *Racial Discrimination* in September 1975 which argued that

the problems with which we have to deal if we are to see genuine equality of opportunity for coloured youngsters born and educated in this country may be larger in scale and more complex than had been initially supposed . . . the Government is convinced, as a result of its review of race relations generally and of the working of the legislation, that a fuller strategy to deal with racial disadvantage will have to be deployed than has been attempted so far. (Home Office, 1975)

Both the government and the opposition were agreed that new legislation was needed, and a new Race Relations Bill was published on 3 February 1976. This new Bill represented a considerable advance on previous legislation. It extended the definition of discrimination to include not only direct discrimination but also indirect discrimination where unjustifiable practices and procedures which apply to everyone have the effect of putting people of a particular racial group at a disadvantage. It allowed individuals who felt they had been discriminated against on racial grounds to take their case to the county court in all cases except in employment where they could go to industrial tribunals. Also, it abolished the Race Relations Board and the CRC and established instead a Commission for Racial Equality (CRE) with greatly increased powers of investigation and enforcement to enable it to make wider strategic use of the law in the public interest (Race Relations Act, 1976).

The Bill was supported by the Labour and Liberal parties and was not opposed by the Conservatives. Roy Jenkins, once again Home Secretary, introducing the Bill, stated that the growing black population born and bred in Britain was entitled to full rights and equal treatment and that racial discrimination was not only morally repugnant but a social and economic waste. Significantly, he added that the success of the legislation depended on the leadership of government and Parliament and on the response of society as a whole (*Hansard*, 4

March 1976, cols 1547–67). Mr Whitelaw, for the opposition, argued that it was because of the Conservative Party's clear commitment to the principle of non-discrimination and in the interests of racial harmony that he advised his honourable friends not to oppose the Bill (cols 1568–77). Only a handful of Conservatives opposed the Bill, but most Conservatives who spoke argued that strong immigration controls were the *quid pro quo* for strong race relations legislation and that the present controls were not strong enough. There was some recognition, even among strong supporters of controls, that there was a need for more positive measures to combat discrimination. For example Mr Dudley Smith, MP for Warwick and Leamington, said that there was 'a need for a crusade to overcome racial discrimination and to give our fellow Britons who are in the minority a new confidence which they have significantly lacked in recent years' (*Hansard*, 4 March 1976, col. 1594). However, strenuous though unsuccessful efforts were made by the Conservatives to amend the Bill in committee, though eventually it received its third reading virtually unopposed. The CRE was therefore established in an atmosphere which generated high expectations that something substantial was at last being done to combat racial discrimination and to promote equality of opportunity and racial harmony. The CRE appeared to be a much more powerful body than its predecessors, with much greater scope for initiative and enforcement, but the hopes it generated have once again largely failed to be realised. Why have legislative and institutional efforts to reduce racial discrimination proved so ineffective? Why has the CRE, like its predecessors, failed to make a major impact?

THE COMMISSION FOR RACIAL EQUALITY

The CRE was established to perform two major functions: first, to work towards the elimination of discrimination and, secondly, to promote equality of opportunity and good relations between persons of different racial groups. In addition the Commission was charged with keeping under review the working of the Race Relations Act and, when required by the Secretary of State or when it otherwise thought it necessary, to draw up and submit to the Secretary of State proposals for amending it (Race Relations Act, 1976, pt vii, s. 43). The enforcement function was inherited from the Race Relations Board and is carried out by its Equal Opportunities Division, which employs fifty-three staff on formal investigations into racial discrimination. This division also advises individuals who approach the Commission with complaints of discrimination. The promotional function was inherited from the Community Relations Commission and is carried out by the Community Affairs and Liaison Division which co-ordinates the activities of

186 Community Relations Officers in eighty-five local authorities, provides grants to minority organisations who are pursuing greater equality of opportunity between racial groups, and publishes reports and other material to promote harmonious race relations. There is also a General Services Division which includes a small research unit. The Community Affairs and Liaison Division has sixty-three staff. Overall the CRE had 224 staff and a budget of £7,687,000 in 1981–2 (CRE, July 1982).

The merger of the two major functions – promotion and enforcement – in one organisation was highly controversial but it was assumed that both could be carried out more economically and efficiently in one organisation and that firms, local authorities and other organisations would take the promotional work of the CRE more seriously knowing that the Commission had strong enforcement powers behind it.

However, from its inception the CRE had considerable difficulty in establishing its credibility. First, the creation of the CRE itself proved fraught with difficulties as members of the abolished Race Relations Board and Community Relations Commission competed for posts in the new Commission. Accusations were made that whites were receiving most of the senior posts and the new Commission was accused of discrimination by some who had failed to gain positions. In two cases members of the old CRC successfully took advantage of the internal appeals procedure and were given posts in the new body. The publicity surrounding these internal problems provided an embarrassing start for the CRE.

There were also problems concerning the priority and resources that should be given to promotional work and legal enforcement. These problems hindered the development of a coherent strategy co-ordinating the enforcement and promotional work of the Commission and, to begin with, those appointed to the CRE carried on with the work they had done before in enforcement or promotion largely in isolation from each other. The work of the research unit, for example, could have been developed to uncover areas of indirect discrimination and provide statistical evidence to support strategic formal investigations, but no lead was given in working out such a joint strategy and co-operation between the research and enforcement divisions was not developed. The ethos of the two major divisions was also somewhat contradictory and this hindered co-operation. Some members of the promotional side wished the CRE to adopt a vigorous, even an aggressively campaigning style and to foster close links with the black communities, even to the extent of acting on their behalf. Those on the enforcement side felt their role demanded the careful and objective preparation of cases against those accused of discrimination. They had to be seen as fair and unbiased enforcers of the law.

It now seems clear that a higher priority should have been given to the enforcement side of the Commission's work. Formal investigations are inevitably slow, as the Act obliges the Commission to warn those whom it is considering for investigation and to give them time to make representations in their defence. Once an investigation is undertaken, every opportunity must naturally be given for those being investigated to present their side of the case. There is thus considerable opportunity for delay. An organisation may challenge the right of the CRE to investigate them, refuse to provide witnesses and documents until subpoenas have been upheld by the courts, and finally may challenge in the courts the non-discrimination notices that the CRE may issue after its formal investigation is complete.

By the end of 1978, eighteen months after starting work, some twenty-nine investigations into racial discrimination had been started but only one, into Genture Restaurants Ltd, had been completed and a non-discrimination notice issued. By the end of 1979 the number of investigations had risen to thirty-nine and a further three were completed. These were all small investigations into a children's home, a working men's club and a social and leisure club. This slow start did not enhance the credibility of the Commission and after 1979, with the election of an unsympathetic government, there was increasing resistance to the investigatory and enforcement work of the Commission. By the end of 1981 the CRE had started forty-seven investigations and had published reports on twelve. In over half the cases where non-discrimination notices were issued the defendants appealed to the courts against the notices (CRE, 1982, pp. 7–9). In two cases the Home Office and Hillingdon Council challenged the right of the CRE even to begin an investigation and in the latter case this was successful. In 1979 the CRE began an investigation into the London Borough of Hillingdon's treatment of homeless applicants arriving as immigrants at London Airport. The borough challenged the legality of the CRE's procedures. In the autumn of 1981 the High Court upheld the borough's appeal and this was confirmed by the House of Lords in June 1982. The full judgement was given in *The Times* on 18 June 1982.

It is very hard to assess the effectiveness of the work of the promotional side of the CRE but is has involved the enouragement of equal opportunity policies by employers, trade unions and their representative organisations. Advice and training courses are provided for major employers in consultation with such organisations as the CBI, the TUC, the Institute of Personnel Managers and the Manpower Services Commission. A draft code of practice in employment has been published (CRE, 1980) after discussions with the CBI, the TUC, the Department of Employment and other organisations, but still awaits governmental and parliamentary approval. Another major area of promotional work is with local authorities who, under Section 71 of the Act, are specifically charged to eliminate unlawful racial discrimination and to promote equality of opportunity and good relations between persons of different racial groups. However, the CRE has only limited resources and is largely involved with organisations and local authorities which are already favourably disposed to its work. Education, housing and employment policies are the main areas of promotional work, although recently special attention has been paid to the needs of young people and police–minority relations.

A further area of work has been providing assistance to individuals who complain that they have been subjected to racial discrimination and request assistance in pursuing their claims in the courts or in industrial tribunals. In 1981 there were 864 such applications for assistance, most of which received some help. However, the failure rate of such cases, especially those which go to industrial tribunals, is very high and the compensation, which is usually for injury to feeling, is very low. In the 280 industrial tribunal cases reported to the CRE in 1981 only fourteen were successful. In 1981, fourteen cases of discrimination were taken to the County Courts, of which eight were successful. Five County Court cases were settled on terms favourable to the applicants. As under the previous race relations Acts, few claimants feel that the time and effort involved in seeking advice, preparing the case and pursuing it are worth while. In the period 1976–81 there were only seventy-six successful cases in industrial tribunals and only thirty-nine cases reached the County Courts, of which twenty-four were successful (CRE, 1982, pp. 9–10).

The CRE is also responsible for funding local Community Relations Councils and their Community Relations Officers, and for providing funds for project aid and self-help grants to ethnic minority organisations. In 1981 some ninety Community Relations Councils were funded, mainly jointly by local authorities and the CRE. The same difficulties which occurred between the CRC and its Community Relations Councils continued to bedevil the relations between the CRE and the Community Relations Councils. The involvement in political activities of Community Relations Councils and Community Relations Officers has been a major problem and has led to crises over the appointment of officers, as in Wolverhampton in 1979 (Jacobs, 1982, p. 255). The relationship between the Community Relations Councils and their national organisation, the National Association of Community Relations Councils, on the one hand and the CRE on the other is unclear, and attempts are being made to negotiate a new structure. The CRE has attempted to define more vigorously the aims of the Community Relations Councils and the programmes of work for which funding is provided, while the Community Relations Councils are anxious to preserve their autonomy and freedom of action in local communities. The proposed increase in central control has caused considerable conflict between the National Association of Community

Relations Councils and the CRE which could be seen in the evidence submitted to the Select Committee by the former organisation (House of Commons, 1981a, vol. 2, p. 124).

A further problem facing the CRE is the widespread expectation that it should play a leading role at each and every crisis which occurs in the area of race. It is expected to respond with help and assistance when problems occur at the Notting Hill Carnival, in Brick Lane, in Southall, Bristol or Brixton. Publicity over incidents like the virginity testing scandal at Heathrow or the allegations against Mr Rudy Narayan of conduct unbecoming a barrister led to demands for formal investigations into the immigration service, which the CRE agreed to do, and the legal profession, which it did not. Each crisis leads to criticism from all sides that the CRE is a failure for not preserving racial harmony.

The CRE, like its predecessors, was established because of considerable evidence of racial discrimination and the fear that a whole generation of young black Britons would become frustrated and alienated unless strong political measures were taken to give them equal chances of employment, promotion, housing and other facilities which all citizens have a right to expect. However, racial discrimination and prejudice can only be combated effectively if the Race Relations Act and its enforcement agency, the CRE, operate in a favourable political environment and have the full support of government and Parliament. The reverse has been true. The credibility of the CRE has been undermined not only by its internal problems but to a far greater extent by unfavourable changes in its political environment. By the time the Commission began work in June 1977 its creator, Roy Jenkins, had resigned as Home Secretary and from Parliament and left Britain to become President of the European Commission. Also in 1977 the National Front pushed the Liberals into fourth place in both the Stetchford and Ladywood by-elections and gained considerable publicity for itself by provoking violence at Ladywood and Lewisham. In November 1977 Mrs Thatcher was attempting to disengage the Conservative Party from its commitment to the all-party Joint Campaign Against Racialism, and by the end of January 1978 was exploiting the race issue for electoral advantage. In April Mr Whitelaw was outlining to the Central Council the new tough immigration proposals that the Conservatives would introduce if they won the next General Election.

It is often assumed that instances of racial discrimination arise from only a tiny minority of people in this country and that the British people are basically fair-minded and tolerant. If this were true there would have been no need for the Act and the CRE would be operating in a basically favourable environment with little to do. In practice, the political environment is hostile and the Act and the CRE are unpopular, not only with large sections of the Conservative Party but with many of the electorate who, while being generally favourable to positive race relations policies, are uncertain about the need for race relations legislation and the CRE (Lawrence, 1978/9; Crewe and Sarlvik, 1980). 'It is the view of many members of the indigenous community that the CRE has contributed to racial tension while being totally ineffectual in its efforts to promote racial harmony' (Holland, 1980, p. 7). Public indifference to and uncertainty about race relations legislation and institutions can only be overcome by strong government support for such measures and this has not been forthcoming. Neither Labour nor Conservative governments have taken steps to implement an effective policy of equal opportunity in awarding government contracts and have been very slow in developing equal opportunity procedures for recruitment to government departments.

In fact firms and local authorities which are opposed to race relations legislation and have resisted attempts by the CRE to pursue strategic investigations into allegations of discrimination have seen the Conservative government of 1979–83 adopt similar tactics and challenge the right of the CRE to proceed with its proposed investigation of immigration procedures which was initiated in response to the virginity tests scandal. The Home Office, the CRE's supervising department, argued in the High Court that such an investigation was beyond the powers of the CRE. The CRE won the case and has proceeded with the investigation although the court action did result, as is frequently the case, in a considerable delay between the notification of the proposed inquiry and the court's decision (Layton-Henry, 1980b). The fact that the government challenged the CRE at all suggests that it is well aware of the inherent contradictions between the aims of its race relations policy and its immigration policy. As was forcefully written by Bernard Levin in *The Times* on 14 February 1978, 'You cannot by promising to remove the cause of fear and resentment fail to increase both. If you talk and behave as though black men were some kind of virus that must be kept out of the body politic then it is the shabbiest hypocrisy to preach racial harmony at the same time.'

Another indication of the low priority given by the government to the CRE and the general lack of sensitivity in handling race relations occurred in April 1980 when five CRE commissioners were replaced. Four of the seven black commissioners were replaced, and one of the eight white commissioners. No matter what the merits of the individual cases, the impression was created that something of a purge of black commissioners was taking place and there were calls for potential black nominees not to accept places on the Commission. The result was an embarrassing delay in filling the places.

The failure of successive governments to give active support to race relations legislation and institutions in spite of the substantial and continuing evidence of racial discrimination (shown, for example, in the 1981 report of the Home Affairs Committee, *Racial Disadvantage*, House of Commons, 1981b) is adding to the increasing frustration and alienation of the growing numbers of British-born blacks. The present economic recession is bearing particularly hard on young blacks as the unemployment figures for areas like St Pauls in Bristol and Brixton in London show. The Thatcher government is firmly set against intervening on a substantial scale to help inner-city areas, declining industry or minority groups but is waiting for its tough economic strategy to work. The social consequences of its policies are particularly harsh on the least skilled, the least qualified and the least secure, as members of the ethnic minorities tend to be. There is clearly a strong case for a statutory agency to enforce the Race Relations Act, to help individual complainants and to provide advice and expertise to government, local authorities, private employers, schools and other organisations on race relations matters. However, without a strong government lead the impact of such an agency is bound to be minimal in a society where racial prejudice is a normal rather than an exceptional aspect of culture (Lawrence, 1974, p. 46). In this situation black Britons need to exert greater political influence than they have in the past.

CHAPTER 10

The Major Parties and Political Developments since 1974

Race relations and immigration hardly surfaced at all as issues in the two General Election campaigns of 1974. In the February Election the constitutional crisis between the government and the miners, the imposition of the three-day week and the defection of Enoch Powell from the Conservative Party over continuing British membership of the EEC all focused the electorate's attention on constitutional and economic issues. The October Election was very much a replay of the February Election, although the success of the Liberals and the Scottish National Party in the earlier election added further political and constitutional interest. However, in neither Election were race-related issues significant.

After the Election, growing attention began to be paid to the importance of black voters. This occurred for a number of reasons. First, the two General Elections in 1974 were closely fought and their results were indecisive in the February Election and nearly so in October as well. In an electoral system where results are close, as has frequently been the case in Britain since 1945, politicians and party officials have to take account of even small groups of electors. Black voters were a distinctive and expanding portion of the electorate and this expansion was clearly revealed by the publication of the findings of the 1971 census. More accurate estimates of the black population settled in Britain were made possible because the 1971 census identified not only those people born in the New Commonwealth but also those with New Commonwealth parents. The census revealed that there were sixty-one constituencies where black Britons formed over 8 per cent of the population. Election studies had also shown that the registration and turnout of black Britons was rising and that for the Asian population the turnout of registered voters was as high as, or even higher than, the turnout of the native white population (LeLohé, 1979).

These developments encouraged the CRC to publish a special report on the participation of the ethnic minorities in the General Election of October 1974 (Community Relations Commission, 1975). The purpose of this report was to bring to the attention of the major political parties the importance of Asian and West Indian voters in the political process, and to influence the parties to adopt more positive policies towards the ethnic minorities. Rather crudely the report suggested that an indication of the importance of black voters could be obtained by comparing the size of the electoral majority in a constituency with the number of people from the New Commonwealth living in that constituency at the time of the census. This argument is highly unrealistic as it assumes that the black population is similar in terms of age, registration and turnout to the host population. In fact the black population is much younger and less likely to be registered to vote than the white population. Moreover, while the turnout of Asian voters is comparable with that of white voters, it is probable that the turnout of West Indians is lower. (In the Marplan survey of electors in Birmingham Ladywood for the by-election in August 1977 West Indian electors were the least likely to have a firm voting intention – 63 per cent. They provided the highest number of *Don't Knows* – 37 per cent. A significant number refused to answer the question – 15 per cent – and 11 per cent said they would not vote.) However, the report argued that in these constituencies the ethnic minority voters were sufficiently numerous to influence the outcome of the election. There were seventy-six such constituencies in February, and eighty-five in October, but in order to eliminate those with freak small majorities, the report concentrated on the fifty-nine seats which returned MPs with smaller majorities than the constituency population born in the New Commonwealth, in both elections. The point was emphasised that in the February Election twenty-nine of these seats were held by the Conservative Party, of which thirteen were gained by Labour in the October Election. Thus thirteen of the seventeen Labour gains made in October 1974 were in seats where the majority was less than the black population. The report implied that the failure of the Conservative Party to appeal to Asian and West Indian voters could have played a major part in helping the Labour Party to victory in both general elections. The evidence that Asian and West Indian voters had supported the Labour Party to a far greater extent than the white electorate in 1974 was overwhelming, but the report also argued that in the past, when other parties had attempted to appeal to black voters by nominating black candidates or making other efforts to gain their support, this had had a fair amount of success. In spite of its erroneous assumptions this report gained considerable publicity and made a significant impact on politicians and party officials.

Labour MPs and officials had been aware for some time that black voters might be crucially important in a number of seats and in many constituencies had made efforts to contact community leaders and organisations in efforts to mobilise the black electorate. Efforts to recruit Asians and West Indians as individual party members had been less vigorously pursued, although in a number of areas where the ethnic minorities were electorally important such as parts of London, Nottingham and Bradford, local Labour Parties had nominated black candidates for local council seats.

CONSERVATIVE INITIATIVES, 1974–79

On the Conservative side the 1971 census returns, the Nuffield election studies (Butler and Kavanagh, 1974; Butler and Kavanagh, 1975) and the CRC report, all emphasising the growing electoral importance of black voters, came as a rude shock. Most Conservatives had assumed that Asian and West Indian voters were concentrated in inner-city constituencies or working-class suburbs like Southall, which would have returned Labour MPs with or without black voters. The realisation that black voters were important in urban marginals in Lancashire, Yorkshire, the Midlands and Greater London caused Conservative Central Office to decide on a major initiative to alert the party to the importance of the ethnic minority vote and to make direct efforts to woo black voters. In January 1976 Andrew Rowe was appointed director of a new Central Office Department of Community Affairs which was specifically charged with promoting the party among target groups in the electorate. These target groups were groups to which Central Office felt special attention should be paid either because the party was lacking support among them or because it was losing support. Examples of such groups were young voters, skilled workers and black voters. Mr Rowe established an Ethnic Minorities Unit whose role was to educate party members about the growing electoral importance of Asian and West Indian voters and to influence party policy so that a more favourable party image could be presented to these voters. One of the first initiatives of the new unit was to create an Anglo–Asian Conservative Society and an Anglo–West Indian Conservative Society in order to recruit Asians and West Indians directly into the party through specialist associations with a national structure and therefore with direct representation on the area and national committees of the National Union of Conservative and Unionist Associations. Since these societies were centrally sponsored it was impossible for constituency associations to refuse them local recognition, but the fact that specialist associations needed to be created suggested not only that local action in contacting and recruiting members of the ethnic minorities was lacking, but also that little would be done without strong prodding from the centre.

These two ethnic minority societies were formed with the help of two Conservative councillors. Basil Lewis, a West Indian from Hornsey, had been elected as a Conservative councillor for Haringay Borough Council in 1968. He played a major role in establishing a base for the Anglo-West Indian Conservative Society in Hornsey. Narindar Saroop, a Conservative councillor in Kensington and Chelsea and a Conservative parliamentary candidate in 1979, helped to found the Anglo-Asian Society and became its first chairman. The Conservative Party gave a high priority to the Anglo-Asian Society as it was widely felt that Asian businessmen and professional people such as doctors and accountants could be successfully recruited into the Conservative Party. Asian cultural and religious values seemed well attuned to Conservative principles and provided a basis for appeal. The Conservatives also felt that they had a strong basis of support among East African Asians as it was a Conservative administration which had accepted its responsibilities and allowed many of them to come to Britain after their expulsion from Uganda. Mrs Thatcher agreed to become honorary president of the Anglo-Asian Society and, in order to impress Asian leaders with the support all sections of the party were giving to this new initiative, fourteen honorary vice-presidents were appointed, including William Whitelaw, Lord Carrington, Michael Heseltine, Winston Churchill and John Biggs-Davidson.

This more positive trend towards the ethnic minorities by the Conservative leadership was also apparent in the largely favourable response of the Shadow Cabinet towards the Race Relations Act (1976) which they decided not to oppose, despite considerable backbench disquiet and resentment at the new powers proposed under the Act. However, the positive approach to black voters within Britain remained predicated on tough immigration controls. At the annual party conference in October 1976, Mr Whitelaw, the opposition spokesman on Home Affairs, in his reply to the debate on immigration stated that every immigrant now here should be treated as an equal and welcome member of our society. However, he also argued that a harmonious and multi-racial society could only be promoted if a policy was followed which was clearly designed to work towards an end of immigration as seen in the postwar years. He reaffirmed Conservative commitments to admitting wives and children of heads of families settled in Britain before 1 January 1973, the date the Immigration Act (1971) came into force, and also to the UK passport holders in East Africa. A future Conservative government, he promised, would introduce a new British Nationality Act to define clearly those who belonged to the UK (Conservative Central Office, 1945–83a, *Annual Conference Report*, 1976, pp. 40–7). The statement of Conservative aims, *The Right*

Approach (Conservative Central Office, 1976), which was published in the same month as the conference, emphasised the tough Conservative approach to immigration controls; and it specifically demanded a reduction in immigration which it stated had 'increased by a very substantial amount under this government'. It suggested a register of dependants, an idea also mentioned by Mr Whitelaw in his conference speech, and argued that there must be a clearly defined limit to the number of immigrants to be allowed into Britain.

The Conservative Party was thus facing two ways on race and immigration issues in 1976. On immigration there were indications of continuing support for tough controls and moves towards even tougher controls than those envisaged by the 1971 Immigration Act. The demands for an immediate reduction in immigration, for a register of dependants and for a new Nationality Act linking right of abode in the UK to citizenship were indications of this trend. In contrast the party appeared to be adopting a softer approach to race relations within Britain, recognising that black Britons were an established and growing political reality, part of Britain's future; and that the party needed to become more attractive to Asian and West Indian voters. The establishment of the Anglo–Asian and Anglo–West Indian Conservative Societies were important innovations in Conservative Party organisation. The decision not to oppose the Race Relations Act (1976) showed an awareness of the extent of racial discrimination and the need for tough measures to combat this in order to prevent the alienation of the ethnic minority population. Mr Whitelaw personally gave strong support to the Federation of Conservative Students' campaign against racialism in the autumn of 1977 and this also suggested that the Conservative Party was firmly opposed to incitement to racial hatred and the activities of the National Front. This appeared to be confirmed by the party's involvement in the Joint Committee Against Racialism (JCAR). This committee was formed in the autumn of 1977 and included the Labour and Liberal Parties, the British Council of Churches, the Board of Deputies of British Jews, the National Union of Students, the British Youth Council and leading immigrant organisations. The Labour and Conservative parties were each invited to nominate one of two joint chairmen, and apparently successful efforts to include the Conservative Party and appoint John Moore, MP, as joint chairman with the Labour nominee Joan Lestor, MP, were vetoed at a late stage by Mrs Thatcher. She was appalled when she discovered that the party was involved in an anti-racist movement which might involve joint activities not only with the Labour Party but with groups on the far left as well. The divisions within the Conservative Party were revealed dramatically when the Executive Committee of the National Union insisted on continuing Conservative participation in the JCAR despite

Mrs Thatcher's opposition and a statement issued by Lord Thorney-croft, the party chairman, earlier on the day the decision was made, indicating that the party would not be involved. Such a move by the National Union against the wishes of the party leader was un-precedented. Mrs Thatcher's veto of John Moore's involvement was subsequently confirmed and instead Mrs Shelagh Roberts, a prominent Conservative from outside Parliament, was appointed as joint chairman (Layton-Henry, 1978b).

This controversy over Conservative participation in the JCAR was quickly followed by two events which indicated that the Conservative leadership was once again hardening its public stand on immigration. On 10 January there were reports in *The Times* and the *Guardian* that Keith Speed, a junior opposition spokesman on Home Affairs, was preparing a report for the Shadow Cabinet on ways of reducing immigration. On 30 January 1978 Mrs Thatcher gave a television interview to Gordon Burns on Granada's *World in Action* programme during which she claimed that people were rather afraid that this country and the British character might be swamped by people with a different culture. She said the Conservative Party should hold out the prospect of an end to immigration except in compassionate cases and suggested that the neglect of the immigration issue was driving some people to support the National Front. She stated that she wished to attract to the Conservative Party voters who had been supporting the National Front (Granada Television, 1978).

Mrs Thatcher was well aware that the private polls conducted for the Conservative Party showed that there was strong support among the electorate for tougher controls on immigration. She was also under pressure from some backbenchers and close colleagues who felt that immigration was an issue which could be exploited to the electoral advantage of the party, and who were determined that Mr Speed's proposals would be very tough. Mrs Thatcher was annoyed by the participation of sections of the party in anti-racialist campaigns, though these could not be opposed too strongly as the party could not support racialism and the JCAR did command support from a wide spectrum of parties and organisations. Mrs Thatcher was, however, determined to impress the electorate that she was responsive to popular anxieties over immigration and that the Conservative Party would bring New Commonwealth immigration to an end. Her statement on television received considerable publicity and showed dramatically how the immigration issue could still provoke an enormous popular response despite the existence of tough control legislation under the 1971 Immigration Act. In January 1978, before her interview on television, the support for the Conservative and Labour Parties was equal at 43.5 per cent of the electorate. Only 9 per cent of this sample mentioned immigration as one of the two most urgent problems facing the country. In February 1978 the Conservatives had shot into a 9 per cent lead over Labour (48 per cent to 39 per cent) and 21 per cent mentioned immigration as one of the two most urgent problems facing the country (NOP, 1978).

By exploiting the immigration issue so dramatically Mrs Thatcher regained the political initiative which at this time appeared to be slipping away from the Conservatives to the Labour government. She also ensured that the Shadow Cabinet would agree to tough new proposals on immigration. The initiatives taken by Central Office to attract and recruit black voters were undermined but Mrs Thatcher's judgement was that the Conservative Party had far more to gain electorally by responding to the concerns of white voters anxious about immigration. The tough new proposals on immigration outlined by Mr Whitelaw at the meeting of the Central Council of the Conservative Party on 7 April were the logical consequence of Mrs Thatcher's initiative.

The Conservative Party thus entered the 1979 General Election campaign committed to toughening up immigration controls. The manifesto emphasised the traditional dual approach to race and immigration, namely that racial harmony within Britain was dependent upon effective control of immigration. It stated that:

> The rights of all British citizens legally settled here are equal before the law whatever their race, colour or creed, and their opportunities ought to be equal too. The ethnic minorities have already made a valuable contribution to the life of our nation, but firm immigration control for the future is essential if we are to achieve good community relations. It will end persistent fears about levels of immigration and will remove from those settled, and in many cases born here, the label of immigrant. (Conservative Central Office, 1945–83b, *Party Manifesto*, 1979)

The manifesto went on to list a number of specific commitments which were intended to reduce immigration. These were:

1   We shall introduce a new British Nationality Act to define entitlement to British citizenship and the right of abode in this country. It will not adversely affect the rights of anyone now permanently settled here.
2   We shall end the practice of allowing permanent settlement for those who came here for a temporary stay.
3   We shall limit entry of parents, grandparents and children over 18 to a small number of urgent compassionate cases.
4   We shall end the concession introduced by the Labour government in 1974 to husbands and male fiancés.

5   We shall severely restrict the issue of work permits.

6   We shall introduce a Register of those Commonwealth wives and children entitled to entry for settlement under the 1971 Immigration Act.

7   We shall then introduce a quota system, covering everyone outside the European Community to control all entry for settlement.

8   We shall take firm action against illegal immigrants and overstayers and help those immigrants who genuinely wish to leave this country – but there can be no question of compulsory repatriation.

The Conservative Party did not emphasise its policies on immigration control during the election campaign though Mrs Thatcher confirmed in a radio phone-in programme that she stood absolutely by her earlier statement that people felt swamped by immigrants, and reiterated the tough proposals the Conservatives intended to introduce. However, while immigration was not an issue in the campaign, Mrs Thatcher had made it clear where the Conservative Party stood on the issue and her stand was popular with most of the electorate. The very substantial swings to the Conservative Party in areas where previously the National Front had done relatively well suggested that Mrs Thatcher was successful in winning many of these voters for the Conservatives (Layton-Henry and Taylor, 1979–82).

In constituencies where there were substantial numbers of ethnic minority voters the Conservatives made modest efforts to appeal to them. The Anglo–West Indian Society was formally launched in February 1979 to help attract West Indian support for the Conservative candidates in the marginal seats of Hornsey and Croydon Central. The Anglo–Asian Society attempted to do the same in marginals with large numbers of Asian voters. In addition two Asians stood as Conservative parliamentary candidates: Narindar Saroop in Greenwich and Farriq Saleem in Glasgow Central. Both of these seats remained safely Labour. Conservatives efforts to attract support from the ethnic minorities were unsuccessful and there was a swing among these voters to Labour against the popular tide which swept the Conservatives to office. Given the impact and emphasis of Mrs Thatcher's initiatives this divergent trend was not surprising.

THE LABOUR PARTY AND RACE SINCE 1974

In the early 1970s a number of developments occurred which caused the Labour Party to change its strategy on race relations and immigration issues and to adopt a more positive approach towards black voters and against public manifestations of racialism. First, the

Labour Party moved into opposition from 1970 to 1974 and was no longer responsible for legislation and administration. It was thus freer to adopt a more radical position, but even so its opposition to the Immigration Act of 1971 was made less credible by the legacy of the Labour governments of 1964–70, particularly the Commonwealth Immigrants Act of 1968. Labour's support for the Conservative administration's acceptance of the Ugandan Asians similarly served to remind socialists of the way their government had treated the Kenyan Asians. Secondly, the early 1970s saw a shift to the left in the Labour Party both on the NEC and more widely in constituency parties and the trade union movement (Hatfield, 1978). This provided a stronger basis for a more principled stand to be taken on sensitive electoral issues like immigration. This was to lead to a divergence between the Labour government of 1974–9 and the Labour Party in the country. Thirdly, the growing activity of the National Front and its exploitation of issues like the entry of the Ugandan Asians demanded a response from the major party on the left and provided a focus for anti-racist activity.

The Labour government which came to office in February 1974 was not committed to specific policies on race relations and immigration but Roy Jenkins, once again Home Secretary, embarked on a programme of cautious reforms. In April he announced an amnesty for illegal immigrants who were Commonwealth citizens or citizens of Pakistan who were adversely affected by the retrospective operation of the 1971 Immigration Act. In June the restriction imposed by the Labour government in 1969 on the admission of husbands and fiancés of women settled in the UK was lifted. In February the following year the quota for UK passport holders was raised from 3,600 to 5,000. In September 1975 the White Paper on *Racial Discrimination* (Home Office, 1975) was published, which proposed the extension of the Race Relations Act 1968, and the following year the new Act was passed and the CRE was established. These actions did not go unchallenged by Enoch Powell and other opponents of liberal race and immigration policies who were mainly right-wing Conservatives. Powell was constantly on the offensive, demanding detailed immigration statistics and castigating the Home Secretary when it was announced, at the end of 1975, that the immigration statistics had been incorrectly compiled over a number of years. At the beginning of 1976 the Labour government was coming under increasing parliamentary pressure over the rising level of immigration and, speaking on the second reading of the Race Relations Bill, Jenkins was forced to admit 'that there is a clear limit to the amount of immigration which this country can absorb and that it is in the interests of the racial minorities themselves to maintain a strict control over immigration' (*Hansard*, 4 March 1976, col. 1548). Also Alex Lyon, the Home Office minister responsible for immigration, was dropped from the government in April, allegedly for being too liberal in his administration of immigration: on 24 May he was criticised by Jonathan Aitken for his past liberal approach (*Hansard*, cols 35–7). In May a major debate on immigration and emigration took place during which Enoch Powell leaked details of a confidential report on immigration from the Indian sub-continent prepared by a Foreign Office official. The Hawley Report suggested that the Home Office estimates for dependants entitled to come to Britain were far too low, that there was a substantial illegal immigrants industry in India helping migrants to come to Britain and that arrangements in India were too generous for intending migrants (*Hansard*, 24 May 1976, cols 49–51). Under mounting pressure, Jenkins announced the establishment of a small parliamentary group under Lord Franks 'to look into the feasibility and usefulness of a register [of dependants] with all the problems and evidence available to them from official sources' (*Hansard*, 5 July 1976, cols 972–87). After the publication of the report in February the following year the government concluded that such a register would not be practicable, desirable or a basis for certainty. However, in March 1977 the government amended the immigration rules to prevent men being accepted for settlement through marriages of convenience and in April published its Green Paper, *British Nationality Law: Discussion of Possible Changes* (HMSO, 1977). This Green Paper contained the government's suggestions for the reform of the nationality and citizenship laws; in particular it contained the suggestion that there should be two forms of British citizenship: the first, UK citizenship for those with close ties with the UK, and the second, British Overseas citizenship for those who were citizens of the UK colonies. These proposals once again foreshadowed Conservative legislation and a number of the Labour government's proposals were incorporated in the Nationality Act, 1981, passed by the Thatcher government. The Labour Party has subsequently modified its position on nationality and is now committed to repealing the Conservative Act and substituting its own non-discriminatory legislation which is more liberal than the Green Paper proposals.

In spite of even greater pressure from the Conservatives in 1978, after Mrs Thatcher's 'swamping' initiative, the government rejected the controversial unanimous report on immigration from the parliamentary Select Committee which was published in March. This report recommended tighter controls on immigration from the Indian sub-continent, an end to amnesties for illegal immigrants, a system of internal controls of immigration and a register of dependants. There were some liberal recommendations such as speeding up immigration procedures for dependants so that families could be reunited more quickly, but on balance it was a restrictive report. Some of the Labour members of the Select Committee appear to have supported the recommendations for electoral reasons as well as wishing to preserve the Committee's tradition of unanimity (House of Commons, 1978; Layton-Henry, 1979).

Outside Parliament in the constituencies, in the unions and on the NEC, pressure was growing for a stronger response to the National Front and a more campaigning stance against racialism. The publicity surrounding the arrival of small numbers of Asians from Malawi in May 1976, the exploitation of this by the National Front and the significant electoral support for the National Front in the local elections worried the NEC. In Blackburn the National Party, which had broken away from the National Front, won two seats on the district council. This success of the far right shocked members of the NEC, particularly Barbara Castle, the MP for Blackburn. She was determined that the Labour Party should act more vigorously as it was clear that the National Front and the National Party were attracting former Labour voters. Also the Blackburn result showed that the threat was no longer confined solely to London and the Midlands.

These developments strengthened the position of those on the NEC who had been pressing for a Labour campaign against racialism, and the NEC agreed to launch such a campaign jointly with the TUC in September 1976. The aim was mainly to educate Labour Party members and trade unionists concerning the evils of racialism and the implications of the neo-fascist policies of the National Front and other far right groups. An additional incentive for positive action was the launching, also in 1976, of the Conservative Party's Anglo–Asian Society. This alerted the NEC to the danger of taking Asian and West Indian votes for granted. Some members of the NEC were concerned that a sustained Conservative initiative might attract substantial numbers of Asian voters. Moreover there was an additional danger that if the Labour Party continued to emphasise firm support for immigration control and failed to combat publicly the activities of the National Front, black voters might become sufficiently disillusioned with both the major parties to nominate candidates from their own communities in areas where they were electorally strong.

There was a major debate on racialism at the annual party conference in September and calls on all sides for a major offensive against the far right. Conference also passed a resolution demanding the repeal of the 1968 and 1971 Immigration Acts (Labour Party, *Annual Conference Report*, 1976, pp. 213–14). The annual conference was again debating racialism in 1978. This time the NEC opposed a strongly worded composite resolution which condemned the Select Committee report, opposed all Immigration Acts and supported the right of blacks to organise self-defence groups. This resolution was lost and a more moderately worded resolution was remitted to the NEC for further consideration (Labour Party, *Annual Conference Report*, 1977, pp. 312–23).

The Labour Party devoted relatively little space to immigration and race relations in its 1979 election manifesto. Its proposals emphasised the need to strengthen the legislation protecting the minorities against discrimination and racialism. It promised that the next Labour government would:

(a) Give a strong lead, by promoting equality of opportunity at work throughout the public sector;
(b) Help those whose first language is not English;
(c) Monitor all government and local authority services to ensure that minorities are receiving fair treatment;
(d) Consider what measures may be necessary to clarify the role of the Public Order Act and to strengthen and widen the scope of the Race Relations Act;
(e) Review the 1824 Vagrancy Act with a view to repealing section 4. (Labour Party Manifesto, 1979, p. 29)

Since moving back into opposition the Labour Party has once again polished up its radical credentials on race and immigration issues and has strongly opposed many of the initiatives taken by the Conservative administration.

THE THATCHER ADMINISTRATION

The Conservative victory in the General Election of May 1979 was won by a party committed to tough policies on immigration control and more anxious to appeal to anti-immigrant voters than to the ethnic minorities. In contrast to the substantial national swing to the Conservatives, black voters swung to Labour, despite their already overwhelming levels of Labour voting. For black voters, race relations and immigration issues remain of paramount importance, so much so that it is possible to regard this as ethnic voting (Crewe, 1983).

The new Conservative government was determined to fulfil its manifesto promises and tighten the immigration rules. However, this proved easier to promise than to implement. The government found that there were considerable administrative and political problems in tightening rules which were already very strict. The commitment, for example, to end the concession introduced by the Labour government in 1974 to allow husbands and male fiancés the right to enter the UK for settlement was intended to prevent the entry of Asian men for settlement by means of the arranged marriage. Mr Whitelaw had argued that substantial evasion of immigration controls was taking place and that this had been a substantial source of primary immigration by Asians into the UK. In 1973 200 husbands or fiancés had entered Britain and by 1976 this had risen to 6,300 (*Hansard*, 4 December 1979, col. 254). It was quickly realised, however, that the closing of this source of immigration would affect the rights of white British women engaged or married to foreign citizens who might wish to return to the UK to settle with their husbands. Some Conservative spokesmen argued that it was normal for a wife to settle in her husband's place of residence and assume his nationality. Organised groups of British wives mushroomed in a number of countries, including Egypt and the USA, to lobby the government. Women's groups within Britain protested strongly against the unequal treatment of women under the new rules. A large number of Conservative MPs saw the Home Secretary to voice the concerns of their constituents. When the new rules were debated on 4 December, as many as nineteen Conservatives abstained. When the final statement of changes in the immigration rules was published on 20 February 1980 there were additional changes to take account of criticisms. For example, the right of entry to husbands or fiancés was allowed providing their wives or fiancées were born or had one parent born in the UK and the primary aim of the marriage was not settlement. Also elderly dependants were allowed to enter the UK providing they were wholly maintained by their children or grandchildren. These final provisions were debated and approved by Parliament on 10 March when the government had a majority of fifty-two. There were only five abstentions (Layton-Henry and Taylor, 1979–82). The government has similarly found that its attempts to liberalise the rules as a consequence of the Nationality Act provoked a revolt from its right wing who felt that the government was failing to implement its manifesto commitments (*Hansard*, 28 January 1981, col. 942). A number of specific commitments in the manifesto have in fact been dropped, notably the register of dependants and the proposal for a quota for all immigration outside the European Community.

THE NATIONALITY ACT

The major commitment that has been implemented was the promise to introduce a new British Nationality Act which was passed into legislation in 1981. The government hoped that by tying the right of abode and settlement in the UK to a clear definition of citizenship it would be able to make immigration control less arbitrary and less controversial and also to avoid criticism of racial discrimination in the operation of the immigration rules.

The Bill the government presented, however, proved to be highly controversial. It proposed three categories of citizenship: British citizenship, citizenship of the British Dependent Territories and

British Overseas citizenship. British citizens would be persons who had a close personal connection with the UK either because their parents or grandparents were born, adopted, naturalised or registered as citizens of the UK or through permanent settlement in the UK. One controversial proposal was that as a general rule British citizenship would descend only to the first generation of children born abroad to British citizens born in the UK. This is important to many expatriate Britons spread around the world and also adversely affects the status of children born abroad to British citizens not born in the UK. The Bill also proposed that children born in Britain whose parents were of uncertain status, for example because of illegal immigration or overstaying their period of residence, should not automatically be entitled to citizenship. Persons marrying a British citizen would be able to apply for citizenship after three years' residence. Citizenship of the British Dependent Territories would be acquired by those citizens of the UK and colonies who had that citizenship by reason of their own or their parents' or grandparents' birth, naturalisation or registration in an existing dependency or associated state. The third category, British Overseas citizenship, was essentially a residual one with virtually no rights. It was intended for those citizens of the UK and colonies who did not qualify for either of the first two categories and related mainly to holders of dual citizenship who lived in Malaysia. British Overseas citizens would not be able to pass on the citizenship nor would they have the right of abode in any British territory. In reality it was an invitation to those British subjects permanently settled abroad and with no close connection with the UK to acquire full local citizenship as quickly as possible. This was a further indication that the British government wished to divest itself of its remaining imperial commitments. As this citizenship could not be passed on to descendants, some children might be born stateless if their countries of birth refused them citizenship.

The Home Secretary, Mr Whitelaw, introduced the Bill on its second reading and argued that under the immigration laws it would not adversely affect the position of anyone lawfully settled in the UK. He claimed that it did not discriminate on racial or sexual grounds, and that it provided the comprehensive and logical overhaul of our citizenship legislation that has so long been required and which it was the absolute duty of the UK government to introduce (*Hansard*, 28 January 1981, cols 931–41).

Despite the fact that the Labour opposition was itself committed to a revision of the nationality law and that many of the Conservatives' proposals were foreshadowed in Labour's Green Paper, Mr Hattersley for the opposition gave the Bill a very hostile reception. This was the first major parliamentary test for Roy Hattersley since becoming Shadow Home Secretary. He decided to use this opportunity to make a principled stand against the Bill. He said that the opposition would oppose the Bill at every stage, that it was racist and sexist and was in reality an Immigration Control Bill dressed up as a Nationality Bill. He argued, 'What we need is a positive statement of nationality based on objectively defined principles, clear of all racial considerations. From that statement of nationality a non-discriminatory immigration policy should then flow' (*Hansard*, 28 January 1981, cols 941–50). Mr Hattersley suggested that the Bill was racist as British citizens of New Commonwealth origin whose children were born abroad might lose their automatic entitlement to citizenship, and this would discriminate against many of his constituents who might wish to have their children with their mother or relatives, for example in Pakistan. The residential qualification for marriage partners who wished to become citizens discriminated against women who might have to wait a lengthy period before admittance into the UK. He argued that all who were born in the UK, whatever their status, should have an automatic entitlement to citizenship. He also stated that the third category proposed in the Bill was a sham and that the government should have discussions with Commonwealth governments to regularise the status of people who would come into this category, but that if their countries of residence refused to give them full status they should be offered British citizenship which would entitle them to entry and abode in the UK.

The Liberals also opposed the Bill, and David Steel described it as the latest in a long line of shabby measures reducing the basic rights of the ethnic minorities and discriminating against them (*Hansard*, 28 January 1981, col. 954). Much of the debate was taken up with MPs making representations on behalf of dependencies like Gibraltar, later granted full citizenship, Hong Kong and the Falklands. (It is likely that as a result of the Falklands war with Argentina the Falkland islanders will be granted full British citizenship.) Some Conservative right-wingers made it clear that they wanted stronger immigration controls and Alex Lyon queried Hattersley's generous offer to accept British passport holders in Malaysia and Singapore. Some Conservatives argued that it was unjust to distinguish between children born abroad to British citizens by birth and those born abroad to British citizens by naturalisation or registration. There was considerable support for the view put forward by Roy Hattersley that each dependency should have its own citizenship rather than the common citizenship proposed in the Bill for British Dependent Territories. The second reading was passed with a government majority of fifty.

After the second reading, on 6 February 1981 the Home Secretary announced two major amendments: first, that any child born in the UK who did not acquire British citizenship at birth might acquire citizenship after ten years' continuous residence, irrespective of the status of the parents; and secondly, citizens by naturalisation or registration would be allowed to transmit citizenship to children born overseas in the same way as British-born parents. These amendments went some way to meeting criticism of the Bill but there remained considerable opposition from legal groups, the churches, ethnic minority organisations, civil rights groups, the CRE and campaigning organisations like the Joint Council for the Welfare of Immigrants, which for example criticised the Act in *The Times* on 30 September. Despite the criticisms the Bill was enacted towards the end of 1981. The Labour opposition is committed to a major revision of the nationality law (Labour Party, 1981).

If the government hoped that race and immigration issues would die down once it was elected, then it was gravely mistaken. In fact Mrs Thatcher's pre-election promises to assuage people's fears over continuing immigration raised expectations about specific actions the government would take to halt immigration. These expectations have not been fulfilled, to the fury of groups on the Conservative right like the Monday Club, because controls are as strict as is practicable and can only be tightened by breaking commitments to the European Convention on Human Rights. Mrs Thatcher by her public statements in 1978 raised the salience of the issue for the public and the press and increased the insecurity and anxiety of black Britons. It is not surprising, therefore, that race-related issues continued to attract considerable media attention and to provoke emotional responses from white and black citizens. Nowhere has this insecurity been more manifest in relations between the public and the police.

POLICE–MINORITY RELATIONS

From the beginning of the Thatcher administration the role of the police and especially police–minority relations have been a major source of concern. The government has wished to justify its claim to be the party of law and order and has given a high priority to defending and supporting the police. The pay of the police has been considerably improved and police powers are being extended under the Police and Criminal Evidence Bill which was proceeding through Parliament until the announcement of the General Election in June 1983 caused the Bill to be dropped. However, the government's support for the police has not prevented the role of the police from becoming the centre of considerable political controversy.

In the General Election campaign of 1979 the death of Blair Peach in Southall led to considerable anxiety about the role of the Special Patrol Group (SPG) in London, and a major unofficial committee of inquiry was established after dissatisfaction with the failure to determine who was responsible for his death. The riot in the St Pauls area of Bristol in April 1980 after a police raid on a café, and concern over the operation of the 'sus' laws (arrest on suspicion) kept police–minority relations to the fore during 1980. The following year proved even more cataclysmic with the failure of the police to determine how thirteen young black people died in a fire in Deptford in February and accusations of police failure to take seriously the widespread incidence of attacks on black people. The most serious events in 1981 were, of course, the anti-police riots which occurred in Brixton in April and in Toxteth in July. The Brixton riots lasted three days during which 226 people were injured, including 150 policemen, and 200 arrests were made. There was extensive damage to property and twenty-six buildings and twenty vehicles were burnt by rioters (Venner, 1981). The Toxteth riots were even more serious.

The immediate political response to the Brixton riots was one of condemnation of the rioters and support for the police. Mrs Thatcher stated that there was absolutely no justification for riots in a democracy and that her government would ensure that law and order was upheld, that law breakers would be punished and that all citizens would be protected (BBC, 3 May 1981). Mr Whitelaw, the Home Secretary, in his statement to the House of Commons after the riots, said:

> We in Parliament, on behalf of the people of this country, have placed on the police the heavy burden of maintaining peace on the streets and of preserving order and the rule of law. Whatever questions may arise in people's minds about the reasons why this outbreak of violence occurred, there is no doubt in my mind, nor should there be in the mind of any member of this House, that Metropolitan Police officers of all ranks carried out their duty with great bravery and professionalism.

He announced the setting up of an inquiry into the Brixton disorders, under the terms of the Police Act 1964, to establish what happened and to investigate the role of the police. The inquiry would be undertaken by Lord Scarman (*Hansard*, 13 April 1981, col. 21).

Before the Scarman inquiry was complete, an influential and well-publicised report on *Racial Disadvantage* was published in August by the parliamentary Select Committee on Home Affairs. This report was given added importance by the serious riots which had occurred in Toxteth in July. Liverpool was one of the areas the Select Committee had given particular attention to and the members had visited Toxteth in the course of their investigations. The report provided evidence of continuing discrimination and disadvantage among Liverpool's black population despite the fact that most were British born and not immigrants. The Committee reported that:

> The situation of Liverpool's ethnic minority population is, however,

of particular interest because of the way in which patterns of disadvantage in employment, education and housing, so far from disappearing with the passage of time have, if anything, been reinforced over the years to the extent that Chinese or Asian 'newcomers' are in a better position than Liverpool's indigenous blacks. If we cannot combat racial disadvantage in our other cities now, we will soon have a dozen Liverpools but on a far greater scale.

The *Liverpool Black Organisation* warned the sub-committee that 'What you see in Liverpool is a sign of things to come'. The Select Committee added, 'We echo that warning' (House of Commons, 1981b).

The Scarman Report into the Brixton disorders of 10–12 April (Scarman, 1981) was published in November. The major focus of the inquiry had been to establish what happened and to investigate the role of the police in Brixton. Partly in response to the threat of a boycott by black organisations, Lord Scarman agreed to investigate the underlying causes of the riots but this formed only a relatively small part of his inquiry, which concentrated on the role of the police, policing and law reform. The report gives the impression of being well prepared and well balanced. After a short description of the social conditions in Brixton – inner-city deprivation, unemployment and discrimination, which Scarman argues cannot provide an excuse for disorder – the course and pattern of the Brixton disturbances are described in detail. The disorders are described as communal disturbances arising from a complex political, social and economic situation and they contained a strong racial element. Putting it bluntly, Lord Scarman found that the riots were essentially an outburst of anger and resentment by young blacks against the police (Scarman, 1981, p. 45).

Lord Scarman was satisfied that police forces generally recognise the significance of good relations with the community they police and that the Metropolitan Police at district command level and above do not lack awareness of the need for good community relations. The police in Lambeth had not, however, succeeded in achieving the degree of public approval and respect necessary for the effective fulfilment of their function and duties. Among the reasons for this loss of confidence were the collapse of the police liaison committee in 1979, hard policing methods which caused offence and apprehension to many, lack of consultation about police operations, distrust of the procedure for investigating complaints against the police, and unlawful and, in particular, racially prejudiced conduct by some police officers. The police had to cope with a rising level of crime in Brixton and to retain the confidence of all sections of the community. Lord Scarman concluded that, while nothing can excuse the unlawful behaviour of the rioters, both the police and community leaders must carry some responsibility for the outbreak of disorder. Broadly, however, the police response to the disorders, once they had broken out, was to be commended, not criticised (Scarman, 1981, pp. 126–8).

The report recommended reforms in police recruitment, training, supervision and methods of policing. The aims of these were to secure more recruits from the ethnic minorities, better relations with the minority communities and to avoid the recruitment of racially prejudiced people into the police force. The report recommended that racially discriminatory behaviour should be a specific offence in the police discipline code (Scarman, 1981, p. 130). On law reform, Lord Scarman concluded that stop-and-search powers were necessary to combat crime, but that an independent element in the police complaints procedure should be quickly introduced to improve public confidence. Finally, he recommended that the Public Order Act, 1936, should be amended to include a requirement of advance notice of a procession to the police and the deletion of 'serious' from the public order test. He suggested that the Act might also be revised to enable selective bans to be placed on racist marches.

On the social questions relating to racial disadvantage Lord Scarman endorsed the findings of the Select Committee report on *Racial Disadvantage*. He argued that there was a lack of a sufficiently well co-ordinated programme for combating the problem of racial disadvantage, and stated that if racial disadvantage was to be effectively redressed positive action, presumably by the government, was necessary.

The Scarman Report is a diplomatic report in that all parties can find aspects with which they agree and disagree. It puts the blame for the disorders on both the police and local community leaders. The direction and policies of the Metropolitan Police were found not to be racist but instances of misconduct were found to occur on the streets. The contention that Britain is an 'institutionally racist' society is rejected although nowhere in the report is a definition of institutional racism provided. Elsewhere in the report Lord Scarman admits that 'it is unlikely, however, that racial prejudice can be wholly eliminated from the police so long as it is endemic in society as a whole' (Scarman, 1981, pp. 11, 79).

In the debate on the Scarman Report, Mr Whitelaw, as Home Secretary, reported his acceptance of Lord Scarman's recommendations on police training, liaison arrangements with local committees and the need to reform police complaints procedures (*Hansard*, 10 December 1981, cols 1001–8). There was some reservation about including racially prejudiced behaviour as an offence in the police code and opposition to making automatic dismissal (which Scarman had in any event rejected) the penalty for such an offence. On Lord Scarman's support for the Select Committee's report on *Racial Disadvantage*, the government promised a detailed reply in a White Paper which, when it was published, in fact was to reject most of the Select Committee's recommendations (Home Office, 1982). Mr Whitelaw also announced that the government would conduct an experiment into ethnic monitoring in the Civil Service. In an effort to show that the government was responding positively he also referred to the small increase in the government's contribution to the urban aid programme which had earlier been announced by Mr Heseltine. Opposition speakers in the debate tended to focus on economic deprivation and unemployment as the fundamental causes of the disturbances and urged the government to take action to promote economic recovery, which they argued was the only sure remedy for the disorders. Roy Hattersley, opposition spokesman on Home Affairs, also called on the Home Secretary to implement all the recommendations on the police and to revise the Public Order Act to enable selective bans to be placed on racist marches (*Hansard*, 10 December 1981, cols 1008–16).

The police response was initially positive and even before the Scarman Report was published the Police Federation announced that it would wholeheartedly support a new independent body to investigate complaints against the police (Runnymede Trust, *Bulletin*, December 1981). However, it quickly became clear that the Police Federation was opposed to the introduction of a specific disciplinary offence of racially prejudiced conduct on the grounds that it was already covered by the existing Police Disciplinary Code, a view supported by the Police Superintendents' Association. They were not prepared in the interests of fostering good community relations to allow the offence to be specifically incorporated in the Code. The Association of Chief Police Officers told the Home Affairs Select Committee that they were opposed to statutory liaison committees. The chairman of the Police Federation attacked Lord Scarman's criticism of saturation policing to stop street crime and argued that operations like 'Swamp 81' were necessary. On 10 March 1982 the Metropolitan Police issued statistics on recorded crime in London for the previous year which included breakdowns by race and which purported to show that blacks were disproportionately involved in street crime. In spite of the fact that it was well known that statistics of reported crime are very unreliable, it was clear that the publication of figures in this way was part of the response by the police to the criticisms of their actions contained in the Scarman Report. It is clear that the police wished for better equipment to deal with rioters and wider police powers, and were unwilling to accept reforms which would make them more sensitive and accountable to local communities. A further indication of a greater willingness by some police officers to become involved in politics occurred at the Conservative conference in October 1982 when Inspector Basil Griffiths, deputy chairman of the Police Federation, spoke at a fringe meeting organised by the Monday Club. He said, 'There is in our inner cities a very large minority of people who are not fit for salvage . . . the only way in which the police can protect society is quite simply by harassing these people and frightening them so they are afraid to commit crimes' (*The Times*, 7 October 1982). The presence of a senior member of the Police Federation at a meeting organised by a group associated with extreme policies on racial issues seems a major break with police traditions of political neutrality. It showed a total lack of sensitivity to the importance of police relations with the ethnic minorities.

It is impossible to exaggerate the importance of the police as an institution contributing to the legitimacy and authority of the state. The police are highly visible symbols of authority. They are close to the community they serve and are far closer to the public in their everyday lives than local councillors, magistrates and Members of Parliament. A major factor contributing to law and order and to the stability of society in general is respect for the police. In fact the legitimacy of the political system rests largely upon a positive evaluation of these institutions which intervene between the government and the citizen. Local government, the courts, the electoral process and Parliament are examples of such institutions, as are the police. The legitimacy which these institutions inspire contributes to the legitimacy of the system as a whole, and if the decisions of these institutions are widely accepted and obeyed without the need for significant inducements or sanctions, their legitimacy will be high. When an institution has a high level of legitimacy its actions are respected and have public support, and even when individuals are dissatisfied with specific decisions which may be seen as wrong or unfair, they are accepted as legitimate. Appeals against such decisions will be made through accepted channels to superior bodies. Research into political socialisation suggests that the policeman is an important representative of authority outside the family and crucially important in influencing the relationship between young people and the wider system of authority in society (Easton and Dennis, 1969). If young people or a particular section of the community come to distrust, despise or reject the police, then the legitimacy of other institutions is likely to be questioned and undermined as well. The establishment of trust and respect between the police and the ethnic minorities, and particularly between the police and young blacks, is of crucial importance if alienation and future conflict are to be avoided. It is thus very disappointing that the response of both the police and the government to Lord Scarman's recommendations has been so lukewarm.

CHAPTER 11

The Political Future of Black Britons

There are a large number of ways in which the growing population of black Britons may be linked to the wider political system. The first involves a process by which black Britons will be gradually integrated into the traditional class structure of British politics. This process assumes that as the ethnic minorities lose their immigrant status they will increasingly be accepted as British, albeit black British, and be incorporated predominantly into the working class but also into the middle class. As this occurs, class issues of employment, housing and standard of living will become dominant, supplanting issues related to race and immigration. The black population will become linked to the major parties as members and supporters in much the same way as the white population. They will thus be incorporated into mainstream British politics (Lawrence, 1974; Miles and Phizacklea, 1977a). It has been widely argued that this process is in the best interests of the ethnic minorities themselves, both because class-based institutions are best able to defend the interests of their members (Rex, 1979) and also because it would be an indication of acceptance and political integration. Thus the Home Affairs Select Committee has argued that 'it is by successful participation in the political system rather than through separation or special representation that the political future of Britain's ethnic minorities must lie' (House of Commons, 1981b). Some commentators have suggested that only by emphasising class-based issues and class conflict can white nativism and racial prejudice be suppressed and the rise of racist parties and policies be avoided (Freeman, 1976). The integration of the ethnic minorities into the class structure and the major parties not only assumes increasing participation by black workers in the trade unions and the Labour Party and by black businessmen and professionals in chambers of commerce, professional associations and the Conservative Party, but also assumes a willingness by these organisations to accept, even encourage, their participation and involvement. This is particularly the case regarding the major parties whose members will have to accept black people as full members, adopt them as candidates and persuade their supporters to elect them to local and national positions. It also assumes that the major parties will respond to the particular interests of the ethnic minorities and allow them to influence party policy.

A second possibility is that racial prejudice and hostility will remain a powerful force in British society and that substantial level of racial discrimination and disadvantage will persist. This might encourage the development of a racial black consciousness and solidarity among members of the West Indian and Asian communities despite their widely differing cultures and countries of origin. Such black unity would presumably be most marked among the immigrant-descended population rather than among the first generation of New Common-wealth immigrants, as their expectations of fair and equal treatment would be higher. However, if British Asians and West Indians continue to face common experiences of social rejection, unemployment, police harassment and racial attacks, this could forge a common black identity as black Britons are forced into a situation of defensive confrontation with white society. Black Britons would then have to defend their own interests through their own organisation in conflict with the white working class as well as with the white bourgeoisie. As Rex and Tomlinson (1979) argue, 'What is being expressed in immigrant politics is not the simple and straightforward class struggle within capitalism either in its reformist or its Marxist version. What we are considering is the political formation of an immigrant under-class.' Other writers have also argued that defensive black political organi-sations are likely to develop as racial consciousness grows among black Britons (Moore, 1975). Politically there are a number of ways in which black solidarity might be expressed, for example by support for black candidates no matter which group or party nominated them, or by support for ethnic-based political organisations or groups. A further possibility is a mixture of class radicalism and racial consciousness so that 'far left' parties might make special efforts to recruit and mobilise members of the ethnic minorities, seeing them as the most exploited and therefore potentially the most revolutionary section of the proletariat. If such efforts were successful, such groups might be seen as vehicles for black radicalism rather than working-class radicalism, even though those parties themselves might not wish to be so identified.

A third explanation of the relationship between black Britons and the political system, and one which has gained considerable influence, is the view that black migrants have been linked to the polity through buffer institutions which have undermined their effectiveness (Katznelson, 1973). The argument is that New Commonwealth immigrants were regarded in a paternalistic, neo-colonial way as people with special needs and problems requiring special help. Institutions were therefore created by successive governments to deal with race-related issues outside the traditional political arenas. This was done partly with the deliberate intention of preventing racial issues from becoming a source of conflict between the major parties (see Chapter 4). Organisations like the NCCI and the CRC were therefore created to manage race relations. The national and local committees of these organisations provided officially sponsored arenas for whites and blacks to meet to negotiate over the special needs and interests of blacks. However, because these institutions were created by the government and were dependent on public funds they were subject to considerable limitations. Their functions and aims were defined by the government and their activities were circumscribed so that they could not, for example, engage in party politics. Membership of these organisations was open at the local level to whomsoever wished to participate and they were encouraged to be as widely representative of local institutions as possible, which guaranteed an influential role for major white-dominated local organisations which would act 'responsibly'. At the national level membership was appointed by the Home Secretary. Thus a paternalistic arrangement was established, giving black Britons special institutions but an implicitly inferior status. The result, it is argued, was a loss of political influence and loss of access to mainstream political institutions. Race relations issues were deflected from the major political arenas of party politics, pressure groups and Parliament. They were managed in élitist, unrepresentative institutions which allowed politicians to claim they were working positively for integration when in fact racial distinctions were being perpetuated unnecessarily and these institutions provided only ineffective avenues for political participation. They were not rooted in the black community and so were unrepresentative of the mass of the black population; they were not independent and therefore could not articulate black frustrations and demands. They were not effective in achieving significant reductions in the levels of racial discrimination or prejudice. In fact some would argue that the creation of these institutions was a double mistake because not only were they ineffective but they also gave the impression to the white population that black people were receiving special treatment, and this was a source of resentment and hostility. If this argument is correct, that black Britons have become linked to the political system indirectly through weak and ineffective institutions, akin to a form of indirect colonial rule, then as frustrations grow with their ineffectiveness revolts might be anticipated as blacks fight to break these links and try to establish viable forms of political influence through their own independent institutions or through institutions representing their common interests with other groups.

A fourth major possibility is that there will occur growing disenchantment, alienation and withdrawal from the political process

altogether. This process might involve widely held feelings that black
minority interests are always going to be subordinated to white majority
interests and that the opportunities for blacks to be influential will
always be negligible. In this situation many members of the ethnic
minorities could become politically marginalised and be pushed to the
periphery of politics. This political marginalisation of black Britons
could result in large numbers avoiding political activity and throwing
their energies into family or employment pursuits, local community
activities or religious revivalism. Rastafarianism, a movement which
specifically rejects white society and looks to a return to Africa, is an
extreme example of religious withdrawal.

Another result of alienation and withdrawal could be a form of
smouldering apathy where an apparent quiescent acceptance of
everyday discrimination and disadvantage in fact conceals pent-up
resentments, bitterness and anger which occasionally break out into
outbursts of sporadic violence, perhaps precipitated by incidents like a
racist attack, a police raid or a clash with supporters of the National
Front or British Movement. The violent outbursts in the St Pauls area
of Bristol in 1980 or the riots in Brixton and Toxteth in 1981 might be
cited in support of this view.

A fifth possibility, perhaps the most likely, is that the diversity of the
British Asian and West Indian communities will be reflected in a
variety of relationships with British political processes and institutions
and that taking any one model ignores the complexity of the
relationships involved. Different groups and individuals may adopt
different strategies or be caught up in a variety of forms of political
action depending on the issues involved. Also, in order to maximise
their influence, they will be involved in a number of strategies
simultaneously so that involvement in the major parties, for example,
does not preclude direct action as well. Similarly the unity of ethnic
minority communities is likely to vary depending on the issues so that
Sikhs, for example, may act independently on religious issues using a
variety of strategies such as the CRE and the courts if discrimination is
involved, as well as the lobbying of local parties, politicians and
Members of Parliament. They may also use peaceful direct action such
as marches and mass lobbying of Parliament. On immigration and
nationality issues where all the Asian communities are particularly
affected, for example through cultural traditions like arranged
marriage, the Asian communities are likely to join together to exert
joint political influence. Protest against racial attacks and the activities
of far right-wing groups will draw support from the whole of the ethnic
minority communities and allies from the wider political community as
well. Such emotional and explosive issues are likely to provoke a more
vigorous, even violent, political response. Members of the ethnic
minorities are thus likely to be involved in a whole range of political

action and activities, from participation in the traditional mainstream political parties to various forms of direct action, some of which might appear irresponsible or even illegitimate to members of the white community (the riots in Brixton and Toxteth in 1981 being the obvious examples). A crucial factor, which has already been emphasised, determining the nature and effectiveness of black political participation, is the openness and responsiveness of political institutions to black demands. The efforts by the political parties to woo and mobilise black support and to accept participation from members of the black communities is likely to be critically important. If political institutions specifically, and the white community in general, reject black participation and neglect black interests, then the ethnic minorities will be forced to adopt alternative means of exerting political influence.

ELECTORAL POLITICS

There is considerable evidence to show that black Britons are participating in British electoral politics, though at present this does not represent a straightforward integration into class politics. Black Britons are gradually being integrated into working-class and middle-class institutions. The high rate of trade union membership among black workers, the membership of professional associations and the election in 1982 of two Asian businessmen to the Council of the Institute of Directors are all examples of this process. However, politically members of the ethnic minorities have distinctive priorities and interests which make them act politically rather differently from their white neighbours. Also there are considerable differences between Asian and West Indian communities and between the various Asian communities as well. This makes it difficult to generalise about the political behaviour of black Britons as a whole.

In the 1950s and 1960s the electoral registration and turnout of New Commonwealth immigrants was assumed to be very low. Even as late as 1970 the CRC found that under-registration among West Indians was 37 per cent, among Asians 27 per cent, and in contrast only 6 per cent among whites: (Community Relations Commission, 1975, p. 14). In 1979 the CRE found that under-registration had declined to 23 per cent for West Indians and 18 per cent for Asians, and was stable among whites at 7 per cent (Anwar, 1980, pp. 35–6). Under-registration suggests a lack of interest and involvement in electoral politics but this is not borne out by the turnout rates of those, particularly Asians, who are registered. Detailed monitoring of Asian turnouts in Bradford have shown that Asian voters have consistently higher turnouts than whites in both local and national elections (LeLohé, 1979). The CRE confirmed these findings in the General Election of 1979. In some areas

Asian turnout was phenomenally high – 91 per cent in the wards monitored in Leicester South (a highly marginal seat which Labour held against the national swing) – compared with 60 per cent among whites. Nationally the CRE study found Asian turnout to be above the national average. West Indian turnout appears to be lower than average and closer to the turnout for whites in inner-city areas, which tends to be significantly below the national average (Crewe, 1983). A pre-election survey carried out by the Harris polling organisation for the television programmes *Black on Black* and *Eastern Eye* between 24 and 30 May 1983 and based on samples of 527 Asian and 469 Afro-Caribbean respondents found 61 per cent of Asians absolutely certain to vote but only 33 per cent of Afro-Caribbeans absolutely certain to vote. A further 23 per cent of Asians and 18 per cent of Afro-Caribbeans said they were certain to vote (Harris Poll, 1983). These replies confirm that Asians are far more likely to vote than Afro-Caribbeans and suggests that the latter have very low rates of turnout.

All electoral studies of the voting intentions and behaviour of black voters show substantial levels of support for the Labour Party and negligible support for other parties. Thus in spite of the Labour Party's uneven record on immigration control it gains the support of an overwhelming proportion of ethnic minority voters. Even middle-class Asians and West Indians give overwhelming support to the Labour Party as Table 11.1 shows.

This massive level of support for the Labour Party cannot be explained simply by the youthfulness or the working-class nature of the black electorate. It must represent a strongly negative perception of the

Table 11.1   *The Labour Share of Two-Party Support by Class and Age within Ethnic Groups*

	White %	West Indian %	Asian %
Social class			
A, B, C1	24	90	86
C2	49	94	93
D, E	63	99	97
Age			
16–34	48	96	90
35–54	43	92	93
55+	40	100	100
All	44	95	92
(N)	(1,416)	(233)	(256)

Source: NOP, *Immigration and Race Relations*, February 1978.

Conservative Party, as the major realistic alternative to Labour, on such issues as immigration, race relations and law and order. The better perception of Labour on 'ethnic' issues reinforces class support for Labour among working-class blacks and overwhelms class considerations for middle-class black voters. However, this NOP poll was taken immediately after Mrs Thatcher's 'swamping' speech in January 1978 and it may therefore exaggerate Labour support among black voters. It also ignores non-voting. Surveys conducted by Gallup Poll Ltd before the 1979 General Election show a rather different distribution of support.

Table 11.2 *Voting at the 1979 General Election by Class within Ethnic Group*

	White				West Indians				Asians			
				Non-				Non-				Non-
	Con	Lab	Lib	Voting	Con	Lab	Lib	Voting	Con	Lab	Lib	Voting
Social class												
A, B, C1	57	20	9	15	17	41	7	35	25	42	6	28
C2	40	35	5	20	11	49	8	32	28	50	3	19
D, E	32	38	5	25	15	48	3	35	25	50	0	25
(N)		(10,024)				(106)				(108)		

Source: Layton-Henry and Studlar 1983.
Note: Data are five pooled 1979 pre-election surveys conducted by Social Surveys (Gallup Poll Ltd). Figures may not add to 100 per cent due to rounding.

Table 11.2 confirms that support for the Labour Party is the predominant choice among West Indians and Asians of all classes, while among the white electorate Labour support is closely related to class. However, it shows that while the Conservative Party only obtains very small levels of support among West Indians, they do achieve support from a quarter of the Asian electorate. Liberal support is rather less than the white average but the numbers in the sample on which these percentages are based are tiny (six for West Indians and three for Asians). In the General Election of 1983 the Gallup Poll found that these distributions of support were confirmed with the Labour Party being by far the most popular choice (64 per cent), above the Conservatives (20.5 per cent) and the Alliance (14.9 per cent). However, non-voting is generally higher for West Indians and Asians than for whites and this is markedly the case for West Indians of all classes. Non-voting is thus a significant factor reducing the electoral impact of non-whites.

One surprising factor, given the residential concentration of black voters, is the lack of success of black candidates standing as independents or as candidates of fringe parties. Even in Southall, where the ethnic minority population (not electorate) was 30 per cent in 1979, the two Asian independents and the Asian Socialist Unity candidate achieved a combined share of the vote of only 2.3 per cent. The best achievement by ethnic minority candidates standing for minor parties or as independents was at the Ladywood by-election in August 1977. At this by-election Raghib Ahsan (Socialist Unity) gained 534 votes (3.5 per cent); James Hunte (Independent) gained 336 votes (2.2 per cent); and Kim Gordon (Socialist Workers Party) gained 152 (1 per cent). This by-election, however, occurred under circumstances which were exceptionally favourable for ethnic voting. The Labour government nationally was very unpopular and the local Labour Party was found to have nominated an election agent who was a former member of the British Movement. He was quickly replaced when this was discovered but not before the Socialist Unity candidate had gained considerable publicity by exposing this extraordinary fact. The National Front was engaged in provocative and violent campaigning locally and nationally, and received considerable publicity during violent clashes which occurred during the Lewisham march a few days before the by-election as well as from the clashes which occurred in Ladywood during the by-election campaign itself. The conditions for non-Labour ethnic voting were exceptionally favourable, but even so the Labour candidate held the overwhelming preponderance of the ethnic minority vote (Layton-Henry and Taylor, 1977/8).

The major parties thus offer the best hope for black candidates to gain election to local and national office. Since black voters are overwhelmingly Labour one would expect that the Labour Party would be the natural vehicle for politically active and ambitious blacks. Gradually there has been a small but growing involvement of Asians and West Indians in the Labour Party which was encouraged during the 1970s by the NEC. There had always been some political participation in the Labour Party: for example, David Pitt, now Lord Pitt, was the Labour parliamentary candidate for Hampstead as early as 1959 when he was a Greater London councillor, but significant involvement is more recent and is still on a small scale. Moreover, it varies enormously between constituencies. However, as registration and electoral participation have increased, so individual members of the ethnic minorities have become involved in party politics. Also local parties, sometimes with an eye to factional advantage as well as to electoral success, have attempted to recruit and mobilise black voters in areas of substantial immigrant settlement. The involvement of Asians and West Indians in the Labour Party is most noticeable in the Greater London area, and sixty-seven Labour councillors of Asian or West Indian origin were elected to London borough councils in May 1982. Black Labour councillors did exceptionally well in Brent, where twelve were elected, followed by seven in Ealing and six in Newham (Commission for Racial Equality, 1982). Outside Greater London there are relatively few black councillors and these have been elected in cities like Birmingham, Bradford, Leeds and Leicester. This small progress at local level is even more apparent at the national level where no blacks have yet been elected to the House of Commons and even candidatures are a rarity. The reluctance of constituency parties to adopt black candidates is not surprising given the widespread belief that black candidates are an electoral disadvantage (Bochel and Denver, 1983) and the small number of winnable seats which become available. In the 1979 General Election there was only one black Labour parliamentary candidate. This was Russell Profitt who stood for the safe Conservative seat of the City of London and Westminster South. He was later selected for the safe Labour seat of Battersea South, which unfortunately disappeared under the re-organisation of parliamentary constituencies in 1982. Profitt was unable to gain selection to the new Battersea seat over the sitting Labour MP for Battersea North. In the General Election of 1983 there were six Labour candidates from the ethnic minorities but only one of these had any chance of being elected. This was Paul Boateng, the candidate for West Hertfordshire. He was defending a highly marginal seat which on its new boundaries had a 'notional' Labour majority of 700 votes. He was heavily defeated in the Conservative landslide and came third, behind the winning Conservative and the Alliance candidate. There was no doubt that in the General Election Labour held the overwhelming majority of West Indian and Asian votes, but as the pre-election survey by the Harris polling organisation found, only 61 per cent of Asians and 33 per cent of West Indians claimed they were absolutely certain to vote. This suggests that there are considerably fewer seats where the ethnic minority vote is decisive than is suggested by, for example, the Runnymede Trust (FitzGerald, 1983).

Gradually, however, as Asians and West Indians become more experienced in Labour Party politics and more willing to participate, and as safe Labour seats in areas of black settlement become available, the first black MPs will be elected and the numbers of black Labour councillors will also rise significantly. This will, however, be a slow process and under the British electoral system it is likely that, in common with most minorities, black Britons will remain under-represented.

As far as the other major parties are concerned, their efforts to attract and recruit black voters have met with relatively little success, although the Conservatives claim to be attracting about 25 per cent of the Asian vote. The Conservatives have attempted to recruit Asians and West Indians through their Anglo–Asian and Anglo–West Indian societies. In 1982 the Anglo–Asian Society had twenty-five branches and 2,000 members. The Anglo–West Indian Society had six branches and 200 members. These societies are affiliated to the National Union which enables Conservative Asians and West Indians to have separate representation at all levels of the National Union and at the party's annual conference. However, Conservative Asians and West Indians have considerable difficulty in being fully accepted in many constituency associations. In attempting to stand as candidates and gain election to local councils, Conservatives from the ethnic minorities have much more difficulty in jumping the second hurdle. The party is short of candidates in inner-city areas and local parties may welcome Asians or West Indians as candidates in these areas, but they have little chance of being elected. In the elections to the London boroughs in May 1982 only four Asians and one West Indian were elected as Conservative councillors. Parliamentary nominations are as difficult to achieve as in the other major parties. In the General Election of 1979 two Asians stood as Conservative candidates, both for safe Labour seats (Greenwich and Glasgow Central). Interestingly, they did not appear to suffer from the prejudiced voting that black parliamentary candidates from the other major parties have experienced in the past. This may be a sign that black candidates are now more acceptable to white electors (LeLohé, 1981). There is bound to be a strong temptation for non-Labour parties to nominate ethnic minority candidates in areas with substantial proportions of non-white voters in the hope of splitting the Labour vote and gaining recruits. This is now beginning to happen, so that in the General Election of 1983 Birmingham Conservatives adopted two Asian candidates in seats with high proportions of ethnic minority voters. These were Mrs Pramila Le Hunte in Ladywood and Mr Paul Nichalls in Small Heath. Neither made a significant impact in these very safe Labour seats. The Conservatives also had non-white candidates in North Durham and Newham North West.

The Liberals and now the Social Democratic Party have also attempted to attract and recruit members of the ethnic minorities. The Liberals have, more consistently than other parties, adopted policies attractive to the ethnic minorities on race relations and immigration (Taylor, 1980). They have generally had one or two minority candidates at recent General Elections but apart perhaps from Rochdale, where Cyril Smith has worked hard to woo Asian voters, they have had little success in gaining ethnic minority support. In the 1983 General Election the Liberal/SDP Alliance fielded eight candidates from the ethnic minorities. The best known was Gus Williams, a West Indian who stood as the Liberal/Alliance candidate for Birmingham Perry Barr. He made little impact in a constituency where the popular Labour MP, Jeff Rooker, substantially increased his majority. In past elections Liberal candidates from the ethnic minorities have tended to perform very badly (Steed, 1974). In the 1983 General Election there does not seem to have been any improvement even though the Alliance was hoping to increase its support from the ethnic minorities because of its positive policies on citizenship, immigration and civil rights, and also owing to the fact that one of its major leaders, Roy Jenkins, was the architect of so much of the race relations legislation.

RACIAL CONSCIOUSNESS

There has been considerable speculation that the continuing experience of racial discrimination and social rejection of non-whites in Britain will encourage black unity and consciousness among the British Asian and West Indian communities. There are clearly widespread feelings, particularly among West Indians, that they are subject to racial discrimination and police harassment and that these are major factors contributing to their lowly position in the labour market, to their high levels of unemployment and generally to their low status in British society (Kettle and Hodges, 1982). These feelings of social rejection and discrimination cause most West Indians to identify themselves as black before British and cause many to stress their African ancestry. There is so far, however, no common group identity or ideology which has been forged in their struggle with white society and finds expression in organised political activity. There is, as yet, no widespread rejection of British society and institutions, though many observers feel that this will come eventually unless strong positive action is taken to remedy the genuine grievances of British blacks. An overwhelming majority (83.3 per cent) of Henry's (1982) sample of West Indians in Birmingham felt that their people should take part in British politics, even though over 20 per cent of his sample were not in fact registered to vote. There is thus evidence to suggest that experience of discrimination and social rejection lead to feelings of resentment which in turn are more likely to result in apathy and withdrawal from political activity by West Indians rather than organised group activity on a community basis. This is supported by the 1983 Harris poll data which suggested very high levels of non-voting among West Indians. Pearson (1981) found a lack of formal organisation among West Indians in his study, as did Pryce (1979) in Bristol. Lawrence (1974) and Henry (1982) more recently found considerable suspicion and mistrust between Asians and West Indians. The latter were resentful of Asian commercial success which they saw in the large number of Asian shops in inner-city areas. This they considered to result from the strong cultural and religious identity of Asians which they continued to maintain in Britain and which West Indians believed motivated them to succeed. Organised political activity on a communal basis is thus more likely among the various Asian communities which have a wealth of social, religious and communal organisations in which they participate at high levels. At present organised political activity by Asians is taking place in both communally based organisations like the Indian Workers Association and more broadly based organisations like the Anti-Nazi League. There is little evidence, however, of the growth of black unity and racial consciousness across the Asian and West Indian communities. The geographical concentration of specific ethnic minority communities like Punjabi Sikhs in Southall makes specific communal organisation easier, but the geographical dispersal of the various ethnic minority organisations makes cross-community organisation more difficult. Moreover, the greater satisfaction, confidence and acceptance of British Asians make the likelihood of black unity less, and this is reinforced by mutual suspicions between Asians and West Indians themselves and, for example, between West Pakistanis and Bangladeshis. There is thus the strong possibility that the Asian and West Indian communities will relate to the political process in rather different ways, with Asians being more involved on a group basis and being relatively more effective than West Indians who participate more as individuals. It is likely that West Indians will be more apathetic, alienated and disenchanted with their experience in Britain, and these feelings may increase if they feel relatively less successful than Asians in business, education and politics. The disorganisation, withdrawal and apparent apathy of these black Britons may thus conceal considerable feelings of resentment at their social and economic situation which may lead to increasing black solidarity, especially among the young. The most likely outcome, if discrimination and social rejection continue, is that their smouldering apathy will result in occasional outbursts of violence, as in Bristol and Toxteth. This may force politicians to remedy the long-standing neglect of inner-city areas for, despite the much-publicised inner-city programme, they have in fact done little to attack or remedy urban decline in these areas.

BUFFER INSTITUTIONS

The third model outlined above, that New Commonwealth immigrants have been linked to the British polity through buffer institutions like the Commission for Racial Equality, which have undermined the political effectiveness of black Britons, is a model which I consider to be historically important but which is now rapidly becoming irrelevant. There is no doubt that the National Council for Commonwealth Immigrants and its local organisations performed this role, as did their successor organisations, the Race Relations Board and the Community Relations Commission. Many able black professionals were involved in these institutions and their energies may have been deflected from organising strong, independent black organisations, but it is hard to believe that more than a small proportion of the talent of the ethnic minorities was deflected in this way. The Commission for Racial Equality remains a buffer institution attracting criticism for the government's racial policies which would otherwise be directed straight at the Home Office and the Cabinet. However, the local Community Relations Councils and the CRE are not the major focus for black political activity nor do they any longer prevent racial issues from becoming a serious source of conflict between the major parties. The inter-party consensus on race relations and immigration that existed before the 1970s has now been broken. While the CRE and the local CRCs are only one avenue for blacks to consult and seek redress for grievances, a host of independent organisations have been created to campaign for black rights, and many blacks approach their MPs directly. The argument that special institutions like the CRE reduce the political influence of blacks and result in loss of access to mainstream political institutions can be reversed. It can equally well be argued that black Britons can do both: appeal for assistance to the CRE and their local MP or campaign through pressure groups like the Joint Council for the Welfare of Immigrants, or the National Council for Civil Liberties, or through a local Labour Party. Increasingly black Britons are also organising within trade unions to campaign for their specific interests and lobbying local councils for fair housing and employment policies.

It seems clear that none of these simple explanations alone will account for the relationship of black Britons of the political process. Individuals and groups will adopt a variety of strategies depending on their goals and their estimate of the likely success of the strategies open to them. Moreover, individuals and groups will use a number of different strategies at the same time. Ambitious and able people will work as individuals in the major parties while at the same time attempting to encourage group consciousness among their particular community to give themselves a strong community base. They will also be involved in direct political action when a major crisis, such as the New Cross fire, seems to demand a particularly powerful response. It is thus impossible to predict exactly what the political future of black Britons will be as the evidence is contradictory and the future actions of parties, governments and politicians are unknown. For many, political support and integration in the major parties, especially the Labour Party, is a realistic option and it is encouraging that all the major parties are making some effort to recruit and create opportunities for black Britons. For many others the opportunities and prospects look bleak in declining inner-city areas, with high levels of unemployment and subjection to racist attack and police suspicion. For these, alienation, apathy and withdrawal may well result. The danger is that politicians may see smouldering apathy as merely apathy and take no action or too little action to remedy discrimination and disadvantage until hurriedly forced to do so by spontaneous violent outbursts.

REFERENCES

Abbott, S. (1971), *The Prevention of Racial Discrimination in Britain* (OUP).
Almond, G. and Verba, S. (1963), *The Civic Culture* (Princeton University Press).
Anwar, M. (1979), *The Myth of Return: Pakistanis in Britain* (Heinemann).
Anwar, M. (1980), *Votes and Policies: Ethnic Minorities and the General Election 1979* (Commission for Racial Equality).
Attlee, C. R. (1937), *The Labour Party in Perspective* (Gollancz).
Ballard, R. (1979), 'Ethnic minorities and the social services', in V. S. Khan (ed.), *Minority Families in Britain* (Macmillan), pp. 147–64.
Baumgart, W. (1982), *Imperialism* (OUP).
BBC1 (1981), 'Nai Zindagi Naya Jeevan', verbatim report of an interview between Mahendra Kaul and Mrs Thatcher (3 May).
Beetham, D. (1970), *Transport and Turbans: A Comparative Study in Local Politics* (OUP).
Benewick, R. (1972), *The Fascist Movement in Britain* (Allen Lane).
Bethnal Green and Stepney Trades Council (1978), *Blood on the Streets: A Report on Racial Attacks in East London*.
Billig, M. (1978), *Fascists: A Social Psychological View of the National Front* (Academic Press).
Birch, A. H. (1967), *The British System of Government* (Allen & Unwin).
Bochel, J. and Denver, D. (1983), 'Candidate selection in the Labour party: what the selectors seek', *British Journal of Political Science*, vol. 13, pp. 45–60.
Bradley, I. (1978), 'Why Churchill's plan to limit immigration was shelved', *The Times* (20 March).
Braham, P. (1982), *Migration and Settlement in Britain* (OUP).
British Nationality Bill, Session 1980/81 (HMSO).
Brockway, F. (1964), 'Why I lost Eton and Slough', *Tribune* (23 October).
Butler, D. and Kavanagh, D. (1974), *The British General Election of February 1974* (Macmillan).
Butler, D. and Kavanagh, D. (1975), *The British General Election of October 1974* (Macmillan).
Butler, D. and King, A. (1965), *The British General Election of 1964* (Macmillan).
Butler, D. and Pinto-Duschinsky, M. (1971), *The British General Election of 1970* (Macmillan).
Butler, D. and Rose, R. (1960), *The British General Election of 1959* (Macmillan).
Butler, D. and Stokes, D. (1974), *Political Change in Britain* (Macmillan).
Butler, Lord (1973), *The Art of the Possible* (Penguin).
Cabinet Papers (1950), *Coloured People from British Colonial Territories*, Cabinet memorandum by the Secretary of State for the Colonies, CP (50) 113, 18 May (Public Records Office).

Cabinet Papers (1951), *Immigration of British Subjects into the United Kingdom*, CP 128/44, February (Public Records Office).

Cairns, H. A. C. (1965), *Prelude to Imperialism: British Reactions to Central African Society 1840–90* (Routledge & Kegan Paul).

Carlyle, T. (1849), 'Occasional discourse on the nigger question'; reprinted in T. Carlyle, *Critical and Miscellaneous Essays*, Vol. IV (Chapman Hall, 1899).

Castles, S. and Kosack, G. (1973), *Immigrant Workers and Class Structure in Western Europe* (OUP).

Clutterbuck, R. (1978), *Britain in Agony* (Faber).

Commission for Racial Equality (1977–82), *Annual Reports*.

Commission for Racial Equality (1979), *Brick Lane and Beyond: An Inquiry into Racial Strife and Violence in Tower Hamlets*.

Commission for Racial Equality (1980), *Code of Practice for the Elimination of Racial Discrimination and the Promotion of Equality of Opportunity in Employment*, (consultative draft).

Commission for Racial Equality (1981), *Racial Harassment on Local Authority Housing Estates: a Report prepared by the London Race and Housing Forum*.

Commission for Racial Equality (1982), 'Black councillors in the Greater London boroughs', *New Equals*, no. 19 (Autumn).

Community Relations Commission (1969–76), *Annual Reports*.

Community Relations Commission (1975), *Participation by the Ethnic Minorities in the General Election October 1974*.

Conservative Central Office (1945–83a), *Annual Conference Reports*.

Conservative Central Office (1945–83b), *Conservative Party Manifestos*.

Conservative Central Office (1949a), *Imperial Policy* (June).

Conservative Central Office (1949b), *The Right Road for Britain* (July).

Conservative Central Office (1976), *The Right Approach* (October).

Crewe, I. (1975), *The Politics of Race* (Croom Helm).

Crewe, I. (1983), 'Representation and the ethnic minorities in Britain', in N. Glazer and K. Young (eds), *Ethnic Pluralism and Public Policy* (Heinemann), pp. 258–83.

Crewe, I. and Sarlvik, B. (1980), 'Popular attitudes and electoral strategy', in Z. Layton-Henry (ed.) *Conservative Party Politics* (Macmillan), pp. 244–75.

Cross, C. (1968), *The Fall of the British Empire* (Book Club Associates).

Crossman, R. (1975), *Diaries of a Cabinet Minister*, Vol. 1 (Hamish Hamilton & Jonathan Cape).

Crossman, R. (1977), *Diaries of a Cabinet Minister*, Vol. 2 (Hamish Hamilton & Jonathan Cape).

Curtis, L. P. (1968), *Anglo-Saxons and Celts* (University of Bridgeport Press).

Daniel, W. (1968), *Racial Discrimination in England* (Penguin).

Deakin, N. (1965), *Colour and the British Electorate 1964* (Pall Mall Press).

Deakin, N. (1968a), 'The politics of the Commonwealth Immigrants Bill', *Political Quarterly*, vol. 39 (January–March), pp. 24–45.

Deakin, N. (1968b), 'Racial integration and Whitehall: a plea for reorganisation', *Political Quarterly*, vol. 39 (October–December), pp. 415–26.

Deakin, N. (1969), 'The British Nationality Act of 1948: a brief study on the political mythology of race relations', *Race*, vol. xi (July), pp. 77–83.

Deakin, N. (1970), *Colour, Citizenship and British Society* (Panther Books).

Deakin, N. (1972), *The Immigration Issue in British Politics* (unpublished Ph.D thesis, University of Sussex).

Deakin, N. and Bourne, J. (1970), 'The minorities and the general election of 1970', *Race Today*, vol. 2, no. 7 (July), pp. 205–10.

Defoe, D. (1899), 'The True-born Englishman', in H. Morley (ed.), *The Earlier Life and Chief Earlier Works of Daniel Defoe* (George Routledge & Sons), pp. 175–218.

Dummett, A. (1976), *Citizenship and Nationality* (Runnymede Trust).

Dummett, A. and Dummett, M. (1969), 'The role of government in Britain's racial crisis', in L. Donnelly (ed.) *Justice First* (Sheed & Ward), pp. 25–78.

Ealing Community Relations Council (1981), *Racialist Activity in Ealing 1979–81* (August).

Easton, D. and Dennis, J. (1969), *Children in the Political System* (McGraw Hill).

Fielding, N. (1981), *The National Front* (Routledge & Kegan Paul).

FitzGerald, M. (1983), *Ethnic Minorities and the 1983 General Election*, May, (Runnymede Trust).

Foot, P. (1965), *Immigration and Race in British Politics* (Penguin).

Foot, P. (1969), *The Rise of Enoch Powell* (Penguin).

Freeman, G. (1976), 'Immigrant labor and working class politics: the French and British experience', *Comparative Politics* (October), pp. 24–41.

Freeman, G. (1979), *Immigrant Labor and Racial Conflict in Industrial Societies: The French and British Experience 1945–75* (Princeton University Press).

Garrard, J. A. (1971), *The English and Immigration* (OUP).

Glass, R. (1960), *Newcomers: West Indians in London* (Allen & Unwin).

Goldsworthy, D. (1971), *Colonial Issues in British Politics 1945–51* (OUP).

Granada Television (1978), Verbatim report of part of an interview with Mrs Thatcher by Gordon Burns. Extract by courtesy of *World in Action* (30 January).

Griffiths, P. (1966), *A Question of Colour* (Leslie Frewin).

Grimble, A. (1952), *A Pattern of Islands* (John Murray).

Gupta, P. S. (1975), *Imperialism and the British Labour Movement 1914–64* (Macmillan).

Hailsham, Lord (1975), *The Door Wherein I Went* (Collins).

Hall, S., Critcher, C., Jefferson, T., Clarke, J., and Roberts, B. (1978), *Policing the Crisis* (Macmillan).

Hanna, M. (1974), 'The National Front and other right-wing organisations', *New Community*, vol. 3, no. 1–2, pp. 49–55.

Hansard: see *Parliamentary Debates*.

Harris Poll Ltd. (1983), *Pre-election Survey for Black on Black/Eastern Eye* (May).

Hartley-Brewer, M. (1965), 'Smethwick', in N. Deakin (ed.), *Colour and the British Electorate 1964*, (Pall Mall Press), pp. 77–105.

Hatfield, M. (1978), *The House the Left Built: Inside Labour Policy Making 1970–75* (Gollancz).

Hattersley, R. (1972), 'Immigration', in C. Cook and D. McKie (eds.), *The Decade of Disillusion: British Politics in the 1960s* (Macmillan).

Heineman, B. (1972), *The Politics of the Powerless: A Study of the Campaign Against Racial Discrimination* (OUP).

Henry, I. (1982), *The Growth of Corporate Black Identity among Afro-Caribbean People in Birmingham* (unpublished Ph.D thesis, University of Warwick).

Hewitt, C. (1974), 'Policy-making in postwar Britain: a national level test of elitist or pluralist hypotheses', *British Journal of Political Science*, vol. 4, no. 2, pp. 187–216.

Hill, M. and Issacharoff, R. (1971), *Community Action and Race Relations: A Study of Community Relations Committees in Britain* (OUP).

Hindell, K. (1965), 'The genesis of the Race Relations Bill', *Political Quarterly*, vol. 34, no. 4, pp. 390–405.

Hiro, D. (1973), *Black British White British* (Monthly Review Press).

Holland, P. (1980), *The Quango Death List* (Adam Smith Institute).

Holmes, C. (1978), *Immigrants and Minorities in British Society* (Allen & Unwin).

Home Office (1967), *Committee on Immigration Appeals, chairman Sir Roy Wilson*, Cmnd 3387 (HMSO).

Home Office (1975), *Racial Discrimination*, Cmnd 6234 (HMSO).

Home Office (1977), *British Nationality Law: Discussion of Possible Changes*, Cmnd 6795 (HMSO).

Home Office (1981a), *Ethnic Minorities in Britain: A Study of Trends in their Position Since 1961*, Home Office Research Study No. 68 (HMSO).

Home Office (1981b), *Racial Attacks: Report of a Home Office Study*, November (HMSO).

Home Office (1982), *The Government Reply to the Fifth Report from the Home Office Affairs Committee 1981–2, Racial Disadvantage* (HMSO).

House of Commons (1975), *The Organisation of Race Relations Administration*, Second special report from the Select Committee on Race Relations and Immigration, Session 1974–6, Vol. 1 (HMSO).

House of Commons (1976), *Commonwealth Immigration to the United Kingdom from the 1950s to 1975 – A Survey of Statistical Sources*, Library Research Paper No. 56 (HMSO).

House of Commons (1978), *Immigration*, First report from the Select Committee on Race Relations and Immigration, Session 1977–8, Vols 1 and 2 (HMSO).

House of Commons (1981a), *Commission for Racial Equality*, First report from the Home Affairs Committee, Session 1981–2 (HMSO).

House of Commons (1981b), *Racial Disadvantage*, Fifth report from the Home Affairs Committee, Session 1980–1, Vol. 1 (HMSO).

Howard, A. (1963), 'The skin game', *New Statesman* (22 November).

Humphrey, D. and Ward, M. (1974), *Passports and Politics* (Penguin).

Husband, Charles (1982), *Race in Britain* (Hutchinson).

Husbands, Chris (1975), 'The National Front: a response to a crisis', *New Society* (15 May), pp. 403–5.

Huttenback, R. A. (1976), *Racism and Empire* (Cornell University Press).

Immigration Act (1971), (HMSO).

Immigration from the Commonwealth (1965), Cmnd 2739 (HMSO).

Institute of Race Relations (1969–71), *Race Today*, Vols 1–3 (Race Today Collective).

Jacobs, B. (1982), 'Black minority participation in the USA and Britain', *Journal of Public Policy*, vol. 2, no. 3, pp. 237–62.

Jenkins, R. (1967), *Essays and Speeches* (Collins).

Jordan, W. D. (1974), *The White Man's Burden* (OUP).

Jowell, J. (1965), 'The administrative enforcement of laws against racial discrimination', *Public Law* (Summer), pp. 119–86.

Katznelson, I. (1973), *Black Men White Cities* (OUP).

Kettle, M. and Hodges, L. (1982), *Uprising: the Police, the People and the Riots in Britain's Cities* (Pan).

Khan, V. S. (1979), *Minority Families in Britain* (Macmillan).

Kiernan, V. G. (1969), *The Lords of Human Kind* (Weidenfeld & Nicolson).

Kiernan, V. G. (1978), 'Britons old and new', in C. Holmes (ed.), *Immigrants and Minorities in British Society* (Allen & Unwin), pp. 23–59.

Kubat, D. (1979), *The Politics of Migration Policies* (Centre for Migration Studies, New York).

Kushnick, L. (1971), 'British anti-discrimination legislation', in S. Abbott (ed.), *The Prevention of Racial Discrimination in Britain* (OUP), pp. 233–68.

Labour Party (1945–82), *Annual Conference Reports*.

Labour Party (1945–83), *Labour Party Manifestos*.

Labour Party (1956), *Labour's Colonial Policy: The Plural Society*.

Labour Party (1958), *Racial Discrimination* (September).

Labour Party (1962), *The Integration of Immigrants: A Guide to Action*.

Labour Party (1972), *Citizenship, Immigration and Integration: A Policy for the Seventies*.

Labour Party (1973), *Labour's Programme*.

Labour Party (1976a), *Immigration and Race Relations*.

Labour Party (1976b), *Labour's Programme*.

Labour Party (1978), *Response to the National Front*.

Labour Party (1979), *Race, Immigration and the Racialists*.

Labour Party (1980a), *Citizenship and Immigration*.

Labour Party (1980b), *Labour and the Black Electorate*.

Labour Party (1980c), *The Tories' Immigration Proposals*.

Labour Party (1981), *British Nationality Law: Our Alternative to Tory Legislation*, September (Labour Party Research Department).

Lapping, B. (1970), *The Labour Government 1964–70* (Penguin).

Lawrence, D. (1974), *Black Migrants, White Natives* (CUP).

Lawrence, D. (1978/79), 'Prejudice, politics and race', *New Community*, vol. 7, no. 1, pp. 44–55.

Layton-Henry, Z. (1978a), 'Race, electoral strategy and the major parties', *Parliamentary Affairs*, vol. 31, no. 3, pp. 268–81.

Layton-Henry, Z. (1978b), 'The Tories in two minds over race', *New Society* (25 September), pp. 399–410.

Layton-Henry, Z. (1979), 'The report on immigration', *Political Quarterly*, vol. 50, no. 2 (April/June) pp. 241–8.

Layton-Henry, Z. (1980a), *Conservative Party Politics* (Macmillan).

Layton-Henry, Z. (1980b), 'Commission in crisis', *Political Quarterly*, vol. 51, no. 4 (October/December), pp. 441–50.

Layton-Henry, Z. (1982), 'Racial attacks in Britain', *Patterns of Prejudice*, vol. 16, no. 2, pp. 3–13.

Layton-Henry, Z. (1983), 'The Importance of the Black Electorate', *Shakti*, vol. 2, no. 5 (May).

Layton-Henry, Z. and Studlar, D. (1983), 'The political participation of black Britons', paper presented at the Fourth Annual Conference of Europeanists, Washington DC (13–15 October).

Layton-Henry, Z. and Taylor, S. (1977/8), 'Race and politics: the case of the Ladywood by-election', *New Community*, vol. 6, nos 1 and 2, pp. 130–42.

Layton-Henry, Z. and Taylor, S. (1977), 'Race at the polls', *New Society* (25 August), p. 392.

Layton-Henry, Z. and Taylor, S. (1979–82), 'Immigration and race relations: political aspects 1–7', *New Community*, vols 7–10.

LeLohé, M. (1975), 'Participation in elections by Asians in Bradford' in I. Crewe (ed.), *The Politics of Race* (Croom Helm).

LeLohé, M. (1979), 'The effect of the presence of immigrants upon the local political system in Bradford 1945–77' in R. Miles and A. Phizacklea (eds), *Racism and Political Action* (Routledge & Kegan Paul), pp. 184–203.

LeLohé, M. (1981), *Ethnic Minorities Candidates and Voter Discrimination in the Local Elections of 1980*, paper presented at the Annual Conference of the Political Studies Association, University of Hull (April).

Lester, A. and Bindman, G. (1972), *Race and Law* (Longman).

Lewis, G. K. (1978), *Slavery, Imperialism and Freedom* (Monthly Review Press).

Little, K. L. (1948), *Negroes in Britain* (Kegan Paul).

London Labour Party (1955), *Problems of Coloured People in London* (September).

Macleod, I. (1968), 'A shameful and unnecessary Act', *Spectator* (1 March).

Macmillan, H. (1973), *At the End of the Day* (Macmillan).

May, R. and Cohen, R. (1974), 'The interaction between race and colonialism: a case study of the Liverpool race riots of 1919', *Race and Class*, vol. 16, no. 2, pp. 111–26.

Miles, R. and Phizacklea, A. (1977a), 'Class, race, ethnicity and political action', *Political Studies*, vol. 25, no. 4, pp. 491–508.

Miles, R. and Phizacklea, A. (1977b), *The TUC, Black Workers and New Commonwealth Immigration 1954–73*, (Social Science Research Council Research Unit on Ethnic Relations, working paper no. 6).

Miles, R. and Phizacklea, A. (1979), *Racism and Political Action in Britain* (Routledge & Kegan Paul).

Miller, W. L. (1980), 'What was the profit in following the crowd: aspects of Conservative and Labour strategy since 1970', *British Journal of Political Science*, vol. 10, no. 1, pp. 15–38.

Milner, D. (1975), *Children and Race* (Penguin).

Ministry of Labour (1948), *Report of the Working Party on the Employment in the United Kingdom of Surplus Colonial Labour* (Ministry of Labour Papers 26/226/7503, Public Records Office).

Moore, R. (1975), *Racism and Black Resistance in Britain* (Pluto Press).

Moore, R. and Wallace, T. (1975), *Slamming the Door: The Administration of Immigration Control* (Martin Robertson).

Mullard, C. (1973), *Black Britain* (Allen & Unwin).

National Committee for Commonwealth Immigrants (1966–8), *Annual Reports*.

National Council for Civil Liberties (1980), *Southall 23 April 1979*.

Nixon, J. (1982), 'The Home Office and race relations policy: co-ordinator and initiator?', *Journal of Public Policy*, vol. 2, no. 4, pp. 365–78.

NOP (National Opinion Polls) (1978), *Immigration and Race Relations*, Political, Social and Economic Review No. 14.

Norton, P. (1976), 'Intra-party dissent in the House of Commons: a case study of the Immigration Rules 1972', *Parliamentary Affairs*, vol. 29, no. 4, pp. 404–20.

Nugent, N. and King, R. (1977), *The British Right* (Saxon House).

OECD (1983), *Continuous Reporting System on Migration,*Sopemi Report 1982.

OPCS (Office of Population Censuses and Surveys) (1982), *Annual Abstracts* (Central Statistical Office).

Orwell, G. (1935), *Burmese Days* (Gollancz).

Pannell, N. and Brockway, F. (1965), *Immigration: What is the Answer? Two Opposing Views* (Routledge & Kegan Paul).

Parliamentary Debates *(Hansard)*, (House of Commons, official reports 1948–82; House of Lords, official reports 1948–82).

Parsons, T. (1969), *Politics and Social Structure* (Free Press).

Patterson, S. (1965), *Dark Strangers* (Penguin).

Patterson, S. (1969), *Immigrants in Industry 1960–67* (OUP).

Peach, C. (1968), *West Indian Migration to Britain* (OUP).

Pearson, D. (1981), *Race, Class and Political Activism: A Study of West Indians in Britain* (Gower).

Pearson, G. (1976), '"Paki-bashing" in a north-east Lancashire cotton town: a case study and its history', in G. Mungham and G. Pearson (eds), *Working-Class Youth Culture* (Routledge & Kegan Paul), pp. 48–81.

Phizacklea, A. and Miles, R. (1981), *Labour and Racism* (Routledge & Kegan Paul).

Political and Economic Planning (1967), *Racial Discrimination* (April).

Political and Economic Planning (1974a), *Racial Disadvantage in Employment* (June).

Political and Economic Planning (1974b), *The Extent of Racial Discrimination* (September).

Political and Economic Planning (1975), *Racial Minorities and Public Housing* (September).

Political and Economic Planning (1976), *The Facts of Racial Disadvantage: a National Survey* (February).

Powell, E. (1969a), *Freedom and Reality* (Batsford).

Powell, E. (1969b), Text of speech delivered to the annual conference of the Rotary Club of London, Eastbourne (16 November 1968), in B. Smithies and P. Fiddick (eds), *Enoch Powell on Immigration* (Sphere), pp. 63–77.

Powell, E. (1969c), Text of speech delivered to the annual meeting of the West Midlands Area Conservative Political Centre, Birmingham (20 April 1968), in B. Smithies and P. Fiddick (eds) *Enoch Powell on Immigration* (Sphere), pp. 35–43.

Proctor, K. P. and Pinniger, J. (1981), *Immigration, Repatriation and the Commission for Racial Equality*, April (Monday Club).

Pryce, K. (1979), *Endless Pressure* (Penguin).

Race Relations Act 1965 (HMSO).

Race Relations Act 1968 (HMSO).

Race Relations Act 1976 (HMSO).

Race Relations Board (1966–75), *Annual Reports*.

Ratcliffe, P. (1981), *Racism and Reaction: A Profile of Handsworth* (Routledge & Kegan Paul).

Rees, T. (1979), 'United Kingdom', in D. Kubat (ed.), *The Politics of Migration Policies* (Centre for Migration Studies), pp. 67–91.

Rex, J. (1968), 'The race relations catastrophe' in T. Burgess (ed.) *Matters of Principle: Labour's Last Chance* (Penguin).

Rex, J. (1979), 'Black militancy and class conflict', in R. Miles and A. Phizacklea (eds), *Racism and Political Action* (Routledge & Kegan Paul), pp. 72–92.

Rex, J. and Moore, R. (1967), *Race, Community and Conflict* (OUP).

Rex, J. and Tomlinson, S. (1979), *Colonial Immigrants in a British City* (Routledge & Kegan Paul).

Richter, D. (1964), *Public Order and Popular Disturbances in Great Britain 1865–1914* (unpublished Ph.D thesis, University of Maryland).

Richter, D. (1981), *Riotous Victorians* (Ohio University Press).

Rose, E. J. B., Deakin, N., Abrams, M., Jackson, V., Peston, M., Vanags, A. H., Cohen, B., Gaitskell, J. and Ward, P. (1969), *Colour and Citizenship* (OUP).

Rose, R. (1974), *Politics in England Today* (Faber).

Royal Commission on Population (1949), Cmnd 7695 (HMSO).

Runnymede Trust (1979–83), *Bulletins, Race and Immigration*.

Scarman, Lord (1975), *The Red Lion Square Disorders of 15 June 1974*, Cmnd 5919 (HMSO).

Scarman, Lord (1981), *The Brixton Disorders April 10–12 1981: Report of an Inquiry*, Cmnd 8427 (HMSO).

Schoen, D. (1977), *Enoch Powell and the Powellites* (Macmillan).

Scott, D. (1975), 'The National Front in local politics: some interpretations', in I. Crewe (ed.), *The Politics of Race* (Croom Helm), pp. 214–38.

Searchlight: The Anti-Fascist Monthly (1982), (Searchlight Publications).

Shyllon, F. O. (1974), *Black Slaves in Britain* (OUP).

Sivanandan, A. (1978), 'From immigration control to induced repatriation', Race and Class, vol. 20, no. 1, pp. 75–82.

Smith, D. (1977), *Racial Disadvantage in Britain* (Penguin).

Smithies, B. (1969), and Fiddick, P., *Enoch Powell on Immigration* (Sphere).

Social Surveys (Gallup Poll) Ltd. (September 1958).

Social Surveys (Gallup Poll) Ltd. (September 1965).

Spearman, D. (1968), 'Enoch Powell's postbag', *New Society* (9 May), pp. 667–8.

Steed, M. (1974), 'The results analysed', in D. Butler and D. Kavanagh (eds), *The British General Election of February 1974* (Macmillan) pp. 313–39.

Steed, M. (1978), 'The National Front Vote', *Parliamentary Affairs*, vol. 31, no. 3, pp. 282–93.

Steel, D. (1969), *No Entry* (C. Hurst).

Street, H., Howe, G. and Bindman, G. (1967), *Report on Anti-Discrimination Legislation*, October (Political and Economic Planning and Research Services Ltd.).

Studlar, D. (1974a), 'British public opinion, colour issues and Enoch Powell: a longitudinal analysis', *British Journal of Political Science*, no. 4, pp. 371–81.

Studlar, D. (1974b), 'Political culture and racial policy in Britain', *Patterns of Prejudice*, vol. 8 (May/June), pp. 7–12.

Studlar, D. (1978), 'Policy voting in Britain: the coloured immigration issue in the 1964, 1966 and 1970 general elections', *American Political Science Review*, no. 72, pp. 46–72.

Studlar, D. (1980), 'Elite responsiveness or elite autonomy: British immigration policy reconsidered', *Ethnic and Racial Studies*, vol. 3, no. 2, pp. 207–23.

Tannahill, J. A. (1958), *European Volunteer Workers in Britain* (Manchester University Press).

Taylor, S. (1978), 'Racism and Youth', *New Society* (3 August), pp. 249–50.

Taylor, S. (1980), 'The Liberal party and immigration control: a case study in political deviance', *New Community*, vol. 8, pp. 107–14.

Taylor, S. (1981), 'Strategy changes on the ultra-right', *New Community*, vol. 9, no. 2 (Autumn), pp. 199–202.

Taylor, S. (1982), *The National Front in English Politics* (Macmillan).

Teear, L. A. (1966), *Colour and Immigration* (unpublished MA thesis, University of Sussex).

Thayer, G. (1965), *The British Political Fringe* (Blond & Briggs).

Times Guides to the House of Commons, 1945–83 (Times Newspapers Ltd.).

Tinker, H. (1976), *Separate and Unequal: India and Indians in the British Commonwealth 1920–1950* (C. Hurst).

Trades Union Congress, 1945–82, *Annual Reports*.

Troyna, B. (1982), 'Reporting the National Front: British values observed', in C. Husband (ed.), *Race in Britain* (Hutchinson), pp. 259–78.

Venner, M. (1981), 'From Deptford to Notting Hill, summer 1981', *New Community*, vol. 9, no. 2 (Autumn), pp. 203–7.

Walker, M. (1977), *The National Front* (Fontana).

Walvin, J. (1973), *Black and White: The Negro and English Society 1555–1945* (Allen Lane).

Waugh, A. (1968), 'The victory of autochthonous racism', *Spectator* (1 March).

West Indian Royal Commission 1938–39 (1945), Cmnd 6607 (HMSO).

Williams, E. (1964), *Capitalism and Slavery* (Andre Deutsch).

Williams, P. (1979), *Hugh Gaitskell* (Cape).

Wilson, H. (1971), *The Labour Government 1964–70* (Penguin).

Wood, J. (1970), *Powell and the 1970 Election* (Elliot, Right Way Books).

Woolcott, D. (1965), 'Southall', in N. Deakin (ed.), *Colour and the British Electorate 1964* (Pall Mall Press), pp. 31–53.

Wright, P. L. (1968), *The Coloured Worker in British Industry* (OUP).

INDEX